A Political Philosophy of Conservatism

Bloomsbury Studies in the Aristotelian Tradition

General Editor:

Marco Sgarbi, Università Ca' Foscari, Italy

Editorial Board:

Klaus Corcilius *(University of California, Berkeley, USA)*; Daniel Garber *(Princeton University, USA)*; Oliver Leaman *(University of Kentucky, USA)*; Anna Marmodoro *(University of Oxford, UK)*; Craig Martin *(Oakland University, USA)*; Carlo Natali *(Università Ca' Foscari, Italy)*; Riccardo Pozzo *(Consiglio Nazionale delle Ricerche, Rome, Italy)*; Renée Raphael *(University of California, Irvine, USA)*; Victor M. Salas *(Sacred Heart Major Seminary, USA)*; Leen Spruit *(Radboud University Nijmegen, The Netherlands)*.

Aristotle's influence throughout the history of philosophical thought has been immense and in recent years the study of Aristotelian philosophy has enjoyed a revival. However, Aristotelianism remains an incredibly polysemous concept, encapsulating many, often conflicting, definitions. *Bloomsbury Studies in the Aristotelian Tradition* responds to this need to define Aristotelianism and give rise to a clear characterization.

Investigating the influence and reception of Aristotle's thought from classical antiquity to contemporary philosophy from a wide range of perspectives, this series aims to reconstruct how philosophers have become acquainted with the tradition. The books in this series go beyond simply ascertaining that there are Aristotelian doctrines within the works of various thinkers in the history of philosophy, but seek to understand how they have received and elaborated Aristotle's thought, developing concepts into ideas that have become independent of him.

Bloomsbury Studies in the Aristotelian Tradition promotes new approaches to Aristotelian philosophy and its history. Giving special attention to the use of interdisciplinary methods and insights, books in this series will appeal to scholars working in the fields of philosophy, history and cultural studies.

Available titles:

Elijah Del Medigo and Paduan Aristotelianism, Michael Engel
Phantasia in Aristotle's Ethics, edited by Jakob Leth Fink
Pontano's Virtues, Matthias Roick
The Aftermath of Syllogism, edited by Marco Sgarbi and Matteo Cosci

A Political Philosophy of Conservatism

Prudence, Moderation and Tradition

Ferenc Hörcher

BLOOMSBURY ACADEMIC
LONDON • NEW YORK • OXFORD • NEW DELHI • SYDNEY

BLOOMSBURY ACADEMIC
Bloomsbury Publishing Plc
50 Bedford Square, London, WC1B 3DP, UK
1385 Broadway, New York, NY 10018, USA
29 Earlsfort Terrace, Dublin 2, Ireland

BLOOMSBURY, BLOOMSBURY ACADEMIC and the Diana logo are trademarks of
Bloomsbury Publishing Plc

First published in Great Britain 2020
This paperback edition published in 2021

Copyright © Ferenc Hörcher, 2020

Ferenc Hörcher has asserted his right under the Copyright, Designs and
Patents Act, 1988, to be identified as Author of this work.

For legal purposes the Acknowledgements on p. vi constitute an extension
of this copyright page.

Cover image: *Prudence and Justice with Six Antique Wisemen* © The Picture Art
Collection / Alamy Stock Photo

All rights reserved. No part of this publication may be reproduced or transmitted
in any form or by any means, electronic or mechanical, including photocopying,
recording, or any information storage or retrieval system, without prior
permission in writing from the publishers.

Bloomsbury Publishing Plc does not have any control over, or responsibility for, any
third-party websites referred to or in this book. All internet addresses given in this
book were correct at the time of going to press. The author and publisher regret any
inconvenience caused if addresses have changed or sites have ceased to exist,
but can accept no responsibility for any such changes.

A catalogue record for this book is available from the British Library.

A catalog record for this book is available from the Library of Congress.

ISBN: HB: 978-1-3500-6718-9
PB: 978-1-3502-5131-1
ePDF: 978-1-3500-6719-6
eBook: 978-1-3500-6720-2

Series: Bloomsbury Studies in the Aristotelian Tradition

Typeset by Deanta Global Publishing Services, Chennai, India

To find out more about our authors and books visit www.bloomsbury.com and
sign up for our newsletters.

Contents

Acknowledgements	vi
Introduction: Prudence and conservatism	1

Part One Prudence in history

1	Ancient and Christian traditions of *prudence*	13
2	Renaissance and early modern *prudentia*	33
3	Late modern *prudentia*	57
	Conclusion of Part One	75

Part Two Prudence in conservative philosophy

	Preliminary remarks	79
4	Agency-constraint	83
5	Time-constraint	93
6	Knowledge-constraint	104
7	The prudent individual's resources: Virtues and character	117
8	The prudent community's resources: Tradition and political culture	133
9	How to find the proper action in politics	148
	Summary: A conservative political philosophy of prudence	162

Notes	167
Bibliography	192
Index of Names	203
Index of Subjects	206

Acknowledgements

This book would not have been written without the help of a number of people and institutions, to whom I express my gratitude.

The idea for the book came from my students at the law faculty of my one-time home university, Pázmány Péter Catholic University, in Budapest.

The writing of the book began during a visiting research fellowship at the Nanovic Institute for European Studies at the University of Notre Dame, South Bend, in 2009. I am grateful to the institute's director in those years, Professor A. James McAdams.

Much of the book's material was discussed in the company of friends with an interest in conservatism in Budapest, all of whom are interested in political theory and philosophy, called Mensa, which has now, unfortunately, been disbanded.

The opportunity to start writing the final version of the manuscript in early 2018 took place at the Institute of Philosophy of the Research Centre in the Humanities of the Hungarian Academy of Sciences. I am grateful to Dr Péter Varga, research secretary of the institute and members of my research group.

The manuscript was finished at the newly founded Research Institute of Politics and Government at the Eötvös József Research Centre, the National University of Public Service in Budapest in early 2019. My thanks to the rector, Professor András Koltay, for inviting me to the university, and my colleagues for our discussions on the final chapter of the book.

I am personally grateful to Professors C. D. C. Reeve, Walter Nicgorski, Iwona Tylek, Günter Figal, Péter Lautner and Attila Simon, who read and commented on individual chapters of the book. Needless to say, any remaining mistakes, factual or conceptual, are mine. I am grateful to Catherine Zuckert, James Hankins, Ádám Potkay, Alexander Nehamas, Sándor Bene, Márton Zászkaliczky and Ádám Smrcz for our discussions on aspects of the project. I was encouraged to go along the road of writing this book by the example of Sir Roger Scruton and Prof. Ryszard Legutko, for which I am very grateful to them.

Special thanks to Ms Andrea Robotka, head of the secretariat of our research institute, who took care of the manuscript's details and prepared the index. Again, any remaining mistakes are my responsibility.

Finally, thanks are due to my wife, Mrs Ildikó Marosi, judge of the Constitutional Court of Hungary, for professional advice as well as her tender help and support in those moments when the project seemed to fall apart.

Introduction: Prudence and conservatism

Justice, from Plato to Rawls, played a predominant role in Western political philosophy. No matter, whether ancient or modern, pagan or Christian, believer or non-believer, political philosophers' preferred choice among the virtues was justice. This book does not want to disown this legacy. Yet, it suggests considering another start: justice being only one among the cardinal virtues in the Greek–Roman–Christian tradition, it proposes taking a look at the other virtues, and their possible role in political philosophy, too. Courage, for example, has been present in political philosophy since Plato's discussion of the warriors in the republic. It famously plays a major role in Nietzsche, Sorel and Jünger, and there was a line of important early modern to modern political thinkers who kept emphasizing its relevance, from Machiavelli to Carl Schmitt and the Straussians. On the opposite side, moderation played a pivotal role in theories of modern liberal democratic rule, too. In these regimes, leaders were and still are expected to be ready to exercise self-restraint, to become an accepted partner in institutionalized politics, and much more so when in power.

Yet, this book will concentrate on the fourth of the cardinal virtues, prudence (*prudentia*). This is a concept which again has its origins in ancient Greece (in Plato's and Aristotle's discussion of *phronesis*), was frequently referred to by Cicero and Christian theorists as well, and the early modern era brought its golden age, with authors such as Lipsius and Gracián among its theorists. The twentieth century saw some efforts to reinvigorate it, by authors such as Gadamer, Ricoeur and Oakeshott. Its recurrence benefited from the rebirth of virtue ethics, but not until the recent boom in political realism, as initiated by Williams and Geuss, did it come into the centre of political thought. Often translated as practical wisdom, its relevance for political realists is that it turns our attention to the practicalities of politics, and within that to the practical abilities of the political actor.

The conception of the present book looks back to an earlier one of its author, entitled *Prudentia Iuris*, published in 2000, aiming to draw the outlines of what was labelled then as pragmatic theory of natural law.[1] While that book was an exercise in legal theory or the philosophy of law, the present book attempts to understand how prudence functions in the neighbouring realm of political thought, where it has not often featured as the main hero of theory.[2] Yet, the last years has seen a reawakening interest in the use of this virtue in political reflection.

In a chapter on theory and practice in politics, Richard Bourke referred to John Dunn's role in directing attention to prudence in political theory: 'John Dunn has written that prudence should stand at the centre of political analysis.'[3] Bourke's article was published in a book on political judgement dedicated to John Dunn, one of the senior members of what came to be called the Cambridge School in the history of political thought. The book was edited by Richard Bourke and Raymond Geuss.[4] While Bourke is a historian, Geuss is a philosopher, and both were closely connected to the Cambridge paradigm in the history of political thought. The book born out of their cooperation hints at the relevance of the political philosophy of the Cambridge School. This connection between theory and history is indicated by the fact that John Dunn is not only a Cambridge-style historian of political thought but also a fine political theorist in his own right.

In their introduction to the volume, Geuss and Bourke characterize Dunn's research into political judgement the following way: it is 'an attempt to rehabilitate the standpoint and the cognitive and practical skills of the political actor'. They add that instead of the institutional or the moral aspect, Dunn becomes increasingly interested in the practical aspect of politics, and proves that political judgement is not to be understood as 'the subsumption of individual cases under pre-given concepts or rules'.[5] Dunn's criticism is double-edged: he is negating both 'the profoundly aberrant quality of political judgement generated by a scientistic political science' and 'a moral philosophy constructed through an essentially apolitical process'.[6] Instead of the dumb quantitative empirical methodology of political science and the moralizing attitude of post-Rawlsian political philosophy, Dunn's aim is to 'treat politics, implicitly or explicitly, as a matter of agency within a more or less refractory practical context', and it is in this context that he concentrates on 'the key virtue of human practical reason occasioned by the treacherous circumstances', namely 'the virtue of prudence'.[7]

In both these points, the present venture shares Dunn's starting points. In other words, it assumes that understanding politics depends on understanding the thoughts and actions of the historically contingent participants of a political situation in a context-dependent and particularized form or, put differently, in accordance with the demands of the here and now. Conversely, it also argues that it should not be seen as an expression of a relativist position as far as basic values are concerned. Rather, it takes the balanced, moderate, Aristotelian position that universal values can only be uncovered from the particular circumstances of specific historical instances, and in this process of interpretation, both poles (the universality of the values and the particularity of the historical instances) have the same relevance.

A combination of present-day political concerns, philosophically inclined political reflection and an interest in the history of political thought characterizes the approach the present volume has chosen when addressing the issue of prudence in political philosophy. It suggests that political reflection could and should be based on prudence as its central category, and that such a de- and recentring of political reflection might offer new – politically conservative and realist – vistas on politics.

However, we need to clarify two further methodological points that are essential to assess the intentions of the present venture. The first point is the connection between political reflection and the history of political thought, while the second touches upon the relationship between political action and reflection, between speech and deed, or in Bourke's Kantian framework, between theory and practice.

Let us start with the relationship between political philosophy and the history of political thought.[8] As Dunn emphasized, political theory should not be conceived as the polar opposite of a historically informed understanding of political reflection. It is a misconception that by bringing in the historical dimension one necessarily loses sight of the specifically political element of the problem. On the contrary, he claims in his essay entitled 'The History of Political Theory' (1996),[9] that 'the political' will not be thrown into the shade by bringing in the historical particularities of political conflicts, just the other way round, it will sharpen the edge of the political agenda by substantiating and contextualizing it. This claim is informative of the present project.

The aim of this venture is to draw the outlines of a political philosophy of conservatism based on prudence, which will also depend on a conceptual history of the concept of prudence, as it was formulated under different regimes in rather different historical and political climates. While the conceptual history of prudence will be reconstructed in the first part of the book, the second analytical part will show in what ways the historically interpreted prudence is connected with a conservative approach to politics. This second part will also attempt to maintain an interaction with the historical interpretation, this way making use of a richer hermeneutic toolkit than that provided by philosophical analysis on its own. Certainly, such a methodological heterogeneity can raise the problem of mixing up the normative and the descriptive dimension of talking about politics. Yet, heterogeneity does not necessarily mean mixing up, or even confusing different components. The present political philosophy of prudence will argue for an understanding of the virtue of prudence, which allows for its historical variability, and yet it claims that there exists a normatively defendable, conservative understanding of prudence, behind the changing applications of the term.

But how about the second point, the one Bourke labels as the debate on theory and practice in politics. The problem itself is politically coloured: the question 'What is the relationship between these levels?' is itself a political question. It wants to define (in certain cases in order to have an impact on) the power relationships between political practice and the reflection on it. Think about the Leninist dictum about the necessarily practical nature of politics.[10] No doubt, Lenin's interest in theoretical questions was no more than an interest in how to get into and then how to preserve power. As American pragmatists would agree, for him the truth of an assertion of political theory was indeed tested by its empirical efficiency. But the problem is more complicated in the case of other political actors, and the connection between the two levels is not so obvious. Consider the Roman emperor, Marcus Aurelius, who also reflected on the relationship between reflection and practice in his *Meditations*. This work by him was definitely not born as a result of simple pragmatic considerations. In fact, it was interpreted as an effort of a student of Epictetus to secure an interface between the two, otherwise isolated realms.[11]

Scholars educated in the German style of *Wissenschaft* had a rather characteristic opinion of this relationship. Perhaps Max Weber is the best-known example of the Prussian view of *Wissenschaft*, including political science. In his 1917 lecture, later published under the title *Science as a Vocation*,[12] he argued that reason and faith, as well as fact and value need to be separated and kept separately. According to his argument, science is a specific approach to reality, based on specific research questions, analytic methods and argumentative strategies and these can only prevail when distanced from ordinary personal interests and political alliances. Weber denied that the results of this methodologically refined, neutral enquiry could really be used by political leaders in their decision-making procedures the same way as the results of natural science research can be used in policy decisions.

Certainly, there is a full spectrum of historical variations between the two extremes of political pragmatist positions of Lenin and Weber, who is searching for a neutral perspective in political science, on the relationship between theory and practice in politics, and not only since the early modern period. The terms of the discourse on the theme were formulated in the early modern period, and reconstructed in Richard Tuck's *Philosophy and Government, 1572–1651*.[13] The research interest of Tuck, an earlier Cambridge-based historian of political thought, is in accordance with the Cambridge paradigm, in uniting a historical interest in politics with a theoretical preoccupation. His aim is to show the shift from the classical humanist position in political thought, which supposed a unity of the virtues both in ethics and in politics, to the more sceptical approach to politics, where the interest of the state (*reason of state*) became an autonomous, in fact, dominant political virtue, in disharmony with the cardinal virtues.[14] The shift speaks about the breaking up of the balance between morality and politics – this break-up is illustrated by the acclaimed turn away by contemporaries from Cicero and by an increased interest in the ideas of Tacitus. At the same time, it tells a lot about the indirect political consequences of changes in the philosophical convictions from one generation to the next, and in this way reminds us of the relevance of the practical and intellectual milieu of political thinking, which might lead to unintended consequences in political convictions, too. Politics, it turns out, is not only influenced by political thought, but it will itself influence political thought – which makes the uncovering of cause and effect in the relationship of political thought and action not much easier.

Besides Tuck, another member of the second generation of Cambridge historians was István Hont, a close friend and colleague of Dunn, who – mainly in his volume of collected essays: *The Jealousy of Trade* (2005)[15] – as a historian of political thought was also influential in bringing together and in dialogue political reflection and the history of political thought. What he achieved was to draw attention to the fact that by deepening our historical knowledge about the ways in which people thought about politics in earlier ages might indeed help us see our own political agenda much more clearly, and even to find adequate answers to the main issues of this agenda. Hont takes the story described by Tuck, and reconstructs its afterlife, in the seventeenth and eighteenth centuries, in the Western world.

It is very telling that by now almost all the members of the originally methodologically, very puritan and positivistic Cambridge School in the history of political thought made their normative 'coming outs', confessing their own political, or at least ideological preferences (which does not necessarily mean partisanship). Although they used to be very consistently purist antiquarians in their historical investigations, promulgating the study of primary sources and strictly condemning the use of anachronistic terminology, in their later career they could not resist turning directly to political analysis. However, the present enquiry does not see a contradiction in this turn or shift in their scientific endeavour. It takes it as an honest admission that writing even in a historical mode about politics is not an 'innocent' or 'neutral' activity, but one that necessarily has its own political dimension. In other words, speaking or writing about politics, every single utterance, even in the historical register, is itself a political deed. What is more, this close connection between talking about politics and doing politics has its particular theoretical relevance: it is an argument in favour of looking at politics not simply as a professional technical activity but rather as a culturally deeply embedded one. Culture is not only historically determined but it also has universal values claims. The admission that a certain pronouncement *about* politics *has* political relevance, while political action has meaning, and that political activity as well as talk about it is historically and culturally embedded, is only an admission of the value-laden nature of politics.

The present account of the political philosophy of conservatism based on prudence is also aware of the political overtone of its narrative. It is looking at the phenomenon of political prudence as experienced in different ancient and classical contexts, from a conservative philosophical and political perspective. It tries to avoid, however, being partisan: its tone is moderated and its presentation is not confrontative. In the first half of the present account, the reader will find summaries of the views on prudence by a selection of classical authors who held different but connected views of the role of prudence in political thought. The narrative's first hero is Aristotle, which is not to deny the relevance of Socrates and Plato in the birth of the political philosophy of prudence, but it suggests that indeed it was Aristotle who first realized that politics needs to be distinguished from the other discourses of practical philosophy, even if they remain closely connected to each other – a conceptual decision that explains Aristotle's accentuated role in this historical narrative of prudence connected with an account of political conservatism. In the first chapter, Aristotle is closely linked to Cicero, Augustine and Aquinas, respectively. Here, the pagan and the Christian version of the group of cardinal virtues is the context, in which prudence appears as a politically relevant virtue. Cicero, and to a certain extent, Augustine, is important in this narrative in another respect, too, in which Aquinas is not: Cicero, as a theorist of the *respublica*, was himself a political agent, and therefore his tremendous influence on the medieval and early modern political discourse also has a message about the *otium–negotium* problem, in other words, on the relationship of political theory and practice in one's individual life. Cicero's political life is a test of the demands of political duty over the intellectual. Cicero's embodied argument (that is to say, the arguments that he presents in the form of his practical activity as a Roman statesman), including his politically motivated death (just as the death of Socrates) succeeds in convincing his posterity that philosophy and politics, *otium* and *negotium*, are not in conflict: 'That philosophical activity is a natural extension of the standard Roman public activities, notably oratory, that marked his earlier career.'[16] Augustine started his career as a politically active professor of rhetoric, but withdrew from public life at a certain point, leaning towards contemplation and religion, and yet as a responsible church leader, had to combine his researches into the depth of Christian theology with political acumen and practical wisdom. Aquinas represents an alternative tradition, in the sense that his interest in politics has nothing to do with his own practice. This difference makes it all the more relevant that all three thinkers keep emphasizing, in an Aristotelian fashion, the importance of the virtue of prudence in politics.

Even more relevant for the afterlife of the Ciceronian model than Augustinian moral theology and Thomistic scholasticism was the rhetorical practice and theory of the Italian Renaissance, and its continuous reference to the Roman legacy. The Italian city states of the fourteenth to the sixteenth centuries employed a number of well-educated humanists, who fulfilled important offices in their respective cities, and their political practice and their written reflections on politics had a rather fascinating interaction. As practising magistrates in cities or employed in princely courts, humanists were certainly aware of the practical side of politics. It was not debatable for them that the virtue of prudence must play a prominent role in politics, even if they might have attributed different meanings to the term. There is an internal shift, as we saw earlier in connection with Tuck, between early and late sixteenth-century notions of prudence, for example – a shift, as we have seen, from a Ciceronian paradigm to that of Tacitus. Machiavelli is, in fact, the threshold between these two discourses. Certainly, the debate if Machiavelli was indeed the sort of asocial monster he is often depicted by his opponents still lingers on. But for us, the theoretically more fruitful question is if the more realistic account of prudence, which learns from the lesson Machiavelli delivered, but which at the same time tries to keep the traditional value structure of the cardinal virtues, as presented both in the pagan Roman and in the medieval Christian tradition, alive, is viable or not, and if so, what is its relationship to latter-day realistic conservative thought. In this respect, highly influential and rather complex authors, such as Lipsius and Montaigne, promise to be crucial for us.

It is noteworthy that the historical account finishes with late twentieth-century authors, such as Bernard Williams and Raymond Geuss, who are taken to represent political realism, a new way of criticizing mainstream theoretical liberalism, and in particular authors such as John Rawls and Ronald Dworkin. Although there are significant differences between the views of Williams and Geuss, by now a remarkable circle of scholarship has developed along the lines they proposed, built on the assumption that constitutional democracy is not a political regime, which can be taken to have eliminated what Carl Schmitt called 'the political' – as was supposed by Fukuyama. According to the recent realist trend of liberalism, if we find this system worthwhile to preserve, there is a need to practically and theoretically defend it – and prudence is exactly the capacity that enables us to act and speak in a politically adequate way. In this respect, the hermeneutic philosophical school of the late twentieth century, as represented by its founder Gadamer, and an important commentator of it, Ricoeur, is just as relevant as the philosophically elaborate British conservative thought of Michael Oakeshott, who was also well versed in the German idealist tradition.

Following the historical overview from Aristotle through Cicero and Aquinas, to early and late modern political realism, the book offers an analytical investigation of the concept of political prudence as the key to understanding conservatism. Initially, it takes an account of the constraints that hinder humans to speak and act in politics in a practically rational manner, alone or in cooperation with the others, in historically determined political situations. The three constraints include agency, temporal and knowledge-constraint.

The first constraint – namely agency-constraint – is connected to the notion of 'the political', which requires, logically and grammatically, a personal or institutionalized agent. The interests of these two types of agency (individual and communal) might be in conflict, of course. In this respect, the issue of sociability – the inclination to cooperate with others – is brought up, together with its opposite, the tendency to look at politics as the expression of conflicting interests in a community or between communities. To dissolve the conflict of the two sides of human nature (the egoistic and the benevolent impulse), the classic Kantian solution of *ungesellige Geselligkeit* (asocial sociability)[17] is discussed, which is followed in the relevant chapter by a short summary of the concept of the person in the Catholic social teaching.[18]

The second constraint – namely time-constraint – is to be understood as the temporal stipulations of human existence. The human concept of time defines the three tenses of prudence, in other words, its orientation towards the past, the present and the future. The virtue of prudence also has an important condition, labelled by Josef Pieper as the 'reality principle': it needs to confront primarily the present moment. But as a historically informed form of knowledge, prudence makes sense of the present as the result of the past and as the cause of the future. Furthermore, the impact of the virtue of prudence on reality is gradual, leading from deliberation to judgement and then to decision, and it will conclude in the proper action. The analysis of time-constraint has a subchapter distinguishing a situation-based universal ethics from a relativist sort of situationism. Finally, the notion of right timing, the Greek concept of *kairos*, is analysed in the context of political decision-making and action.

The third hindrance to a well-informed and free political action – namely knowledge-constraint – concerns the issue of how to get informed in the world of politics. This chapter collects three major causes why knowledge in politics is necessarily both confined and distorted and also, to a large extent, unreliable. The barriers to reliable information in politics are analysed under three headings: 'perspectival distortion', 'situational mutability' and 'value dependence'. However, the chapter warns the reader not to feel overwhelmed by these barriers, because suspending belief in the possibility of obtaining knowledge in politics might have even more disastrous effects. After the barriers, therefore, it offers a short account of the expositions of the operation of practical knowledge by such diverse authors as Michael Polanyi (personal knowledge), Friedrich Hayek (spontaneous order) and Michael Oakeshott (practical knowledge, in the narrowest possible sense).

After the constraints, the book summarizes the resources that can be moved in politics to prepare a practically wise decision and action. First, it looks at the individual's own, personal resources, followed by a summary of the communal resources. As for the individual resources, they include two pillars in the Aristotelian tradition: virtue and character. The chapter investigating these concepts first relies on Julia Annas's book-length overview of the notion of intelligent virtue. Virtue and character, however, are not stable, static things. More precisely, they need to be mobilized in politics. This insight leads to the concept of virtue politics. This concept, born in analogy with virtue ethics, is introduced with reference to Catherine Zuckert's Aristotelian analysis of it, in contrast to some mainstream contemporary directions. A second, more historically oriented version of virtue politics is also considered in the chapter, as presented by James Hankins, in his analysis of the Italian Renaissance humanists' notion of virtue politics. This introduction of the Aristotelian themes of virtue and character will be widened by a presentation of what Aristotle might have meant by moderation (*sôphrosunê*), including this concept's connections with the notions of balance, civility and decorum, also taken from the Aristotelian–Ciceronian tradition. But this is not an aesthetic interpretation of prudence. Self-restraint has a political value, as have the notions of trimming and the art of compromise, concepts that belong to the conservative tradition as it is understood in this book. This time, we will rely on Aurelian Craiutu's path-breaking work on moderation (*sophrosyne, temperantia*) another Platonic–Aristotelian–Ciceronian–Christian cardinal virtue.

The intelligent individual's personal resources, including virtue, character and the art of self-restraint or moderation are no doubt very powerful engines that support the political agent's practical activity. Yet, they will surely not be enough without the further support of the wisdom of the political community to overcome the hindrances caused by the three restraints previously mentioned. It is therefore of the utmost necessity to look at the resources made available for the individual political agent by his or her community. The first level of these communal resources is that of the institutional order arranged in the given community by the valid and legitimate legal norms of the community. It helps to align individual and group interests in an explicit and formalized way. This is called the rule of law in the modern West. Yet, there are further dimensions to the communal resources behind this surface, procedural level. There are unwritten customs and loosely defined traditions that also have an undeniable impact on individual behaviour, and in fact on personal (and communal) identity-formation, as well. Already the life of the Greek *polis* was based on this: on a system of unreflected habits and mores, which were included in their sense of communal order, *nomos*. The ancient Greek concept of *nomos* also included something, which might remind us of the *spirit* of the law, as the concept is developed by Montesquieu. And the most complex level of the communal resources of practical wisdom is nothing else but political culture, the way people think, feel and act together in cooperation or in conflict with one another in a particular political environment. While, undoubtedly, Aristotle was interested in the formal description of the different constitutional regimes of the Greek city states, he was aware of the soft conditions defining a given political arrangement, which is nothing else but political culture as we understand the term. Although this factor might be soft, and might be in a constant flux, no political agent can ignore its existence, although he or she can legitimately make efforts to influence it: to keep the tradition alive, political education is needed. Tradition knowledge is nothing less than a long-term expression of practical wisdom, when practised in an accepted or acceptable manner in the community.

Putting together the three chapters on the constraints of the practically wise political action and the two chapters on the individual's and the group's resources to counterbalance the constraints, we can perhaps make a more convincing effort to answer the simple question: how to act properly, in other words, in a prudential manner, in politics.

The last chapter aims to answer this simple question in a conservative dialect: how to act properly in politics. It tries to distinguish between a perfect and a proper act: while the former is impossible to achieve, the latter is more realistic as an aim. A proper act in the Aristotelian–Ciceronian tradition is connected to *decorum*, and through it to the Greek concept of *prepon*. This historical recapitulation of the term of appropriateness will be followed by a short subchapter on the relationship between prudence and political realism, between Cicero and Machiavelli, arguing that the difference is not to be described as if Cicero was less realistic and more ideological than Machiavelli. Finally, the book's concluding arguments explain the notion of conservative republicanism. It first looks at the early modern framework in connection with the Dutch Republic in its golden age. These final historical parts can be seen as arguments that the proper operation of personal and communal prudence, in fact, has both historically well-defined examples and a well-established explanatory mechanism. In other words, to find the proper act in politics is to see and understand past examples, to confront the moment and to have a strategy for how to proceed in the future. This is done by the political philosophy of conservatism, as determined by the concepts of prudence, moderation and tradition.

Part One

Prudence in history

1

Ancient and Christian traditions of *prudence*

Aristotle's *phronesis*

Raphael's Aristotle

In 1508, Pope Julius II commissioned Raphael to paint the walls of his private library in the Vatican Palace. The four walls were to be decorated according to the Christian humanist programme provided by the pope, representing personifications of theology, philosophy, poetry and jurisprudence, respectively. Philosophy came to be represented in the famous fresco of the School of Athens (Figure 1.1). The view of Aristotle offered by Raphael's School of Athens fresco in the Palazzo Apostolico relied heavily on traditional iconographic elements of the philosopher, and it had a deep impact on later perceptions of the Greek philosopher. Aristotle, a man in full power, surely idealized, is presented here as much younger than his companion and master, Plato, who reminds the viewer of the biblical prophets – or at least of their presentation by Raphael's elder contemporary, Leonardo. The old man's gesturing seems to be intended to reveal his remonstrance. The open right palm of the younger man is turned towards the ground (in this case the steps), in direct opposition to the finger of his companion, which is pointed towards the highest point of the dome. This gesture is usually interpreted as expressing the down-to-earth approach to philosophy characteristic of Aristotle. Plato, however, embodies his doctrine of the primacy of the idea. When interpreted psychologically, a quiet and balanced Aristotle seems to calm down a passionate Plato. They gaze at each other, as if they were arguing with each other. Both hold a book in their left hand: Aristotle his *Nicomachean Ethics* and Plato his *Timaeus*, a book on cosmology that was highly esteemed by practitioners of mathematics and artists of the early modern period. Through their chosen books, Plato is represented as a metaphysician, while Aristotle is fashioned as a moralist. One is interested in eternal problems, the other in earthly and, more particularly, human problems.

This reconstruction of the Aristotelian tradition is going to rely on the conventional interpretation of Aristotle offered by Raphael's fresco, with his calming gesture towards the metaphysical enthusiasm of Plato and (presumably) of the Neoplatonism of Renaissance Italy he embodies. In other words, the plan is to rely on the Greek moralist and his politics (*politikê*), which is the title of his other important book of practical

Figure 1.1 Raphael's 'School of Athens', 1511, Wikimedia Commons.

philosophy, in addition to the one presented by Raphael's fresco. Taken together, Aristotle's *Nicomachean Ethics* and his *Politics* build up a rather elaborate complex of individual and public morality, and, as we will see, together are responsible for a very specific philosophical tradition, lasting through the late medieval and early modern period until the neo-Aristotelian virtue ethical revival of the twentieth century.

Besides *Nicomachean Ethics* and *Politics*, Aristotle's analysis of the Athenian constitution is also worthwhile studying, as it helps us comprehend his relationship to the very tradition of the city state where he spent the bigger part of his life: Athens. This account of Athens' constitution helps to imbed his philosophical ideas in a politico-historical context, without which it would remain the same abstract reasoning on politics he criticized in his master's work, as well as in Socrates's own unwritten teachings. While most of the secondary literature keeps emphasizing Aristotle's connection to the Macedonian court, his engagement with Athens was surely at least as formative and searching as his experience of teaching Alexander. Even if he was a critical analyst of Athenian political history, he was certainly aware of the achievements of this *polis*, despite the fact that he himself experienced the operation of Athens' political machinery in its declining phase. Aristotle tried to draw conclusions from its history for his own practically oriented reflections. After all, one of the key issues that differentiated his position from the Socratic–Platonist tradition was the realist basis of political philosophy: that he was not merely inventing a theory, but he also made an effort to rely on the empirical data and draw conclusions from that collection of data. We will start from the assumption that his theoretical work should be read in the context of his own empirical investigations into politics.

In what follows, a very brief sketch of Aristotle's practical philosophy will be provided, with the concept of *phronesis* or practical wisdom at its centre. Due to the nature of the present enquiry, this will be a rather shorthand overview of the main points – one which approaches its topic with a very definite aim. It will reconstruct Aristotle with the present book's own questions in the background; in other words, it will be an admittedly one-sided interpretation.

Phronesis versus wisdom

While *philosophia* itself, in the Greek tradition, sets theoretical wisdom (*sophia*) at the centre of politics, as we can see in Plato's *Republic* (*Politeia*), Aristotle's *Nicomachean Ethics* makes a great effort to put practical wisdom (*phronesis*) at that centre. It seems therefore appropriate to start our overview of the Aristotelian teaching on *phronesis* with an overview of the two concepts.

It is the famous book VI of the *Nicomachean Ethics* where Aristotle differentiates between the two terms. More exactly, he distinguishes here between five forms of how the soul grasps truth: craft knowledge (*techné*), scientific knowledge (*epistémé*), practical wisdom (*phronesis*), theoretical wisdom (*sophia*) and understanding (*nous*).[1] It is in this context that we can interpret the Aristotelian distinction between *sophia* and *phronesis* – a distinction that was not yet made by Plato.

To be sure, these are not so much forms of enquiry in this context, but rather states of the soul, conceptually distinguished by Aristotle. Of interest, first of all, is that *sophia* loses its primary position in ethics and politics. As the philosopher defines it in *Metaphysics*, *sophia* provides 'a theoretical grasp of the primary starting-points and causes'.[2] In other words, it is 'the virtue of the scientific part of the soul', 'the most exact form of scientific knowledge'.[3] Reeve also adds that 'living in accord with theoretical wisdom is the best kind of happiness' for Aristotle.[4] Yet, he does not directly oppose the two sorts of knowledge: theoretical and practical wisdom. His effort is to reposition *phronesis*, but not to contrast it with *sophia*.

It is his interest in the really practical concerns of politics that leads Aristotle to the recognition of the importance of experience in political matters, and therefore to an investigation of the constitutions of contemporary Greek city states. As a student of politics, he needed the sort of knowledge that is distant from abstract philosophical wisdom, as exemplified by the way of thinking of his master, Plato, and closer to the kind of empirical knowledge Aristotle himself relied on in his researches into what we call today the natural sciences. This difference between his own approach and that of Plato (even if Plato also had some contact with politics in Syracuse) must have been influenced by Aristotle's own, more direct acquaintance with the realities of politics, when he experienced them earlier in the Macedonian court, as tutor to the would-be Alexander the Great, and later in Athens, teaching the sons of the elite families of the city. The experience he gained by being in direct contact with real politics must have played a major part in his decision to initiate a wide-scale research of constitutional data collection with his students, which resulted in the accumulation of the constitutional regimes of 158 contemporary Greek states.

Apparently, Aristotle was not satisfied with the way Plato constructed the ideal constitution in the *Republic*. Rather, he thought that just as the practical politician, so the theorist, too, needs to take into account the particular conditions of a given political situation when thinking about the best possible solution for a particular political problem. It is noteworthy that according to a recent commentary, his *Politics* was more concerned with 'the universalist side of practical wisdom', with 'designing and developing universal laws appropriate to them', while in the *Nicomachean Ethics* 'the particularist side of practical wisdom is more in focus'.[5] This distinction certainly stands, but the important thing for us is to note that Aristotle takes into account hard facts, without which no knowledge (including philosophical knowledge) of politics seems to him possible. And if we are interested in his real view of the power of general provisions, we have to take into account his view in the *Constitution of Athens*, where he is claimed to write about 'the impossibility of including the best solution for every instance in a general provision'.[6] That is why experience gains significance: if the lawmaker cannot foresee the best solution for every future scenario, what is required is to interpret the general clause in a cautious way, which fits the given particular situation. And one can only interpret it in a fitting way by a reliance on experience. This is why practical wisdom is connected to experience – to make the right judgement about the application of a general clause presupposes a prehistory of learning from earlier occasions which were sufficiently similar to interpret them as precedents to make sense of the present dilemma, and to find the right answer to the question it poses by applying the conclusions drawn from these precedents.

This type of knowledge is not formalized. It is not drawn from abstract and universally valid premises. Rather, it is based on a trial-and-error mechanism, which helps to answer the dilemma by developing a sense, which will inspire the individual in the right moment to move towards the best possible choice. It is not simply giving in to a kind of unidentified instinct: rather, what is required is a recognition that politics is indeed like an art, where excellent performance depends on practice, practice and practice.

To put it more succinctly, Aristotle connects knowledge of particulars with experience. In what follows, we will see that both of these categories are connected to social custom and individual habit (*ethos*). Aristotle finishes his lectures in the *Nicomachean Ethics* with the claim that later on, when he talks about the state, it will be done in the mirror of the conclusions drawn from the analysis of the constitutions they have collected. In other words, he stresses that he does not want to improvise as an armchair philosopher is expected to do, but rather tries to react to what he finds outside in the realm of real politics. This effort is based on his seemingly firm belief, according to which the 'undemonstrated sayings and beliefs of experienced and older people or practically-wise ones'[7] who kept confronting their ideas with reality, are much more worth listening to than philosophers taking their ideas out of the blue. That is to say, confronting ideas with facts of real life can help to sustain a level of political rationality which is not available to the pure logic of the philosopher. The sum of the collected empirical data of constitutional mechanisms and political arrangements returns in his magnum opus on politics, in book V of *Politics*, where he compares different constitutions to find out which is the best possible, as distinguished from the absolute best.

Certainly, Aristotle's description of constitutional life is much wider than our present-day concept of a constitution suggests. In Reeve's interpretation, he affirms that finally it is our habits which determine the type of life we, as a political community, lead. More exactly, as Reeve's introduction to Aristotle's *Politics* explains 'our habits do still largely determine our conception of the good',[8] and of course, as he quotes from Aristotle, 'it is not easy to alter what has long been absorbed by habit'.[9] In other words, it is habits that will determine our judgements of what is good, and through that also our practical choices. But how can we alter habits? Or once a certain habit is established within a community, can anything be done to break it? Aristotle seems to imply that, in fact, habituation – the education that helps would-be citizens to inculcate certain habits and to avoid others – is one of the key determinants of political life. For example, he argues that if emotions are properly habituated, they will be able to 'listen to reason'. In other words, the individual's virtue is largely dependent on what is inculcated in him or her, or how his or her soul is habituated. As politics is compared at some points by Aristotle to *techné*, what is required, in fact, is not convincing people by argument, but rather through training and experience.

Although sceptical of the use of general rules in his ethics, Aristotle is famous for his high esteem of the law in his ideal *polis*. It is remarkable, however, that when at one point he compares the effect of the law and of habit, he claims that habit has much stronger effects: 'The law has no power to secure obedience except habit; but habits can only be developed over a long period of time.'[10] The city state can only ensure that it will be run by practically wise leaders in the long run if proper habituation of its citizens is guaranteed. Habituation can lead citizens to act virtuously for their own sake, simply because it gives them pleasure to do so, and it is only the virtuous statesmen who can hope to govern their city as we expect from a *phronimos*.

But how do social customs come into the picture? Aristotle stresses that habits build up a certain political and constitutional climate, in other words, a political tradition. This tradition is a constant point of reference in Aristotle's descriptions, as when certain institutions, for example, the Athenian Boule, are legitimized by their roots in tradition. Greek law was much less developed than Roman law, and it was not so systematically recorded in written form as was the case in Roman law with the Roman law collections. Tradition, therefore, had an unrivalled significance in that social context. Tradition kept its significance in constitutional discourse in modern times, too, in countries such as Britain, and in the Hungarian Kingdom, where a historical constitution instead of a statutory one was cherished. In these cases, the unwritten constitution meant and means not much more but the rule of tradition. Aristotle, too, referred to the ancestral constitution in his historically rooted investigation into the institutional framework of the Athenian constitution: 'The peace terms specified that the Athenians should be governed by their ancestral constitution.'[11] British constitutional discourse kept the concept of the ancient constitution up until the end of the Enlightenment in the late eighteenth century. This overlap between the Aristotelian vocabulary and what can be regarded as the prehistory of British conservatism might have played its part in the birth of a political Aristotelianism with a conservative bent. But, to finish this part of the summary of what is relevant for the present project in Aristotle's political thought, the following quote shows how the concept of tradition was used to legitimize an institution in the Aristotelian narrative: 'Homicide trials ... were to be conducted in accordance with traditional practice.'[12] In the present context, this statement means that tradition-based practice had priority over any innovations in Athenian criminal law, too.

Pericles as an example of the ideal *phronimos*

When explaining what exactly he means by the term *phronesis*, Aristotle provides only a short circuit explanation, by referring to an example of a statesman who is practising the virtue of *phronesis*. He claims that practical wisdom involves 'reason, a practical one, concerned with what is good or bad for a human being.'[13] This claim is underlined by a reference to 'Pericles and people of that sort', 'because they have a theoretical grasp on what is good for themselves and for human beings, and we think household managers and politicians are like that.'[14] It might sound a bit confusing that Pericles is mentioned here as one who has a theoretical grasp of something, but this is because of the teleology of Aristotle's conception of right action. But this theoretical side of Pericles's character is balanced by the stress on the fact that his reason is practical. In fact, practical wisdom seems to coincide in this description with practical reason, which is not surprising considering that *phronesis*, as we have seen, is an intellectual virtue for Aristotle.

To know what is good for man, in other words, to have practical reason is not to lose sight of the common good as the final aim of one's activity. For if that aim – in the case of politics, the aim of the common good – would be left out of the picture, instead of practical wisdom we would only have cunning or cleverness. In this context, cleverness (*deinotés*) is described as the ability to allow our decisions to hit the centre of a proposed target. But it does not help to decide if the target is the right one or not, it simply prepares the ground to act in a decisive and efficient way. The major difference between practical wisdom and cleverness is that the former points at a deliberately chosen aim, the good, while the latter does not consider the aim at all, it only wants to hit the target, no matter what it is. While this second ability can lead us astray, the first one would never do so, as 'it is impossible to be practically-wise without being good.'[15]

It is also remarkable that the *phronimos*, the person endowed with the virtue of *phronesis*, knows what is good both for himself and for the whole community. Here, we return to the Aristotelian continuity between ethics and politics: if someone is practically wise, he knows what is good for himself, but the same pattern works in the case of the statesman who knows what is good for the whole of the community. One should not be surprised at this similarity. We are aware, after all, of Aristotle's definition of the human being as a *zóon politikon*, in other words, a political animal: 'A human being is by nature a political animal.'[16] If so, his particular existence is embedded into that of the community.

Aristotle's reference to Pericles as the ideal *phronimos* does not mean that he liked him as a political leader. In fact, he found Pericles's populist democratic measures dubious, for, as he saw them, they eroded the traditional institutions of the *polis*. Aristotle specifically mentions in the *Constitution of Athens* that Pericles 'deprived the Areopagus of some of its powers'.[17] He also mentions that Pericles was paying for those who served in the *dikastéria* (jury courts), and this led (according to some, as Aristotle claims) to the decline of the quality of the *dikastai* (the ancient Greek term for judges), as well as to the 'beginning of the corruption of the *dikastai*'.[18] It is more remarkable, however, that even if Pericles was not Aristotle's favourite statesman, as far as his own political priorities were concerned, he did use him as the typical example regarded as practically wise by ordinary Athenians, who embodied the virtue of *phronesis*, as explained in the *Constitution of Athens*: 'Throughout the period of Pericles' ascendancy the state was run reasonably well.'[19] This choice of Aristotle is most probably due to the high esteem in which Pericles was held by ordinary Athenians even after his death. Aristotle, as we saw, relied heavily on what he regarded as common sense. He certainly had other favourites, including Solon, of whom he gave a favourable description, and for example Hippias, of whom he said: 'A natural politician and a wise man.'[20]

However, Aristotle's presentation of the practical wisdom of Pericles is not too specific and detailed, and therefore it cannot really serve as the example that explains the concept of *phronesis* itself. The relevant conclusion we can draw in this context of his reference to Pericles is that he indeed does not want to conceptually dissect the term *phronesis*, and rather leaves it in this opaque form, as that something which is embodied by Pericles.

But Aristotle's discussion allows us to take two further steps. First, his conceptual distinction between and comparison of knowing what is good for the individual and for the community invites us to present his views on the relationship of the individual to the community and vice versa. And second, in his description of another practically wise politician, Solon's political activity, Aristotle offers us his views on conflict, competition and cooperation within the *polis*. These issues – the relationship between the individual and his or her talent, and how to negotiate inner-city conflicts in order to foster cooperation – will be recurring themes in this book's analytical account of the prudential conservative paradigm.

Cicero's *prudentia*

Speech and deed for Cicero: The Roman political context

The basic difference between the viewpoint of Cicero and that of his Greek forerunners is that he was an active politician, trained in the actual battlefield of rhetoric and politics,[21] while the Greek philosophers, including Aristotle, reached political problems from their respective philosophical standpoints, that is to say, from the point of view of making and teaching philosophy. And this is a crucial difference in the context of the virtue of prudence, and more generally for conservatism, even if in ancient Athens making and teaching philosophy was not yet outside the realm of civic engagement, as it would be later, for example, in the medieval university, or at least when the modernized university model was established by Humboldt. Cicero, as one commentator characterized him, was no 'starry-eyed philosopher', but a 'clever and hard-headed politician with his feet planted firmly on the ground'.[22] He was and remained a statesman, a *rector rei publicae*, as he called himself, even when he wrote his theoretical pieces.[23] He used the term *rector* to describe the professional politician at his best (even if he took it as the standard to which his own achievements would be weighed), following once again a Platonic inspiration. In Plato, the ideal ruler of the *polis* is an expert, who has a special knowledge of the art of governing (*techne politike*), but who is most of all a morally excellent figure, whose elevated aim is to defend the interest of the citizens of his city. Cicero's *rector* is similarly an ideal type, who presents an example for the other citizens, and through that acquires a sort of *auctoritas*. He is skilful in governing, relies on his *prudentia* to hinder civil unrest and his most important task is to preserve the political community in the form it had when he took office. For Cicero, the *rector* is and remains an ideal, and though he refers to heroes of the Roman past by this name, he does not mention any names as examples of a *rector* from his own time.[24]

It is not often mentioned, but Cicero uses another term for a statesman, *politikos*, taken directly from Greek.[25] In Cicero's text, the sense of *politikos* can sometimes turn negative, when political praxis turns unprincipled and dishonest.[26] However, in most cases, it is not pejorative at all. On the contrary, it emphasizes the prudential dimension of politics. As in the Greek original, it recalls the connection between the political agent and his *polis*, it reminds one of the obligations of citizens and adds weight to the demand for citizen participation in routine civic affairs. But perhaps even more directly, it refers to hard cases, emergency situations and political crises, when the *politikos* is able to act efficiently with a cool head. More often, it relates to 'a person who takes extraordinary action in a time of political crisis'.[27] In other words, the real power of Cicero's *politikos* is visible when he has to act in an emergency situation.

By the time Cicero had finished his final works, he had been forced to leave the political arena. However, his writings are not devoid of certain political relevance. Although there are those who claim that his *Republic* is more a philosophical dialogue and less a political pamphlet, it is Cicero himself who reminds his correspondent in one of his letters that he chose to deal with past figures in his *Republic* 'to avoid giving offence in any quarter', which is interpreted by Zetzel as an explicit reference to the political engagement of the author.[28] There can hardly be any doubt that if someone took the top offices of the Roman Republic, when in retirement he simply writes philosophical pieces, he remains to a certain extent still politically active. The more so that Cicero was known as the best rhetor of his time, which meant that people were aware of his abilities to raise even political passions by his words. It is at this point, and connected to Cicero, that an important topic of this book needs to be addressed, which is the fact that speech and act in politics come so close to each other that in a number of cases they grow together, as if they belonged to the same field of human behaviour. When politicians give speeches, they might have a very direct aim in mind that they want to achieve with their talk. And vice versa: political acts can be so expressive that they turn out to have a communicative power as well. In other words, utterances, such as speeches addressed to particular audiences and even informal conversations when they result in certain acts (such as shaking hands or signing treaties), should be regarded as speech acts. Even the texts we have inherited from earlier ages can preserve their communicative power, and they let us understand them better, if we reconstruct the political environment and climate in which they were born.

This is an important issue for our story: the fact that Cicero was both a rhetor and a statesman calls attention to the connections between his political words and his political actions. Certainly, already in ancient Athens, orators were looked on with deep suspicion by philosophers. Plato criticized the Sophists when they raised passions regardless of principles and values, for political reasons. In ancient republican regimes in general, orators or – as they were called – demagogues had very important public functions, and those who could speak obtained power, while in these face-to-face political cultures no power could have been exercised if not supported with the power of words. One can hardly resist the suspicion that Cicero's own political predicament made him sensitive to the issue 'whether anything can be accomplished by words rather than deeds'.[29] The issue was pressing for Cicero, who was generally considered as the most able public rhetor in Rome of his time. And yet, after his dismissal from the political arena, he became hesitant, and started doubting the efficiency of words. Cicero admitted: 'In this time of trouble for the state, would that it was possible for me to devote my energies to and accomplish the work of a *politikos*.'[30] To put it differently, he had to realize that he had failed the test of being a *politikos*. And still, it is indeed remarkable that he examined his own output by examining his words and deeds together.

If Cicero predominantly lived an active life both as a successful public orator and as a politician, the political circumstances may have played a major role in his intellectual development and in the form his philosophical agenda took shape. As we saw, he was aware of the political implications of his words and that politics is, to a large extent, pursued by words. If we want to interpret his words properly, we have to take into account their political context and try to understand them as directly related to the political circumstances, or sometimes even as deeds in political interaction. In this sense, he is closer to Socrates talking to an audience in the agora, than to the role of the speculative philosopher, exemplified by Plato.

Let us see the main political challenges Cicero had to confront. Cicero had a very strong ambition to excel and be glorious. His character and education did not predestine him for military service, even if as a youngster he had tasted camp life. Rather, he was to earn fame and political influence as a lawyer. Through one of his early orations, he made the dictator Sulla angry, requiring him to leave Rome and travel abroad. It was during this period of his life that Cicero deepened his knowledge of Greek life and language and Greek philosophy, rhetoric and religion in particular, making him the most influential bridge in his age between the cultures of Rome and Athens.

On his return, Cicero went through the routine offices of the *cursus honorum*, the usual path for eminent Romans who wanted to become leaders of the country. Coming from a non-noble and undistinguished family, who were not even of patrician standing, he was a *homo novus* and had to fight more to get the positions for which he dreamed. He was first a *quaestor* in Western Sicily, where the inhabitants turned out to be very grateful for his services. His accusation of Verres established his reputation in a wider circle. But coming from the *equites*, he was not accepted by the *optimates*, and therefore, even his cautious plans to reform the state while preserving its constitutional arrangement were doomed to fail. And yet, as far as his individual career was concerned, he achieved all the major posts: after being a *quaestor*, he became *curule aedile* at the age of thirty-seven, *praetor* at the age of forty and finally *consul* at the age of forty-three. In 63 BC, his court victory led to the execution of the Catilinarian conspirators, making him an outstanding popular leader, honoured with the title of *pater patriae*. Yet, without the support of any of the major factions, he could not achieve what he really wanted (moderate reforms), and instead incurred the hatred of a number of influential opponents. He appears to have committed a major tactical mistake in not accepting Julius Caesar's call in 61 BC to join a leadership group, with him, Pompey and Crassus, a judgement that would be easier to make today than in his day, because we know the consequences which, of course, Cicero did not at the time of his decision. This decision was determined by Cicero's fears that the republican era was over because of the authoritarian methods of Caesar. This was a rather stormy period, and most probably Cicero's mistake was a false judgement about his own political power. In 58 BC, once again he had to leave Rome because the leader of the *populares* introduced a law threatening exile to anyone who executed a Roman citizen without the necessary procedure – and Cicero did exactly that against the conspirators. He was well aware of the political causes that led to the legislative acts responsible for his exile, explaining it with 'the defection of Pompey, the hostility of the senators and judges, the timidity of equestrians, the armed bands of Clodius'.[31]

Although public support was raised in his favour, and Atticus and his own wife were also quite active in helping Cicero return, it was Pompey's invitation that brought him back to Rome, although neither Pompey nor the *optimates* gave him their full support. Even after his return, Cicero could not find a way to re-enter politics. In fact, he was soon forced to retire from public life. Still, he reluctantly supported Pompey, and was thus surprised with the news of Caesar's assassination. After the assassination, Cicero returned as *princeps senatus*, fighting the other strong man, Antony, who represented the case of Caesar. Unfortunately, Antony won over Octavian and Lepidus, and the three men formed the second triumvirate. Antony also convinced Octavian that Cicero, his long-time opponent, needed to be killed, prompting his murder in 43 BC.

Obviously, Cicero had quite a successful career, even if he was unable to save the republic and it ended on a tragic note. But the point we must keep in focus is that all his writings did not make him forget the public nature of his career, in which his writings usually played a strategic role. If he wrote a lot during his period of *otium*, his writing exercise was still linked closely to his political strategy. Words and deeds served the same ends.

Tradition, experience, education

At the time of the conception of his *Republic*, Cicero must have had the feeling that, in fact, partial and individualistic interests were threatening the republican regime of Rome. In a way, his writing was thus meant as an SOS, expressing his worries about the survival of the republic. Of course, the book could not directly attack those in power, the two remaining members of the first triumvirate, Caesar or Pompey. It is for this reason that the framework story of the *Republic* was pushed back in time. In this way, he could also introduce a very important topic: the significance of the past in a political regime, in other words, of tradition.

In accordance with the general practice, Cicero presents past heroes as real models, and as standards to which present leaders can be compared. In the lost fifth part of the *Republic*, according to Augustine, he recalls a line of the poet Ennius: 'The Roman state stands upon the morals and men of old.'[32] In other words, to honour the past, it is not enough to claim that the statesmen of the past were better. What needs to be shown is that their morality, too, excelled. And most importantly: we can and should learn not only from the deeds of the heroes of the past but also from their morals. His protagonists represent ancient republican values. The reader of Cicero's text could not avoid comparing the description of ancient morals and the men of the past with his own time's morals and men: 'Before our time, ancestral morality provided outstanding men, and great men preserved the morality of old and the institutions of our ancestors.'[33]

By creating this direct connection between public morals and individual achievements, Cicero wants to introduce a reference to communal traditions into the public discourse of his day. The idealized picture of the ancestral customs has both a critical impact and an edifying effect. By comparing the present with the past, Cicero wants to establish a necessary link between the two. In other words, he stresses that the present is dependent on the past. This is an undoubtedly conservative attitude much before the establishment of modern conservatism as an ideology. In the *Republic*'s – no doubt idealized – world, no individual talent or character can disregard the teachings and standard of the past. But, Cicero claims something stronger, as well. The tradition, in other words what is inherited from the past, what has been handed over by our fathers, needs to be updated to meet the demands of the day – it needs constant vigilance and updating.[34] In Cicero's judgement, this tradition was not cared for, renewed (*renovare*) or preserved, and this is the reason why political culture (*mores*) necessarily declined. Institutions do not operate on their own – they require the contribution of the virtuous statesmen, who preserve the morals of the past. 'Not cared for and followed, the ancient ways, even it seems the structure and mode of operation of the res publica, drop from sight and are no longer understood.'[35]

In order to keep a vigilant eye on tradition, the political community has to provide adequate education to its would-be citizens. What is required to fulfil this duty is a proper institutional form to hand over past experience to the new generation. As Cicero reports, Cato Major refers in this connection to the utility of education as 'the benefit of experience and the passage of time'.[36] In particular, education helps to give substance to the statesman's understanding and to lend form to his character. Taken together, understanding and character serve as the foundation of prudence. The prudent statesman, however, is characterized not only by his intellectual skills and knowledge of the nature of politics but also by his way of life, his defence of basic values and the moral standards of his political community. To form the character of the politician to achieve these excellences is the aim of the educational process, which has to take place in politics, and which is fostered by Cicero's own writings.

Honestum, decorum and *prudentia*

In addition to his views on politics, one should not disregard Cicero's moral philosophy. Cicero's views on human nature are complex. To use later distinctions, his view of human morality is neither rationalistic nor emotion based, as it is neither utilitarian nor deontological. Let us label it – for brevity's sake – as based on a kind of practical 'judgement of taste'.[37] This term is used here to refer to a view of the morally right action described in aesthetic terms: 'Overall virtue or right (*honestas*) is understood by Cicero as essentially propriety or appropriateness.'[38] By this definition of virtue as propriety (*decorum*), Cicero seems to imply an ideal of proportionality, which could be compared to the golden mean (*mesotes*) in Aristotle's practical philosophy. As there, here too, human action is compared to an arrow: its function is to hit the target. To do so, it needs to find the most streamlined form, the one that will lead straight to the desired aim. But, as shown already by Plato, it is very difficult for the human agent to hit the target with his action, because human passions easily distract our attention, and do not allow us to keep our attention focused to implement our plans.

In the context of finding the proper action in a given situation, the Ciceronian teachings on the use of rhetoric might be relevant. After all, it is in his rhetorical theory that Cicero refers to the relevance of raising human passions: in ancient rhetoric, non-philosopher audiences are less easily convinced through logical argumentation than by manipulating their desires and sentiments. In order to fuel the passions of his audience, the orator needs to tune into the wavelength of his listeners, and this means to be able to intuitively 'feel' the reactions of the audience.[39] While for Aristotle maintaining a sober mind during the process of deliberation in order to manipulate others is the role of the orator's virtue of moderation, Cicero has a special term for this function: *verecundia* (moral sensibility, feeling of shame). According to Nicgorski, it is a term for Cicero which is 'the basis and source for not only the specific virtue of temperance but also morality and right itself'.[40] It is an inner sense of rightness, as far as moral and aesthetic qualities are concerned, quite close to what will be called 'moral sense' in a much later age.[41] This latter is a term which – originally even for Kant – had a lot to do with the aesthetic capacity of taste, as it was worked out in the court culture of the medieval, Renaissance and early modern period. One should recall here Gadamer's teaching of the humanistic concepts of judgement and taste – the two connected to each other and both referring to one of the ancient and the Christian cardinal virtues, namely prudence. If it is a sense-like attribute, *verecundia* also connects the judgement of propriety to external standards, and more exactly, to the standards of nature. In other words, the fact that we have something like this moral sensibility even if we do not reflect on it, is in connection with this inner capacity which helps us to find what is proper. The act in accordance with *decus* means to act properly and vice versa. Before we have a concept of truth, we have a sense of truth, before we have a sense of 'sympathy',[42] we have an inner feeling of sympathy, because we sympathize with those who suffer. This is true because of our inner natural social capacity of *verecundia*.

Cicero seems to imply that we have two levels of relation to right and wrong. First there is a 'natural sense of right and wrong', and second, when we reflect on it consciously, the 'comprehensive right (*honestas*) or overall virtue'.[43] These two levels are in harmony with one another. The innate and the culturally polished are in tune with each other. The sphere of nature is in this sense parallel with the sphere of morality, even if in certain respects nature has priority. Notwithstanding, there is nothing rigid about its operation in Cicero's vision. On the contrary, values are 'determined with reference to human needs, wants, ordinary pleasures, practices, and traditions'.[44] Certainly, Cicero remains a natural law thinker, with no inclinations to become a philosophical relativist. Yet, he finds flexibility in determining right and wrong actions in particular situations rather important. In moral deliberation, what is required is the application of the general principles of human deeds in their particular contexts.

It is in connection with a flexible judgement of right and wrong that Cicero also arrives at the distinction between wisdom and prudence: 'The foremost of all virtues is wisdom – what the Greeks call *sophia*; for by prudence, which they call *phronesis*, we understand something else, namely, the practical knowledge of things to be sought for and of things to be avoided.'[45] Yet, the distinction is not used by him systematically: the two terms are close enough to each other and he, just like Plato, does not seem inclined to cut them away from each other, even if that was suggested by the Aristotelian tradition.

As with *honestum*, Cicero seems to distinguish two senses of the term 'prudence'. First, there is a general sense of the virtue of prudence, where it is one of the traditional excellences of a practically wise person, in the ordinary choices of his life. Nicgorski refers to Cicero's definition 'of prudence in general as excellence "in the choice of goods and evils", in knowing what is to be sought and what is to be avoided'.[46] But for us, here, it is more important to look at what he calls political prudence (*civilis prudentiae*). Cato defines it the following way: the essential element of it is 'to see the paths and turns of commonwealths, so that when you know in what direction any action tends, you can hold it back or anticipate it'.[47] As Nicgorski interprets it, the term means 'a quality of being able to discern political good and evil and choose the one and, thus, avoid the other'.[48] This can only be done if the prudent statesman is able to influence the others' actions to prevent certain political changes, thereby preserving, but if necessary, 'reforming and improving in a timely manner the existing political community'.[49] In other words, in civil prudence, Cicero's teachings of a moral sense applied to politics are connected with his teachings of the tradition-based wisdom of the community. In this sense, 'aesthetic' sensibility in moral decision-making is widened to include a kind of *sensus communis*, a common sense – not only of the community of which he is a member but also of humankind. In this way, an even wider circle is drawn – one that connects the individual through his community to nature, and right moral decisions both to the (positive) law of the community and to the natural law. This way, the prudent statesman is attuned to the norms established by the traditions of his community and through that, to the norms of humanity, or humaneness – even if it is left to our own judgement to tell which statesman is, after all, prudent, and which is not. The judgement of taste is based on a balance between the individual and his community. Yet, to establish a harmony between communal morals and the laws of nature will be the difficult lesson that Cicero bequeaths on Christian Europe, one that will be directly addressed both by medieval Christian moral theology and by early modern humanism.

Augustine's two cities

The two cities and the two sorts of prudence

While Rome and Athens had very different political cultures, no doubt, Christianity meant a radically new departure in the history of Western political thought, compared to the ancient world. The Christian teaching of the church was, for example, incompatible with the ancient conception of religious worship and communal religious bond. However, in certain respects the connection between ancient Rome and Christian Europe was much closer than between Rome and Athens – after all, Christian Europe imagined itself as a direct inheritor of the Roman Empire.

One of the most important bridges between these two cultures was the work of the bishop of Hippo, St Augustine. Augustine was 'very much a Roman of his times'.[50] Born on the peripheries of the realm, he had the fortune to live after Carthage in Rome, and after Rome in Milan, the seat of the emperor, he served as the municipal professor of rhetoric.[51] There, he had first-hand experience of how politics worked, and his reconversion to Christianity under the influence of Ambrose is interpreted as a reaction to it. His retirement can be interpreted as a choice of contemplative life in the Aristotelian sense, instead of struggling for worldly success. Yet, as a priest first, and later as bishop of Hippo, he was again responsible for a community, and this responsibility returned him to the *vita activa*. As an eyewitness to the fall of the empire, he perceived his main task as providing a spiritual shelter for its victims. By critically and self-critically commenting on the Sack of Rome by Alaric the Visigoth's troops in 410 BC, he was engaged in preparing the ground for the new kingdom, the Christian kingdom of God. It is in this context that we can make sense of his conceptual opposition between the earthly city and the City of God, published in his opus magnum, *De Civitate Dei*, written between 412 and 426 BC.

As a well-educated person and as a professor of rhetoric, Augustine constantly refers to Cicero and other thinkers of ancient Rome.[52] He is taking over some parts of their teaching of moral virtue. Nevertheless, as a Christian, he makes it clear that a believing Christian can only follow the teachings and example of Christ. Yet, given the fact that through the original sin of Adam and Eve, humankind has been expelled from Paradise, no one is actually able to follow Christ through his or her own will, without divine grace. In fact, human beings' fallen nature leads them to pursue individual self-interest, destructive passions, lust and the misuse of power – character traits which lead to the establishment of the earthly city, *civitas terrena*. Nevertheless, the mercy of God is expressed as a form of predestination, which helps certain individuals receive salvation, even if they are themselves sinners. These elected spirits, live or dead, join in the City of God, *civitas Dei*. Let us see how the two cities compare in Augustine's words: 'Two cities, then, have been created by two loves: that is, the earthly by love of self extending even to contempt of God, and the heavenly by love of God extending to contempt of self. The one, therefore, glories in itself, the other in the Lord.'[53]

Although humans' fallen nature does not allow them to save their own souls, Augustine thinks that human virtues are still useful among the conditions of the *civitas terrena*.

Parallel with his theology, in his ethics, more properly in his account of the virtues, Augustine works out two layers of human action. The early writings still rely on the Stoic views of Cicero on the virtues, and in particular on prudence: Augustine accepts that indeed prudence can choose between the good and the bad, and as a virtue it would never fail to do so.[54] But in his later theory, Augustine changes his position, due to his interpretation of Paul's Letter to the Romans 8:7. The King James Bible translates this sentence as follows: 'Because the carnal mind is enmity against God: for it is not subject to the law of God, neither indeed can be.' The Latin translation for carnal mind has here *prudentia carnis*, a mistranslation of the Greek original, but accepted by Augustine, so he requires a more nuanced interpretation than that provided by Cicero, to save prudence as a virtue. His solution is that *prudentia* can only choose correctly if the mind is set on God, in the sense of *consuetudo* or *habitus*, a set disposition. As Augustine interprets it, prudence is a neutral technique that can serve good or bad purposes, in the first case it is *prudentia spiritus*, in the second it is *prudentia carnis*. Only its right orientation towards God can guarantee good choice. As he puts it: 'For the usual definition of prudence is to seek good and avoid evil. Wherefore the Apostle rightly names it the "prudence of the flesh" when one seeks these lesser, transient goods instead of major ones.'[55]

In politics, again in harmony with his theology, instead of the heroic virtues of ancient Rome, Augustine advocates the Christian virtues, most importantly the virtues of avoiding violence and war. This is in the spirit of Christ, as established in the New Testament. Augustine does not want to work out direct political teachings. And yet, the conceptual distinction between the two paradigms of the city (with all the misunderstandings of later generations) had a tremendous impact on how politics was perceived in Christian Europe.

This is because what Augustine was doing – in accordance with the narrative of the Bible – by the distinction between the two cities was separating and intermingling the temporal and the eternal order at the same time. The separation is clear: no one can enter the City of God by his own will, while the earthly city will always remain the city of sin, because of the original sin. Even martyrs and saints are sinful, even if they are saved by grace. However, Augustine makes it clear that we all have our own responsibility, and this is even more true of leaders, no matter whether religious or temporal, who take responsibility for their community. Christianity has a lot to do in this sphere, according to the bishop of Hippo. As he puts it, churches are 'sacred lecture-halls for the peoples of the world'.[56] When he considers political problems, it is usually in his scattered writings, letters and sermons, and he always tries to solve particular cases. Augustine's procedure is to rely on the scripture to make sense of his own experience, and to rely on experience to interpret the scripture.[57] The scriptures 'offered broad guidelines' to help him decide individual issues, but there always remained 'room for discretion and for initiative'.[58] This is in accordance with the contemporary application of the law in the Roman Empire: 'The extent to which a law was promulgated and followed was partly up to the local governor and partly up to the initiative of the local communities.'[59] This method of decision-making guaranteed that his political thinking was 'not static, rigid or idealistic, but instead flexibly pragmatic'.[60] This Christian pragmatism came from Augustine's recognition that 'politics is indeed the art of the possible', leading him to a kind of political rationality that was 'neither utopian nor revolutionary'.[61] This fine balance in the application of a Christian ethics in matters political helps him to remain within the confines of realism, while his writings radiate the message that 'without an ethics grounded in faith and humility, political society, in his view, has little hope to offer'.[62] In other words, the combination of the gentle virtues, a non-destructive ethical demand and perseverance combined with a certain flexibility remains Augustine's main message for the later generations: 'In short, we dearly wish not to abandon Christian gentleness; but also to avoid leaving any destructive examples in the city for others to imitate.'[63]

While Cicero remained a constant reference point, certainly, Aristotle was not unknown to medieval authors. In addition to his works on logics and – thanks to the translation of Boethius – his *Categories* and *De Interpretatione*, from the twelfth century, further works of Aristotle came to be translated. By the time of the other towering Christian thinker of the Middle Ages, Aquinas attended a course on liberal arts and philosophy at the University of Naples, the natural philosophy of Aristotle was already part of the curriculum.[64] In Paris, the reception was a bit more problematic: it was only between 1252 and 1255, in other words when Aquinas as a young Dominican friar was studying theology there that the teaching of Aristotle was officially accepted. Universities were keen to embrace all earlier knowledge that was suitable for integration into a Christian curriculum of philosophy, including authors of Judaism and of an Islamic background.[65] However, the reception did not prove easy, as it required the reframing of contemporary science, which was founded on Platonic principles. Nevertheless, some of the best minds helped the reception, including Augustine, who wrote twelve commentaries on different works of Aristotle. Aquinas's master, Albert the Great was also keenly interested in the philosopher's work.

Aquinas dealt with different aspects of the Aristotelian corpus, but we will only refer to his works in the field of practical philosophy. One should make it explicit that besides the scripture and Augustine, Aristotle is the author most often referred to by Aquinas. For our purposes, the *Nicomachean Ethics* is one of the most relevant works in Aquinas's reception of Aristotle. This work was commented and/or translated by Robert Kilwardby, Robert Grosseteste and Albert the Great as well. The *Super Ethica*, a lecture series by the last author, was important for Aquinas's own reading of Aristotle. As Albert saw it, in accordance with Aristotle, 'the happiness natural to man is that coming from life in society'.[66] Albert's realistic interpretation of Aristotle denies that the human intellect would be ready to exercise divine contemplation. For that, no less than a theophany is required, and that is not something the human mind could achieve on its own. Nevertheless, 'by the habitus of wisdom the human intellect is prepared for philosophical contemplation'.[67] In addition to forms of contemplation, he also talks about a third, even lower level of happiness, civil happiness, the source of which is nothing else but prudence in Albert's scheme.

As we will see, Aquinas does not fully agree with the views of his master at this point. In his value hierarchy, contemplation as such remains the top value. But he seems to accept Albert's important claim, according to which prudence has a further role, that of 'perfecting the order given by natural reason'.[68] In order to see how these elements fit together in Aquinas's philosophical structure, I provide a short overview of some of the most important points of his practical philosophy, from the perspective of the present investigation.

Aquinas's politics of virtue

Aquinas on the natural sociability of man

Just like Aristotle, and not independently from him, Aquinas very explicitly pronounces his thesis about the natural sociability of man. He claims: 'Man is by nature ... a social and political animal, living amid a multitude of his kind, more so, indeed, than is the case with all other animals.'[69] This is the command of nature, in other words, of the world of necessity. The natural logic behind the command is that this world is not habitable for a single man, as all alone he 'could not sufficiently make his way through life. It is, therefore, natural for man that he live in the companionship of many of his kind.'[70] Aquinas convincingly argues that other animals are equipped with the necessary armament to earn their living, and defend themselves by them. Human beings, however, have no such obvious weapons, such as strong teeth, horns or claws, they are neither fast nor eagle-eyed. This is why for them to be together with others is of vital importance. Together, they can solve problems that alone most of them would not be able to do. As evolutionary biologists would put it, sociability is a condition for human survival.

In other words, sociability in Aquinas's vocabulary is not a kind of romantic feeling, nor the formal rhetorical exercise of the humanist. Rather, for Aquinas it means an ability to think, feel and act together with the others, thereby enabling the whole group and its members to survive.

Cooperation is vitally important for humans, which is exactly why they become sociable creatures. The fact that they are able to do what they are required to do is connected to their special capacity to think rationally and to communicate effectively.

Kinds of prudence (personal, domestic, political and regnative prudence)

To rule a community is, in an important way, similar to ruling oneself. Both are made possible by the practical use of reason, that is to say, by practical reason. In this respect, Aquinas refers to Aristotle when he writes that 'political prudence and prudence are the same habit, but their essence is not the same'.[71] There is no room here to elaborate on the Thomistic notion of *habitus*. Let it suffice to quote the following summary: 'We are always creatures of habit, either good or bad. Nature inclines us toward good habits, but it is not without our own efforts, the promptings of our parents, and the precepts of the law that we are able to acquire the proper habitual disposition.'[72] For our present purposes, it is more important to concentrate on the different layers of the term 'prudence' in Aquinas. Let us, therefore, first of all, see how Aquinas distinguishes the three levels of prudence: the personal, the domestic and the political level, as far as their communal effects are concerned: 'Prudence simply so-called, which is directed to one's own good; another, domestic prudence, which is directed to the common good of the home; a third, political prudence, which is directed to the common good of the political community or kingdom.'[73]

These three levels of prudence belong to three different scales of human community. The minimal size of a community is the individual taking care of his or her own interest. This is labelled personal prudence. Yet, as we have seen, this scale is only given logically for Aquinas, in real terms the individual is already born into a community. The medium level is, therefore, the family, while the third level is the perfect political community. While the family's level is that of domestic economy, prudence is only properly called political prudence when it 'is directed to the common good of the political community or kingdom.'[74]

In connection with these layers, the following two remarks are made. First of all, Aquinas is dealing here with what was important for Aristotle, too: the right size or scale of the perfect community. The Greek thinker has already built on the natural linear development of the community, from family, to village, to *polis*. In fact, Aquinas, too, seems to rely on this sort of levelling. Also, his categories resemble Aristotle's original division of practical philosophy: ethics dealing with the right action of the individual, economics with the good of the household, while politics relates to the good of the perfect political community.

Secondly, we should note that for Aquinas, too, personal prudence is closely tied to political prudence, while at the same time they are also clearly distinguished. He refers to Aristotle: 'It belongs to a good man to be able to rule well and to obey well.'[75] This is the view, that to be virtuous, one needs to have experience of ruling and being ruled. Yet being ruled is the state of a good man, while it is the specific virtue of the citizen to know both sides of ruling and being ruled. Further, the ruler, who in Aristotle's *Politics* also had to experience what it means to be ruled by a ruler in order to learn how to rule, in Aquinas acquires a specific form of prudence: political prudence – this way St Thomas seems to consider the meaning of differentiating between the virtue of the citizen and that of the ruler: 'The virtue of the ruler and that of the subject differ specifically.'[76] This seems to be a slight shift from the more community-based (today we would call it, with Cicero's term, more republican) approach of Aristotle to the more monarchic view of Aquinas. Although Aquinas does not talk about empires, he surely had to provide a theory for the medieval kingdoms – a form of political community quite distant from Aristotle's *polis*. Interestingly, for Aquinas a complete community is achieved by a city and even more, by a province, which means that he does not apply the term only to a large kingdom, according to the medieval practice. And yet a perfect community, even if it is only a city or a province, requires in his view a proper ruler: 'He who rules a complete community that is, a city or a province, is justly termed king.'[77] This is not a fundamental difference between Aristotle and Aquinas: after all, monarchy is the perfect form of rule in Aristotle, too. Rather, the shift from the tripartite system of good person, good citizen, good ruler to a duality of being ruled and to rule expresses a different political reality in the background, a shift from the *polis* system to that of the medieval kingdom. As opposed to the face-to-face community of the *polis*, the medieval kingdom is less dependent on the interpersonal relationships of its citizens, and more on the loyalty and obedience of its subjects to the ruler, and on the wisdom and moderation of the ruler. The bipolar system of political prudence in Aquinas is based on the distinction between what he calls the superiority of the ruler's prudence over the political prudence of subjects, which has the aim to help subjects 'so that they may direct themselves in obeying their superiors'.[78] Political prudence is also juxtaposed with prudence, commonly so-called by Aquinas. The difference between the two is that ordinary prudence serves the person's 'own good', while 'by political prudence ... he directs himself in relation to the common good'.[79]

As Aristotle, so Aquinas, too, finds monarchy the most perfect form of government. But this does not mean that his individual ruler should not experience external as well as internal barriers. On the contrary, he considers both external and internal barriers for his ideal individual ruler – a major achievement of his political theory. Externally, the community has responsibility to do whatever they can to prevent the ruler from becoming a tyrant: 'The community ought to provide that certain circumstances should be prevented, so that a king will not become a tyrant.'[80] What Aquinas means by this is no less than an institutionalized guarantee against tyranny – a kind of constitutional safeguard. As he later puts it: 'The government of a kingdom must be arranged so that there is no opportunity given for a king who has been instituted to act as tyrant.'[81] This institutionalized control, however, is supported by an internalized inner control mechanism, namely by the virtue of the ruler. In other words, according to Aquinas, whoever has the potential to become a ruler, should by that time receive an education, which aims to prepare him for the job, by perfecting his character. This is necessary in order to ensure that whoever takes the job, should indeed be able to do the job: 'It is necessary that whoever is elevated to the rank of king ... have the kind of character that makes it unlikely that he would stoop to tyranny.'[82] In spite of his firm belief in the use of institutionalized constraints, Aquinas seems to be more trusting of the internalized control mechanism – in accordance with the ancient teachings of virtue. In particular, in this context he seems to focus on the cardinal virtues and, besides prudence, especially on the virtue of moderation. The reason behind this choice is that he regards tyrannical rule as a kind of deviation from the norm, a product and a further cause of a kind of feverish, sick spiritual state, which is caused by disproportionate attention to private interest, itself an excess.[83] As for Aristotle, for Aquinas, too, the ruler needs to keep the balance between two extremes in every political situation. There is an obvious inclination in human nature that leads rulers to concentrate power in their own hands. This is an excess, that is to say, a failing on someone's part to keep the right balance. In politics, because of this natural inclination, rulers have to struggle hard in order to avoid both pitfalls. Moderation, therefore, operates like an inbuilt mechanism of self-constraint, to keep one's excessive tendencies under control. Compared to the other three cardinal virtues, which demand action, this is a negative one – in this case, the subjects are expected not to do certain things, to avoid giving in to the natural inclination to concentrate too much power in their hands. According to Aquinas's account of it, moderation is a more reliable obstacle to shift from legitimate to unlawful rule than any of the institutionalized safeguards. Which does not mean that one of the two could or should take over the other one's role and function. On the contrary, Aquinas seems to be keen to preserve the dual structure of the state's defensive system. For him, institutions are almost as necessary tools as the excellence of character, also implied in this text, to hinder unlawful activity. But there can be no doubt that his priority is Plato's and Aristotle's virtue ethical approach, which allowed them to give a nuanced picture of human nature and its positive and negative inclinations.

If virtues, and prudence and moderation in particular, might serve to control the excesses of those in power, it is crucial to see the specific virtue of prudence characteristic of rulers. Here, again, Aquinas starts out from a claim by Aristotle suggesting that 'prudence is a virtue which is proper to the prince',[84] which is to say that prudence has specific traits when they are exercised by princes. This is what Aquinas calls regnative prudence, which is the excellence acquired by a ruler in order to be able to rule without excesses. Although governing and command are parts of prudence in all its forms, whenever prudence belongs to the ruler who rules the perfect community, this element of command and governing is more pronounced than in any other forms of its exercise. Therefore, if an individual rules a city or other forms of a perfect community, he needs to have this specific form of prudence, according to Aquinas: 'Prudence in its special and most perfect sense, belongs to a king who is charged with the government of a city or kingdom: for which reason a species of prudence is reckoned to be regnative.'[85] Once we realize that for Aquinas prudence itself has the function to control excesses, we can understand that the specific type of regnative prudence is not an allowance of the ruler to commit evil deeds, but a stricter regime controlling the behaviour of the ruler, exactly because, compared to others, he has got more power over more people's fate. Viewed from this perspective, one can claim that although Aquinas is apparently in favour of the individual ruler as opposed to other forms of constitutional regimes, and though he does not fully trust the control power of legal norms, he is aware of the temptations of power to corrupt human beings' judgement when they exercise princely power, and therefore he demands a stricter regime of prudence to prevail in the character of a princely ruler. In other words, prudence in Aquinas's system is not widening the latitude of the ruler; on the contrary, it operates as an inbuilt control mechanism over the nature and character of the ruler, just like moderation. That is to say, Aquinas presents both prudence and moderation as keys to a virtuous princely rule.

2

Renaissance and early modern *prudentia*

In Chapter 1, we saw the development of the discourse of prudence in the ancient Greek, Roman and medieval European context. First, we recollected how Aristotle established the specific intellectual (and partly moral) virtue of *phronesis*, based on the earlier, but not yet fully terminologically conscious use of the term by Plato. In Aristotle's system of practical philosophy, ethics is closely linked to politics, which makes it understandable why his notion of *phronesis* is partly an individual's intellectual excellence, partly a political and moral virtue. The second phase in the narrative in Chapter 1 touched upon the virtue of prudence as discussed by Cicero at the moment when the Roman republic gave way to Ceasarism. The fact that Cicero wrote in the last moments of the republic in a way resembles Aristotle's late celebration of the *phronetic* Athenian *zoon politikon*, as exemplified by Pericles (even if he was critical of some of Pericles's activity). Aristotle's own position is made the more ironical by the fact that he was the private tutor to Alexander the Great, the would-be emperor of the Macedonian Empire. As was pointed out, the Greek and Roman discourse has important dissimilarities, but the claim was made that *phronesis* and prudence can be seen as belonging to one common way of explaining the practical (and moral) worth of a political agent as opposed to abstract accounts of the ideal state, like that of Plato in the *Republic*.

After the ancient contexts, a third context was medieval European philosophy, as exemplified by Augustine and Aquinas, and their appropriation of Cicero and Aristotle, respectively. While Augustine was still closely linked to the ancient Roman Empire and therefore rooted in its culture, compared to Aristotle and Cicero, St Thomas represented a characteristically different way of thought. His philosophy was fully determined by a Christian theological background, and expressed in a rather peculiar form, later referred to as scholasticism. Opposed to Aristotle, Cicero and partly Augustine, who had a direct interest in or at least a connection to politics, Aquinas was and remained a university professor of theology and philosophy at a medieval university. It is also relevant that his political experience was not that of a citizen of a free *polis* or of a republic, but that of a subject of a medieval kingdom, as well as a protagonist of a Europe-wide institutional system, the church and its academic network. In spite of his own, rather divergent political experiences, he was quite fascinated by Aristotle's practical philosophy of the *polis* and made a good job of integrating Aristotle's legacy into the Christian world view.

The next step is an overview of the humanist recapitulation of the prudential paradigm. As we will see, it was the achievement of – mostly Italian – humanists to integrate the three different episodes (Greek, Roman and Christian) into one overall scheme. And even more importantly, they gave it a sharp edge, which made the teaching politically relevant, too.

The Italian city states

As a preparatory note to set the stage for the Italian theoreticians of prudence, let us recall that the medieval tradition separated Aristotle's teaching of ethics and politics, transmitted by Aquinas and his pupils and taught at the universities by serious professors, from the Ciceronian tradition, which played a more important role in the professional training programmes of *dictatores*, those teachers who taught rhetoric to lawyers and notaries.[1] This latter tradition proved vital for the daily activity of magistrates and leading political elites of the Italian city states, emerging from the medieval political and legal entity of the *comune*. The notaries and other magistrates with a humanistic educational background were responsible for the creation of the characteristic cultural climate of these urban communities. But this sphere of activity, defined by a combination of public service and a recycling of the intellectual heritage of republican Rome, was clearly separated from the world of the university professors, who dedicated their lives to pure intellectual reflection and to presenting their findings to their colleagues and students, without the intention of directly interfering in the public affairs of the city or the state. The way of life of the academic teachers was meant to resemble more the reclusive life of the Christian hermits or monks, while humanists were expected to lead the life of courtiers or the *vita activa* of city magistrates, as the term 'civic humanism', introduced by Hans Baron, was meant to imply.[2]

If we focus on the Italian Peninsula, and more particularly, on the medieval political entity of the Italian city state, we see that it was understood as a commune, a social, economic, political and legal entity of a political community (*communitas*), constructed in order to provide public or common shelter for its members against external threats, including powerful lords, ordinary bandits or bishops and other powerful protagonists of the age.[3] With time, thanks to a trial-and-error learning process, these communities learnt how to organize their lives as self-regulating units, providing their citizens with not only powerful city walls to defend themselves but also certain individual, professional or commercial liberties and privileges, creating an environment for a specifically urban way of life.

From this foundational spontaneous development of self-rule in the early Renaissance grew the cultural practice of the humanists, a group of intellectuals who were not secluded scholars but were engaged in public affairs while concurrently cultivating their intellectual capacities. To show how political engagement and cultural activity were combined in the life pattern of Italian civic humanists, let us concentrate on the Florentine experience.

It was only in the fifteenth century that humanists decided to cross the Rubicon and challenge the knowledge privileges of university professors. To achieve this aim, they appropriated Aristotle for their own purposes. It is at this point that the first hero of this chapter goes on stage, the Florentine humanist and chief magistrate, Leonardo Bruni.

However, to understand the relationship between culture and political engagement among Florentine humanists, one should start out from the example of the founder of that tradition, the chancellor of Republican Florence between 1375 and 1406, Coluccio Salutati (1331–1406). Not an academic scholar, but 'trained in the *ars notaria*', and inspired by the Petrarcan 'humanistic politics of virtue',[4] it was Salutati who first presented proof that humanistic letters could be used as weapons. In his missive letters circulated during the time of the War of the Eight Saints against the pope, his was a personal 'war fought on paper'.[5] In these letters, he worked out the basis for an original Florentine cultural-political 'ideology', relying on the earlier ideology of the ancient Roman republic as well as on the medieval concept of liberty, as it was worked out by people such as John of Salisbury or Ptolemy of Lucca. By applying his erudition to the affairs of the city, Salutati indirectly already argued that humanistic science could turn towards human affairs, including what was labelled by Aristotle as ethics and politics. This suggestion seems to be a Ciceronian criticism of medieval metaphysics in Salutati's programme, one which was directly influenced by Petrarch, his basic source of inspiration. This practical philosophical turn was paralleled by his insistence that it is human will, and not the intellect, which is primarily responsible for human action, as opposed to what medieval Aristotelians supposed. According to the interpretation of Hankins, this change in emphasis was connected with his preference for the active life of the magistrate above that of the contemplative life of the scholar.

Importantly, as he grew older, Salutati the thinker also grew more conservative. Instead of his earlier insistence on the concept of liberty, he turned in his later writings towards the notion of the 'common good', which was to be pursued no matter the actual constitutional regime of the city. In this respect, he came to value the active virtues of political protagonists more, and downgraded (although he did not fully neglect) the significance of institutional safeguards. His practical bent taught him that abstract principles or general claims in politics are not always reliable. Instead, he emphasized the relevance of 'prudence, legality and the common welfare'.[6] A pragmatic, consequentialist approach to political activity became important for him. As he saw it in his later years, hardly any political act can be justified if it leads to armed conflict or even civil war. If the results of one's actions are worse than the state of affairs looked like earlier, than those actions are, most of the time, illegitimate. In other words, he prepared the ground for a more consequentialist version of ethics and politics, bridging the gap between Aristotelianism and Machiavelli's innovations.

If Salutati made good use of the two European pasts, both that of the ancient and of the medieval tradition, his disciple, Leonardo Bruni (1370–1444) became the archetype of the humanist combination of the learned scholar and a man of action.[7] He was famously regarded by Hans Baron as the first civic humanist.[8] He studied law, which was one of the quickest ways to get introduced into the world of city management. It was his father figure and patron, Salutati, who supported Bruni's rapid move up the ladder of the city's bureaucratic hierarchy. He was appointed chancellor of Florence in 1427, a position he kept until the day of his death. Bruni came from a non-noble family; therefore, as far as his social standing was concerned, he was comparable to

Cicero. He, too, finished his political career with writings, which made him even more famous than his political achievements.

From our point of view, however, Bruni's relevance is because he was one of the first humanists who actually learnt ancient Greek, and translated a number of works from Greek. In this way, he became an influential figure of cultural transmission: he could connect the separate phases of the European cultural tradition, the Greek and the Roman experience.

If Salutati represented a cautious defence of republican ideals in the medieval urban context, which shifted towards a conservative–pragmatic position by the end of his career, Bruni's own position was aristocratic and meritocratic, to a certain extent elitist from the beginning. He was not at all such a devout believer in a democratic kind of self-rule as Baron or Arendt's account of civic humanism would imply.[9]

Bruni was fully supported by his forerunner, Salutati, who recommended him to Pope Innocent VII, after which he had the opportunity to serve under and in the court of four different popes. In 1415, by the time he had withdrawn from the high office he had earlier gained in the papal court, he could afford to lead the life of a 'retired literary gentleman'.[10] Following the example of Cicero, who also used the occasion of losing his latitude in politics to turn to writing, he translated Aristotle's *Ethics* and wrote historical pieces and treatises too. Yet, a second return to political involvement came with his appointment to the position of the chancellor of Florence in 1427. In 1436, he became eligible to holding major offices in the city, making him one of the key decision-making magistrates of the city. As Hankins puts it, 'Bruni was thus, like his model Cicero, a man of letters and a *novus homo* (not a member of an ancient Florentine family) who ended his career as a wealthy and influential statesman.'[11] He published a number of significant contributions to the Italian humanist movement. First of all, his translation into Latin of Aristotle's *Ethics* and *Politics* – which was only possible after Bruni learnt ancient Greek with the help of the famous Greek *émigré*, Manuel Chrysoloras, invited to Italy by Salutati. Also, his great history of Florence, which contributed to creating the myth of Florence as the cultural capital of the continent, was exceptionally useful for his city.

As is obvious from this short sketch of some of the main points of Bruni's political and intellectual achievements, he had indeed risen high in both spheres. In other words, both in *vita activa* and *vita contemplative*, he proved his prowess. Our major concern here is, however, how the two interacted in his actual practice – dedicated to accommodating Aristotle and Cicero within the humanist discourse. To see this, we look at the English translation of his early Latin panegyric, *Laudatio florentinae urbis*, most probably produced in 1403–4 (according to Hans Baron). In this piece, 'Bruni works together the translation of Aristotelian praxis into a Ciceronian description of *decorum* with Greek civic panegyric – Isocrates' *Panegyricus* and, in particular, Aristides' *Panathenaic Oration*'.[12] As Hankins characterizes the work, in it the author 'paints Florence as a competitive meritocracy where the virtuous and well-educated rule and vie for honor'.[13] Most importantly, however, for our present purposes, a constant phrase in this work is 'prudence', understood here as a virtue responsible for the famous, well-educated, cultivated and elegant Florentine manner.

In Chapter 1, the citizenry of the city was characterized as 'these citizens surpass the rest of mankind in talent, prudence, glory and grandeur'.[14] Glory and grandeur were obviously part of the Roman republican discourse, but talent and prudence were not so obviously combined. As the point of the term is not necessarily clear in this sentence, the oration clarifies its meaning: 'First – and this is a sign of great prudence – we observe that Florence takes care not to display any outward show. She rather follows the rules of balance and measure than those of foolish and dangerous capriciousness.'[15] There are at least two elements of this explanation worth further reflection. On the one hand, it shows that prudence is closely linked to the Ciceronian notion of *decorum* in Bruni's oration. As the golden mean for Aristotle, apparently it is both a moral category and an aesthetic value. This prudence helps Florence and by it 'she keeps the middle'.[16] A rhetorical tour de force helps to visualize this middle-of-the-road mentality, when it refers to the geographic location of the city by a symbolic use of language 'this city is very prudently located … in the middle between the extremes of fortune … and the dullness of the plains'.[17]

On the other hand, the explanation successfully reframes prudence to fit into the framework of the Roman republican discourse. Foolish capriciousness is easily associated with that sort of moral corruption and luxury-bound individualist view of life, the criticism of which was famously formulated by Cato the Elder in ancient Rome. Balance and measure in this respect is contrasted with disbalance and excess.

By returning to Cato's Roman discourse, virtue is once again in harmony with manliness: it is obvious that prudence cannot do without valour and courage. They are also connected, however, to 'strength of mind'. Apparently, wartime virtues play a prominent role in the everyday life of the Florentines: their walls express their willpower and determination to save their souls and body. But beauty and elegance still preserve their place in this lexicon. In other words, the masculine and the feminine dimension of the city's excellences do not exclude each other in this discourse.

As was mentioned, a Ciceronian inspiration is present throughout the oration. This is made obvious when the term 'virtue' comes up with the term 'humanity', in connection with 'the courage and humanity of the citizens'.[18] The Latin terms used here were *virtus* and *humanitas*, and, of course, *humanitas* is important not only as one that has been popularized by Cicero in *De Officiis* but also as the core idea of the movement, called humanism, of which Bruni is becoming one of the earliest but paradigmatic examples.[19]

We do not have space here to analyse all the relevant points of Bruni's paper, including his arguments against locating one's city near the sea. His criticism of seaport cities had its forerunner in earlier debates of the ideal city, including the corrupting influences of the seaports on the morality of the citizenry, for example in the case of Athens. Bruni's position is clear when stating: 'A prudent community avoids the ports in favor of the harbor of rest, and … it rather abstains from the changing tides, than to subject herself to it.'[20] The interesting thing is that here individual virtue is applied to describe communal achievements – in this sense, the city becomes a particularized agent, a body.[21] This identification of the individual and the city is made possible by Roman law, which took bodies as particular legal entities. Yet, Bruni adds to this identification of individual and public virtues that public virtue depends on the virtues of the individuals who build up the community. Florence is fortunate, as its people can trace back their origins to the Romans: 'Learn, men of Florence, learn to know your root and kin!'[22] And why is that so urgent? The answer is straightforward: 'This city of Rome produced more examples of virtue than all other cities of all ages together.'[23] Interestingly, Roman virtue turns out to be mostly martial virtue: in the urban republican tradition, liberty depends on the capacity of the city to take up arms against potential or actual enemies and defend itself, or even to conquer new territories. And certainly wartime behaviour is by definition cruel – in this sense the fact of identifying virtue and military activity prepares the reader for a stronger claim than the simple identification of individual and communal interest. Bruni is ready to exempt public misdeeds – they 'are not of the same order as private crimes'.[24] This is a shift prefiguring the Machiavellian break with a morally founded politics, and pointing forward to the reinterpretation of *virtù* as power instead of moral excellence. It is not yet a definitive break with tradition in Bruni's case – rather, it is only the opening up of a new possibility. He himself withdraws from this possibility, claiming that Florence is still prudent in the ancient sense of the word: 'Where do you find so much benevolence as had been shown by our city?'[25] With benevolence comes 'charity and mildness'[26] as well – tuning down his own views, and returning with his discourse within the Christian moral framework. And that prepares the ground once again for the use of the term 'humanity'.[27] Yet, some elements are present even here, which will turn out to be crucial for Machiavelli, too: Bruni praises the energy of the city, its courage, its 'love for glory and fame',[28] and connects its prudence with its forceful decision-making potential. Yet, a combination of greatness and ethical behaviour is recovered: 'They do not only want to display great deeds, it is just as important to them to perform them ethically.'[29] In other words, his argument is culminating in the identification of prudence and justice. What is more, this return to an ethical politics is reaffirmed by Bruni's returning reference to aesthetic values – he associates the harmony of the sounds of orchestral musical instruments with the concord of the city. As harmony characterizes the cooperation of musicians, so balance is supposed to play its part in the ideal mechanics of city politics. Laws need to be laid down prudently, achieving 'a certain balance between the several classes'.[30] In the final paragraphs of the essay, Bruni is once again mixing moral and aesthetic values into his political account – just as he did at the beginning of it. With these phrases, Bruni is, in fact, suggesting that besides the hard power of the arms, in other words military virtues, the success of Florence is partly due to its soft power, 'scholarship' and 'commerce' just as much as 'the gentleness of speech', 'beautiful works of architecture' and 'elegance, luxurious lifestyle, wealth, people, wholesome climate, lovely surroundings'.[31] In this way, he is preparing a perception of the city that will play a crucial role in Burckhardt's famous narrative of the Renaissance Italian city as a work of art, and which is again underlining the point that prudential decision-making in Renaissance political thought is quite close to propriety and aesthetic judgement in the discourse on art and culture.

Machiavelli's revolution

If we want to assess the significance of the turn in the history of political thought initiated by Machiavelli's own understanding of the terms 'prudence' and 'virtue', it might be useful to recall three different scenarios in which his achievements were discussed in the literature on him. Let us start, therefore, with a short overview of Machiavellian prudence, and with asking the question how his performance looks in the contexts of Descartes, Baldassare Castiglione and Guicciardini.

The author of a short history of prudence written with a focus on the Machiavellian turn, Eugene Garver suggested that the novelty of Machiavelli's approach to politics and practical philosophy in general is comparable to that of Descartes in the field of theoretical reason.[32] Both of them introduced a new understanding of their subject matter, a paradigm shift, to use a Kuhnian term in a rather simplified way. However, while Descartes's breakthrough was almost immediate and final, Machiavelli's provocative ideas of prudential politics almost immediately came under heavy attack from all circles of the intellectual elite of late Renaissance Italy and Europe, and his legacy is less than dubious. But the comparison does not hold, as Garver points out, for a further reason. While Cartesian theoretical reason offers a clear account of what is achieved by this theoretical innovation, after all, scientific propositions are easy to test in an objective manner, the evaluation of the Machiavellian revision of the prudential paradigm is itself a matter of (more or less prudent) political and moral preferences. 'Prudential reasoning yields conclusions that are always open to further debate because it yields conclusions that are open to further action, and for that reason prudential reasoning will always appear a weak kind of reasoning measured against standards of theoretical reason.'[33] In this view, Garver relies on the Aristotelian understanding of ethics which always stressed that the conclusion of practical syllogisms is a decision about the right action. For Aristotle, to teach *phronesis* means to lead the audience to make the right practical decisions, where rightness depends on the particular circumstances of each and every particular actor and his or her political environment. Garver makes use of this Aristotelian point when he emphasizes that Machiavelli's *phronesis* does not provide general standards to test whether a prudent decision was the right one or not. As he sees it, prudential reasoning is 'halfway between an ethics of principles ... and an ethics of consequences, in which the successful result is all'.[34] Further on, he denies that Machiavellian prudence leads directly to relativism, and to an ethics of anything goes, arguing that there are 'rules applicable to prudence, but they are neither algorithmic, nor heuristic'.[35] As he explains it, prudential rules do not lead directly and faultlessly to the right results ('nothing assures that a prudential action will be correct'[36]). What prudence can achieve is that it 'positions the reasoner for further argument',[37] and it calls attention to the fact that moral and political decisions are not as simple and final as supporters of the algorithmic or heuristic understanding of practical wisdom would suggest.

Another context to fully appreciate the novelty of Machiavelli's understanding of prudence is provided by Victoria Kahn in her account of rhetoric, prudence and scepticism in the Renaissance.[38] Connecting her own interpretation of Machiavelli to Garver's account of the Florentine secretary's use of the concepts of virtue and prudence, Kahn compares Machiavelli's innovation to that of Castiglione. In her view, these two authors represent two different ways of deconstructing prudence. As she sees it, Castiglione succeeded in redefining prudence aesthetically while Machiavelli renewed the political meaning of the term. She is quite critical about both of these attempts: 'Castiglione and Machiavelli represent two versions of the disintegration of this synthesis.'[39] In Machiavelli's hand, as she sees it, 'prudence has become what its critics always feared it would: a technical skill divorced from ethical considerations'.[40] This transformation of ethical considerations into technical issues reminds Kahn of the criticism of Plato's Socrates against the Sophists: Machiavelli's prince is 'the sophist as portrayed by Plato: a master of dissimulation for the purposes of self-aggrandizement'.[41] It is more than telling that, at this point, Kahn's own vocabulary borrows from Castiglione's vocabulary, when he describes Machiavelli's views: dissimulation is part of the art of the courtier in Castiglione's tale – itself merged into the tradition of Boccaccio. But obviously, Kahn's real merit is to show that, in fact, both Castiglione and Machiavelli react on the Quattrocento discourse of the humanists 'proposing revised versions of prudential judgment: on the one hand (i.e. in Castiglione's vocabulary) *sprezzatura*, on the other (in Machiavelli's terminology) *virtù*'.[42] In both cases, she finds it a loss that the moral dimension had disappeared, in one case in favour of the aesthetic, in the other in favour of the political, which makes their views flat and artificial. In this criticism, as we will see in the next chapter, Kahn is following Gadamer's criticism, as worked out in his magnum opus *Truth and Method* – Kahn's reference to technique points in the same direction as Gadamer's criticism, itself inspired by Heidegger. Besides Gadamer, one could also refer here to Harvey Mansfield, who also explains Machiavelli's use of the concept of prudence as transforming it into technical knowledge or expertise: 'In representing prudence as art, in contradiction to Aristotle, he makes prudence morally neutral.'[43]

Finally, let us take a look at the influential comparison Pocock offers in his magisterial *Machiavellian Moment*.[44] Pocock compares Machiavelli to Guicciardini. This is of crucial relevance for our story, as we, too, will turn to Guicciardini after assessing the relevance of the Machiavellian revolution.

In Pocock's reading, Machiavelli's *Il Principe* is 'an analytic study of innovation and its consequences'.[45] As he sees it, if a political actor wants something new and novel, he disturbs the status quo, in other words, he destabilizes the regime. It is in this context of instability and disorder that fortune takes over the rule. The only chance for the 'new prince' to keep his newly acquired power is to mobilize his own virtue to gain control over fortune. It is important in this interpretation that Machiavelli disowns the traditional understanding of virtue and constructs his own concept of *virtù*. This concept means for him 'exceptional and extraordinary qualities … by which form was imposed on the matter of fortuna'.[46] In other words, according to Pocock, Machiavelli's main achievement is explaining the nature of 'delegitimized politics'.[47] As Pocock interprets him, Machiavelli connects innovation with fortune and virtue, thereby creating a conceptual triangle, where each of the three concepts is closely linked to the other two.

Pocock seems to be especially attentive to Machiavelli's conceptual manipulation. In particular, he highlights some of the conceptual pairings that are characteristic of Machiavelli's analytical language. The first pair was fortune and virtue, as we saw, and both of these terms were connected to innovation. While fortune is a power independent of the individual's own realm of influence, through the Machiavellian *virtù*, an innovative force, the proactive political agent can regain control over political events. Without this active power, the new prince is lost: in this way, Pocock points out that Machiavelli argues in favour of a close connection between *virtù* and innovation: 'The only constant semantic association is now that between *virtù* and innovation ... *virtù* is pre-eminently that by which the individual is rendered outstanding in the context of innovation and in the role of the innovator.'[48]

Machiavellian virtue is, however, also closely connected to Machiavelli's prudence (*prudenzia*).[49] In chapter 7 of *The Prince*, for example, Cesare Borgia is presented as prudent and virtuous (*prudente e virtuoso*).[50] In the ancient (Greek and Roman) and medieval (Christian) tradition, prudence (earlier *phronesis*), as we saw, was one of the key (cardinal) virtues, connected with virtuous politics. It is nothing new or surprising, therefore, to say that Machiavelli connects prudence to virtue. However, with his reinterpretation of virtue (in the form of *virtù*), the concept of prudence will also be reinterpreted. If *virtù* becomes a dynamic, manly, active principle, it is logical that compared to *virtù* prudence signifies a more passive ability. *Virtù* and *prudenzia* will stand in this context as audacity and caution. Obviously, as far as this conceptual pair is concerned, Machiavelli gives priority to *virtù*, and has a more critical approach to prudence: 'The cautious man, when it is time to act suddenly, does not know how to do so and is consequently ruined.'[51] In *The Prince*, Machiavelli concentrates on the new ruler who has to rely on his armed forces, because he has yet to establish his authority.[52] We know from Machiavelli's letters as secretary of the city state of Florence that he associated *virtù* more or less simply with military virtue, and this is surely a reference to the Roman understanding of (armed) civic virtue.[53] The history of Rome taught Florentines such as Machiavelli that as soon as the citizens forget about their traditional duty to defend the *patria*, their morals get corrupted and the *libertas* of the city is in danger.

However, in comparison with the ancient Roman understanding of civic virtues, Machiavelli is an innovator. While Roman virtue was based on what could be labelled the politics of tradition, Machiavelli's virtue is to be understood in the context of the politics of action and creation. If *The Prince* is about political innovation, it is about political chaos, which is caused by the simple appearance of the new prince: innovation brings chaos into politics. In other words, Machiavelli turns against the politics of tradition, which was the basis of Roman republican thinking, by his innovation to focus on the new prince instead of the legitimate one. It is in this context that Pocock distinguishes the politics of action, which first destructs and then constructs a new order by its own will power, by its own *virtù*, and the politics of tradition, which is based on a solid moral order.[54] It is at this point that Pocock's opposition between Machiavelli and Guicciardini becomes relevant.

In Pocock's historical narrative, Guicciardini represents that traditional moral order of Florence that is (to be) destroyed by the new prince. While Machiavelli is more or less a newcomer, Guicciardini belongs to that patriciate order, which governed Florence for centuries – no matter what exactly was the format of the actual political regime. This is why Guicciardini becomes the ideal type of prudential political leader, critical of the destructive consequences of the Machiavellian prince's way of exercising power. As Pocock reads him, 'Guicciardini since 1512 had been exploring the theoretical realm of Aristotelian polity and mixed government, and the less remote exemplary realm of the 1494 constitution and the Venetian model.'[55] In fact, Pocock uses the polar opposition between Machiavelli and Guicciardini, and presents his two heroes as embodying *virtù* and prudence, respectively. While Machiavelli seems to identify his own position in political philosophy with that of the *virtù* of the new prince, Guicciardini emerges as the arch-representative of the prudent (but legitimate) ruler. Naturally, Guicciardini is identified with the republican tradition, while Machiavelli's great breakthrough is with his book on non-republican, princely power, yet this is not the basic difference between their theoretical constructions. One of the main points Pocock makes is to differentiate between their respective conclusions drawn from their study of ancient Roman political history and the history of ancient Roman political thought. Machiavelli's original interpretation of these histories claimed that 'the disunion and strife among nobles and people was the cause of Rome's attaining liberty, stability, and power'.[56] These ideas went against Guicciardini's more traditional civic republican view, according to which union and stability (concord) is the guarantee of peace, stability and liberty, while faction leads to internal conflicts and the loss of common liberty. Machiavelli's further statement was that Rome's audacity encouraged that city 'to grow and establish an empire', while Sparta and Venice had the sole purpose 'to maintain its independence'.[57] While the active impetus of *virtù* plays a major role in Machiavelli's account of a successful but aggressive, externally imperial and internally conflict-generating Rome, Guicciardini still defends a concept of politics based on internal stability and external self-defence, which finds the safeguards of liberty in a mixed regime internally, and a peaceful if competitive and powerful coexistence externally.

This opposition, pointed out by Pocock between Machiavelli and Guicciardini, is quite relevant for our agenda. It helps us to show that prudential considerations do not need to lead to a negation of the ancient Greco–Roman and Christian European tradition of a morally sound political order. In its second part, this book considers the realist proposal that the innovations of Machiavelli could be integrated into this tradition without letting them disrupt the whole practical philosophical framework of Christian Aristotelianism. In what follows, Guicciardini is set forth as the proper answer to Machiavelli's challenge from within the Christian Aristotelian framework. He is shown to offer a conservative response to the pragmatic, but potentially disruptive challenge of Machiavelli.

Guicciardini's effort to save prudence

Although Guicciardini had not published anything in his life, and his fame cannot be compared to that of Machiavelli, soon after his death he was widely read in Europe as an accepted authority on questions of politics.[58] Yet, his views were not as scandalous as those of Machiavelli, and therefore his fame did not travel as far and as fast as that of his older compatriot. For us, today, the crucial issue is if and in what sense his position can be understood as an alternative to Machiavelli's radical views. This section will join this line of interpretation and with the help of his *Dialogue on the Government of Florence*, we will look at those efforts of Guicciardini that aimed at rescuing a richer and more tradition-based notion of prudence than the one Machiavelli opted for. This interpretation will rely once again on the analysis of Guicciardini by Pocock in his *Machiavellian Moment*.

Pocock starts out from a rather strong claim: that Guicciardini's 'greater concern with the actual and the practicable' is closely connected with 'his aristocratic conservatism'.[59] In Pocock's reading, Guicciardini in his own way – intellectually armed to the teeth – represents 'the *ottimati* as a politically experienced inner ring' in the government of Florence. This conservatism is in diametrical opposition with the starting point of Machiavelli's thought – after all, it is not based on the needs of the new prince. For him, the primary conceptual connection is not the one between virtue and innovation, but on the contrary, the one between experience (*esperienza*) and prudence (*prudenzia*).[60] According to Pocock, the *Dialogue* is based on this conceptual pair as its basic value. Three of the participants of the debate are younger *ottimati* (Capponi, Soderini and Piero Guicciardini), who came together to listen to an elderly man (Bernardo del Nero), who collected enough experience to share with them his own comments on the recent political situation. He has to judge the political situation of 1494, with its '*mutazione dello stato*'. Bernardo brings the typical conservative view that 'he has found by experience that all *mutazioni* are for the worse'.[61] Even though this might sound a bit simplistic and deterministic, later on Bernardo argues pragmatically and in a detailed fashion 'in favour of conservatism'.[62] The main insight here is that politics is always 'anchored in the concrete and the *particulare*', to which Guicciardini's hero adds that in the standard case the main aim of politics should be 'to ensure the conservation (*conservare*) of the rule of law and the common good'.[63] It is in this context that we can recall Machiavelli's enthusiasm for imperial Rome, while Guicciardini's examples are Sparta and Venice. Instead of an offensive strategy, he prefers a reserved, cautious manner of governance in a strong city. As Pocock points out, 'It is fascinating to observe how he moves in the opposite direction to Machiavelli when faced with the choice between audacity and prudence.'[64] His political agents are not characterized by their virtue, but more by their experience – and this latter can be collected only with spending much time in power, in other words, only by a long-standing elite. Experience helps to appreciate order and stability. Chance or fortune is not to be fought by power after they have taken control over events, rather preliminary measures are needed to exclude their rise: 'So it is necessary that the governors of states should be men of prudence, vigilantly attentive to the smallest accident, and weighing every possible consequence in order to obviate at the beginning, and eliminate as far as possible, the power of chance and fortune.'[65] So chance is not a major player in this framework, prudence (or foresight) has the function to prevent its takeover. Pocock goes as far as to claim that in Guicciardini's conceptual universe *virtù* itself is identified with prudence. It is in connection with this identification that he claims that Guicciardini's politics is a 'politics of maneuver rather than action'.[66] The temporal dimension becomes all-important (among other aspects, *tempo* and *occasione* are to be observed). By gaining time, the prudent actor gains latitude, space for manoeuvre, and it is more important for Guicciardini, the conservative, to rely on experience in handling crisis situations than abstract knowledge or 'innate intelligence'. Virtue is not identified in his conceptual world with power, the city is not such an aggressive political unit as it is in Machiavelli's theory. In fact, Guicciardini's city is disarmed (as opposed to the militarized vision of Rome), and less interested in military intervention and combat. The common good requires peace, stability and cooperation – but it also needs competition. It requires first-hand, practical knowledge of others, to learn the specific demands of particular political settings. This sort of local knowledge can only be attained by long-term experience. Guicciardini is even more particularist than Machiavelli, in this respect he is a follower of Aristotle who was ready to collect – according to tradition – the constitutions of 158 different city states. And when one reads in Guicciardini – almost like in Montesquieu – about 'the nature, the quality, the circumstances, the inclinations and, to express all these terms in a single word, the humours of the city and the citizens',[67] then his particularism brings his views of the determinants of a city close to our present-day concept of local political culture. And the same feature, together with his reliance on usage and tradition, can be easily associated with the customary foundations of politics in the conservative tradition.

One cautionary remark is needed at this point. This preference for stability and order, which characterized the attitude of Guicciardini in most of his writings, was lost by the time the final version of the *ricordi* had been prepared. By that time, his realistic approach to politics had lost all hope of maintaining the ideal balance of Aristotle, and he was unable to take part in governing the city by a mixed government, in accordance with the Ciceronian ideal. By then, his world was overrun by the improvisations of *fortuna*, proving that the world of politics is finally unpredictable. By the end of his life, he thought that the survival of the city states depended on the mercy of external powers, and that he lived already in a post-civic world. The only advice he can give to his readers is to adapt to the environment through prudence – and that the environment had more to do with the values of Machiavelli's *Principe* than with that of his *Dialogue*. It is at this junction that he reaches Machiavelli's separation of morality and politics, when he, too, advices that

> anyone who wants to hold dominions and states in this day and age should show mercy and kindness where possible, and where there is no other alternative, one must use cruelty and unscrupulousness ... because it is impossible to control governments and states, if one wants to hold them as they are held today, according to the precepts of Christian law.[68]

It is here that he gets closest to the concept of a new, specific and autonomous concept: reason of state. His spokesperson claims that it is impossible to live properly in this world as a Christian, and 'in order to talk realistically about things as they are in fact', 'I didn't perhaps talk as a Christian: I talked according to the reason and practice of states.'[69] As Richard Tuck points out, it was this disillusioned Guicciardini who 'had thus launched the principal term in the later political vocabulary, *ragion di stato*'.[70] In what follows, we will see how the term is related to prudence in the texts of some of the key authors of the next half-century.

Prudence and reason of state: Botero and early modern scholasticism

If Machiavelli broke the tradition of ancient and Christian prudence, Guicciardini's own works were interpreted as soon as they were spread in Europe as efforts to reconstruct that very tradition within a city (or civic) republican framework. However, as Tuck claims, in fact Guicciardini contributed to the birth of a new way of thinking and speaking about politics, in a new context – to the so-called reason of state discourse of the newly born territorial state of the sixteenth century. Guicciardini's efforts, however, were not yet pronounced within a framework of a Christian–non-Christian antagonism. It is usually attributed to Giovanni Botero (1544–1617) that an anti-Machiavellian effort was joined with a defence of Christian values, while still some of Machiavelli's points were preserved.

Botero was just as well versed in city and foreign politics as his Florentine predecessors. His practical experience was quite wide-ranging: besides spending years as a professor of rhetoric at Jesuit schools, he worked as secretary and counsellor to prelates and rulers, and could in this way collect numerous insights and fine details from the workshop of late Renaissance Italian real politics. His writings are not unconnected from these realms of experience: his three major works look at the political community from three different angles: the city (*On the Causes of the Greatness and Magnificence of Cities*, 1588), the (territorial) state (*The Reason of State*, 1589) and the empire (*The Universal Relations*, 1591–6). We neither have the space nor the time to discuss how the three works relate to each other (either logically or as far as the spiritual development of their author is concerned), but if we look at the titles of his main works, it is obvious that Botero is aware of the relevance of the Aristotelian problem of scale for the life of political communities. In what follows, we concentrate on his work *The Reason of State* because in it a crucial issue is the relationship between the new concept of reason of state and the more traditional term of prudence.[71] This analysis will be based on the assumption of Höpfl, that 'Botero and Ribadeneira clearly tended to equate reason of state with prudence, but it was not a deliberate strategy'.[72] This equation will be seen here as part of their more deliberate strategy to win back the newly fashionable term of reason of state for Catholic-Christian ways of thinking. Botero will be interpreted here with some of the Jesuit thinkers of his age in the background, as they were also interested in underpinning reason of state thinking with a more traditionally based theory of Christian virtues, and in particular with their own interpretation of the cardinal virtue of prudence as a form of knowledge and even more, as a moral quality.

In his dedication to the Archbishop and Prince of Salzburg[73] in *The Reason of State*, Botero explicitly refers to Machiavelli and Tacitus as the two authors who persuaded him to write this piece. He claims that during his journeys these two names were mentioned most frequently in connection with the rather trendy notion of reason of state. However, as soon as he understood that they were separating reason of state from conscience, his admiration waned. First, he considered writing about the moral corruption introduced by these two authors. However, later he came to the conclusion that instead of simply criticizing them for their mistaken views, it would be better to show 'the true and royal way that a prince ought to follow in order to become great and to govern his people successfully'.[74] In other words, he decided to go for his own version of reason of state, which preserved a number of the novelties of Machiavelli, but kept the ancient Christian moral framework intact.

As opposed to Machiavelli's *Prince*, Botero's starting point is not innovation, but preservation: 'Reason of state is knowledge of the means suitable to found, preserve, and expand dominion.'[75] This is crucial in the sense that it shows that rulers and ruling elites do not usually need to create ex nihilo, but rather they confront the challenge whether their political community and they themselves can preserve and ameliorate the conditions, which prevailed when they took over power, and only try to expand after that first aim is secured. In other words, Botero's interest in the professional techniques of politics has a different aim from that of Machiavelli: he is less interested in the creation of a new political community or in the transformation of an existing political community, and more in the maintenance and conservation of it, and if possible its expansion. This starting position shows that reason of state can be used to achieve a rightly chosen target or political end, which makes it comparable indeed to the operation of prudence.

Given this different end of political activity, the ruler confronts different difficulties here than in Machiavelli. Here, he does not have to rely on sheer power but can use traditional legitimacy, or reputation, as Botero calls it. To earn reputation, he needs to acquire traditional princely virtues, such as justice and liberality. But from our own point of view, the real question is what role does prudence play in Botero's thinking. Already in the second chapter, he addresses the issue. Prudence turns out to be one of the key prerequisites of reputation: 'We now come to those things that lead to reputation; they are principally two: prudence (*Prudenza*) and valor (*Valore*).'[76] In other words, the cardinal virtue of justice is followed by two other virtues: prudence and courage. These two virtues serve right action the following way: prudence gets a clear sight of the situation and advises how to confront it, while valor helps to realize the plan proposed by prudence: 'The former refines the judgment (*giudicio*), the latter emboldens the heart of great personages.'[77] Prudence relates to valour as pen to sword – an important classical reference, which has the rhetorical role of calling attention to the intellectual dimension of ruling. Botero initially gives a short analysis of prudence. It is deduced from history, which is our main source of experience in politics. In other words, here he deals with the relationship between the past and the present – a connection that shows us that this is again a conservative understanding of prudence. Botero's metaphor for indirect, historical experience ('history is the most vast theatre that one can imagine'[78]) is memorable, and connects his views with Castiglione's description of the court as a theatre and later baroque views of the public assembly as a theatre. A further point of connection between the two of them is the relevance attributed to 'the nature, inclinations, and humors of persons',[79] and to rhetoric, in its Aristotelian sense, the basic set of skills to learn about and manipulate the former. Manipulation and the theatre – in other words, Castiglione's counterfeiting legacy – leads the ex-Jesuit Botero to discussions of (dis)simulation. But his attempt to realistically understand human nature is preparation for the appearance of the fourth cardinal virtue. Moderation or temperance means to keep one's own passions in the middle. It turns out to be of crucial importance in matters of 'the arts of peace and war'.[80] It is here, talking about balancing (dis)simulation and self-discipline that Botero tries to marry reason of state and the traditional teaching of the virtue of prudence in his theory of political behaviour.

After grounding his concept of prudence, Botero offers a mosaic of short statements about it, in a fashion resembling Guicciardini's own way of handling this theme in his *Consigli e avvertimenti*, later known as *Ricordi*, of 1570–80.[81] One of the key concepts of these disordered notes is interest, which 'overcomes every other consideration' 'in the deliberation of princes'.[82] This reference makes it obvious that in Botero's mind, prudence is indeed already quite close to reason of state. A further point for him, too, is the relevance of time in matters of prudential considerations. The temporal dimension means first of all a preference for what already exists, in other words, for things that have already proven their utility. In this respect, Botero, too, comes close to the conservative credo. His rhetoric is not too distant from the descriptive language used by the twentieth-century British conservative thinker, Michael Oakeshott: 'Prefer old things to new and the quiet to the upsetting because this is to place the certain before the uncertain and the secure before the dangerous.'[83] At a later point, referring to Livy, he declares 'Nothing is more hateful in governments than to change things which have acquired esteem through their antiquity.'[84] Here, Botero adds to *historia* and experience the concept of custom (deep-seated customs), which, of course, played a major role in the Ciceronian ideology of the Roman republic, and returns in modern conservative thought, too.

And yet, there is an even more Machiavellian line in his thought – of making sense of time in politics: this is the reference to the proper time (*kairos*), right moment and opportunity to act, as key components that determine the result of one's actions.

After these preparations, Botero can already make the important distinction between the right and the wrong forms of cleverness. The wrong form is here called astuteness (*astuzia*) and this is how he distinguishes it from the right form of it: 'In the choice of means prudence seeks the honourable more than the useful, while astuteness takes account only of interest.'[85] This distinction, in fact, goes back to Aristotle, and it had its place in Aquinas, too, but Botero's point is, of course, to reconquest prudence from a non-moral, non-Christian way of using it, which identifies it with pure consequentialism. This is made obvious by the final part of the chapter on prudence, which connects it to true religion as well. Here is Botero's orthodox moment: 'God himself commands the king that he have near him a copy of his holy law and that he observe it carefully.'[86]

It is at this point that we have to turn to the ex-Jesuit Botero's scholastic contemporaries, thinkers of theology and philosophy, who – besides their original mission – also paid special attention to this-worldly power, as it manifested itself in reason of state thinking. According to his researcher, Botero had three sources of inspiration: 'The medieval "mirror for princes" tradition, the Scholastic, and the Florentine (tradition).'[87] The last of them we have already dealt with: we saw Botero's intentions as far as Machiavellianism was concerned, and we also saw how close his views were to those of Guicciardini's on a number of issues. We also saw that Botero and Guicciardini, unlike the innovative Machiavelli, positioned themselves on the (politically) conservative side of the reason of state discourse. It was also mentioned that Botero tried to return to a Christian understanding of reason of state, which connects him to the medieval mirror-for-princes tradition.

Now it is important to say something about his relationship to the early modern period, and particularly to what is called second or late scholasticism. In this respect, the secondary literature usually refers to three authors: the Dominican Francisco de Vitoria (1492–1546), the Jesuit Francisco Suarez (1548–1617) and the Jesuit Robert Bellarmine (1542–1621) who was a classmate of Botero earlier in his Roman Jesuit college.[88] As opposed to Botero, their primary target was not Machiavelli, but a later contemporary, the originator of the reformation, Martin Luther. And beyond handling the charges of Luther, they were participating in a spiritual movement labelled both as counter-reformation and as Catholic revival – in the aftermath of the Council of Trent (1545–63).

There is no space here to present in a detailed fashion the respective ideas of these authors. Rather, let us concentrate on their views on prudence and reason of state – two terms they regarded as rather close to each other. As followers of Aquinas, they were dedicated to the classical interpretation of prudence. Yet, in the traditional Christian version, it used to be more an individual moral virtue and less a term used for a specific political cleverness. But these late scholastic authors were not blind to the new developments in political theory initiated by Machiavelli. On the contrary, they were ready to take his challenge seriously and to answer it. The more so as they served as advisors to secular rulers and to prelates, who also exercised this-worldly power – which made it necessary for them to confront the new trends in political thought.[89]

Höpfl keeps emphasizing that early modern Jesuit theorists had two, in some respect contradictory strategies. They either applied 'a strategy of appropriating and domesticating reason of state for orthodoxy'[90] or some of them were also ready to take a 'more risky strategy: equating reason of state and prudence'.[91] In the first case, the dictates of reason of state were 'softened' to make them acceptable to believers, and compatible with if not the words then the spirit of the teachings of Christ. In the second case, they provided a much more radical interpretation of prudence, in order to make it applicable to those states of affairs where more traditionally understood Christian virtues could not be applied successfully: in states of emergency. The famous Jesuit way of argumentation called 'casuistry' was regarded as necessary to offer clues for Christian rulers in situations that could not be solved along more traditional lines. Höpfl explains: 'To Jesuits it was the merest commonplace that ruling demanded more than merely adhering to general rules, that prudence was this additional ability required to handle circumstances.'[92] The rhetoric of casuistry was nothing less and nothing more than leaving 'ample room for discretion, foresight, judgment, and circumspection, in a word, prudence.'[93]

The danger of this method of cautious withdrawal from political matters together with a bold reinterpretation of more traditional Christian values was to discount their own theological position. Yet, the late scholastic movement in fact never lost position on that ground: with their rhetorical strategies, they could always make compromises when necessary and withdraw in order to push forward at another point of the frontline. The basic concern for them was to give a realistic account of the machinery of politics without giving up their Thomistic moral theology. Ultimately, what they achieved from our point of view was simply this: 'Prudence could thus end up being co-extensive with the whole of statecraft.'[94] Yet, Jesuit thought was perceived by their critics as well as by the laity as drifting rather close to reason of state thinking, in fact they sometimes seemed to vindicate the term.

Early modern conservative prudence: Montaigne

If the early sixteenth century brought with it a reinterpretation of prudence by Machiavelli, creating a new way of thinking and writing about politics, called Machiavellism or 'reason of state' discourse, the second half of the sixteenth century might be seen as an effort to turn back to a more traditional understanding of the term, or at least to try to combine prudence and reason of state in a way that would help to keep it within the Catholic frame of mind. However, the success of the new discourse made it evident that Protestant authors would also be interested in it. In his influential book, Friedrich Meinecke traced back the mostly Huguenot sources of Protestant discussions of reason of state.[95] Apparently, these authors, from Henri de Rohan (1579–1638) to Gabriel Naudé (1600–53), had no scruples about using the Italian discourse in their own context, for their own purposes. Yet, this is beyond the horizon of the present overview. Rather, we will finish the Renaissance humanist episode of the history of prudence with the views of Montaigne and Lipsius who both seem to have got stuck in between the two religious camps, between the Catholic and Protestant factions.

Why the two of them together? In his *Foundations*, Skinner, for example, explained his choice of paring the two of them as follows: 'It was in France and the Low Countries ... that the pure Machiavellian doctrine of *ragione di stato* gained its firmest foothold in the course of the sixteenth century.'[96] Why so? Because of the fierceness and poignancy of the clashes between the two camps, often in the form of civil wars, making it reasonable to give up high hopes of deciding who is right in principle, and to find political solutions in a practical way. Skinner's first French example in this context (of course, Bodin's effort to establish absolute sovereignty remains disregarded for our present purposes) is Guillaume de Vair, but after him it is already Montaigne. Skinner does not share the view of Montaigne in the costume of a Stoic country gentleman, withdrawing from political affairs leading to civil war. Rather, he tries to explain why Montaigne is forced by the urgency of the tragic situation of a bloody civil war to reflect in his essays on the political crisis. His questions to investigate include the potential of 'goodness' in politics, and the place of 'prudence' in theories of government. Skinner quotes Montaigne's dramatic description of the political situation in contemporary France, which is according to all our historical knowledge correct: 'Divisions and subdivisions ... tear our nation apart today.'[97] For Montaigne, the role and function of prudence is to make politics useful 'for sewing our society together, as are poisons for the preservation of our health'.[98]

Skinner's point is elaborated by the literary historian Francis Goyet in an essay on 'Montaigne and the Notion of Prudence'.[99] Admitting that 'in the sixteenth century, prudence is the concept used to think about action and especially political action', and also that Montaigne's political position is rightly characterized as conservative, he provides an assessment of Montaigne's prudence in the context of his being a nobleman, a *prudens* and an 'artist'. While Goyet portrays Montaigne as conservative in politics, he argues that as a writer he proved to be really innovative, identifying his role as that of 'the director of conscience'.[100] In this respect, Goyet, with Fumaroli, finds similarities between Montaigne's position and that of the Jesuits. Goyet also connects sixteenth-century uses of prudence with Machiavellianism, and therefore needs to address the issue of Montaigne's relationship to the famous Florentine author. The point Goyet wants to make is that Montaigne does not reject Machiavelli outright. He being one of those '"political professionals" who populated all the chancelleries and courts of the sixteenth century'.[101] This meant in the case of Montaigne an active engagement on the Catholic side in the political struggles, as 'go-between for the very Catholic Foix clan and their enemy Henri de Navarre'.[102] We learn from him that Montaigne's retreat to his country cottage was only a tactical move, and even his *Essays* should be understood as part of the strategic political game he was playing. It was addressed to that part of the nobility that belonged to the 'middle rank', the mediocrity. Montaigne's writing aims to reconcile and unite his readership: his readers were either noble or mediocre, and their political and moral considerations also seemed antagonistic in the age. As he saw it, what needed to be done with Machiavelli's legacy was not to deny it, but to add a further dimension to it: 'To reconcile the "skillful man" and the "honest man"', in other words the negative (Machiavellian) and the positive (virtue-like) sense of the word prudence. 'Montaigne works therefore to construct an ethical configuration favourable to the reappearance of the ancients' prudence, favourable to its dialectic reappropriation, so to speak, which would integrate Machiavellianism.'[103] In this reappropriation of the ancient concept, the middle rank represents the golden mean of Aristotle, and the virtue of prudence is once again strongly connected to *sophrosyne*, or moderation. Montaigne's aim is to create this new–old ideal in his *Essays*, which mirrors his true self, in other words, in his own narrative he presents himself as the embodiment of his ideal. This effort is based on the very essence of the meaning of prudence: it is a virtue that functions as a substitute for moral rules or political norms: the prudent person 'is himself the rule or *kanon* (of) our actions'.[104] 'The *prudens* is the rule incarnate, in Greek *kanon kai metron*, in Latin *norma et mensura*.'[105]

This insight of Montaigne is crucial for us, and for our overview of the modern history of political prudence: it presents prudence as a norm that is, however, embodied by the prudent person, because it cannot simply be translated into abstract, conceptual language. The individual who acquires the virtue is an example who helps us to understand the norm without becoming able to express it by well-defined categories. The prudent person deliberates in a considerate way, decides correctly and acts in accordance with his or her deliberation and decision, without being able to conceptualize this process in a way to make all of that explicit.[106] His or her form of knowledge is embodied and is not an abstract form of knowledge. To use a later philosophical distinction, it is more like a know-how than a know-what – or, in another register, it is conditioned and habituated action and not the knowledge of the school. In this sense, it comes close to that ancient Greek idea of wisdom according to which – as Hadot reconstructed it[107] – philosophical knowledge is not much more than the choice of a certain form of life. In traditional Latin, the term used in connection with this understanding of prudence is *habitus*, while the accepted Greek term for it is *hexis*. Montaigne, too, relies on the term, in the format of *habitude*. It is through constant learning, in other words through taking the necessary exercises that one can facilitate the acquisition of a virtue. Montaigne's withdrawal from the turmoil of political life was intended to pacify his soul and to moderate his passions. His spiritual exercises, the *Essays*, enabled him to become an exemplary prudent person, a *prudens*. If we rely on the tradition in the context of which we analyse Montaigne, we can identify his aim as following Cicero's *dictum* about '*ars bene vivendi*'.[108]

It is at this point that the closeness between the moral and the artistic stakes of Montaigne's venture becomes more visible. His effort is to become and help others to become politically wiser, but the way to achieve this aim is by forming the perfect practically wise person out of himself. In this programme, the ancient understanding of philosophy, Cicero's notion of practical wisdom and an early modern way of self-formation get in touch with each other. Let us recall Hamlet's effort to find the right decision in a tight political and existential situation in Shakespeare's play – a typical example of the wise prince who wants to act properly. Or let us recall the concept of the 'art of self-fashioning', as analysed by Stephen Greenblatt, in connection with some of the best minds of Renaissance Britain.[109] Greenblatt's notion of self-fashioning is not too distant from the way Castiglione, in his *The Book of the Courtier*, presents the challenge that needs to be confronted by those who want to become successful courtiers in a Renaissance Italian court.

Montaigne adds a political dimension to this early modern engagement with self-formation: to manage oneself is the first prerequisite to managing the affairs of the state, while studying and reflecting on the management of the state is closely connected to an understanding of human nature itself. This truth can be learnt from those ancient historians who were rather sceptical about the human condition. No doubt, their scepticism helped Montaigne to identify his political conviction as conservative. However, when he embarked on the long process of self-formation, which is documented, partly executed and fully illustrated in the *Essays*, he was embarking on a risky voyage of changing his own nature – and politically, the customary ways of managing the state. In this respect, Montaigne's literary effort, aiming not so much at self-understanding, but more at making sense of the human condition, and through that of discovering the real tasks and final barriers of politics, brings him the closest to Machiavelli, whom we described as the arch-innovator of modern politics. In other words, Montaigne's sceptical political conservatism is not devoid of an innovative dimension, which is supported by his moral venture of self-formation, and which unavoidably leads him to an interpretation of the mission of the clever political agent as conserving the existing values of the community by adapting it to the changing parameters of political life.

In this respect, Montaigne seems to admit that Machiavelli was right as far as the necessity for innovation in politics was concerned. Yet, Montaigne's own innovation never turns into a revolution or an aggressive act of transformation. As opposed to Machiavelli's metaphor of rape, Montaigne's own message is better conveyed by the term 'marriage', as far as the relationship of the *Prince* and *Fortune* is concerned. Here, human (male) action is not against the will of the female recipient of it, rather, Montaigne prefers to describe the relationship as a cohabitation, and not as a mastery of one over the other. His idea is political amendment, or 'true reform', instead of the aggressive intrusion into the affairs of the state envisaged by Machiavelli. It is at this point where moderation, self-discipline and the Aristotelian notion of the golden mean become relevant. Montaigne's hero is a real Christian humanist, who, however, has the necessary political experience, through which he acquires practical wisdom. In this respect, his position is not far from that of the Jesuits. Fumaroli argues that Montaigne was close to becoming the 'Loyola of an order without vows or ecclesiastic discipline', while his magnum opus is hardly less than 'the Spiritual Exercises of the Christian nobleman'.[110]

Early modern conservative prudence: Lipsius

If Montaigne's withdrawal from public life together with his opus magnum, the *Essays*, was meant as a complete reshaping of his own public persona, as an exemplum of the ideal realization of the *prudens* in the risky and chaotic world of the French religious civil war of the 1570s and 1580s, Justus Lipsius had a less radical plan with his political masterwork. The *Six Books on Politics or Civil Doctrine* (1589)[111] had a more traditional aim: to argue in favour of the ideal monarchy, as was customary in the earlier mirror-for-princes literature.[112] The *Politica*'s format and genre were rather tricky: as we learnt from the detailed introduction of its recent translator, Lipsius's work was hardly more than a commonplace book, a collection of quotes from mostly ancient authors about the different dimensions of politics, collected into thematic groups. One can easily understand that in a time of rising suspicion on both sides of the religious divide and during the anti-Spanish struggles in the Low Countries, it was safer for the author to put his views into the mouth of accepted ancient authorities. However, as Waszink argues, one should not look at it as an open work of art, inviting free interpretation, without internal limitations. On the contrary, Lipsius, who was an erudite scholar, had a large reservoir of political experience by the time of publishing this book, as by then he was acquainted with the world of politics. We have his own explanation of the genre he chose: 'I have taken the stones and rafters from others; but the construction and shape of the building are mine entirely. I am the architect, but I have collected material from everywhere around.'[113]

Traditionally, Lipsius's philosophical position is described by the following labels: political Tacitism,[114] Neostoicism and reason of state thinking. Politically, it had the function to defend the absolute rule of the prince as the best possible form of politics in an age of internal conflict and religious strife. In what follows, we will concentrate on some of those passages of the *Politica* that described and analysed the notion of prudence – a term that turned out to be crucial in the argumentation. The point to be made is that Lipsius was not at all the kind of republican some of the representatives of political prudence were. On the contrary, his great book represented in its strongest form the idea that a prudent prince embodies the strongest guarantee of both internal and external security and peace, and that his rule is also a safeguard for the survival of both classical and Christian teachings of the role of virtue in politics.

Published in 1589, Lipsius's work served both universalist (scientific) aspirations for truth and very practical (political) purposes. Humanists trusted the ancient classification of human knowledge (based on Aristotle), which distinguished the following three levels: logic, dialectic and rhetoric.[115] While logic was closest to our modern notion of science, dialectic described the sort of knowledge we can gain of 'human affairs', of morality and politics. While the first type is about items, whose qualities are necessary and non-contingent, the truth about human actions cannot be strictly and formally established, yet one can rely on rational argumentation about them, and the truth gained can be expected to be probable. When the philosophical interests of Renaissance humanists turned away from the metaphysics of the scholastic authors and aimed at describing human (moral and social) phenomena, with this shift in research interests a re-evaluation of the category of dialectical knowledge was unavoidable. Lipsius can be supposed to have been influenced by some of the writings, which called attention to the specific nature of dialectic in the age, including Rudolph Agricola's *De inventione Dialectica* (1479). Beyond this shift in scholarly interest, Lipsius also had very practical political targets, which must have had an impact on the rhetorical strategy he chose. His intended audience can be characterized as 'humanist princes and politically experienced humanists'.[116] In other words, he relied on traditional academic knowledge as well as on political experience, and his point was to discuss the conclusions people could draw from the Machiavellian and later reason of state challenge of traditional virtue-based theories of politics. The structure of the book was itself very telling: while the first three books summarized 'the traditional Christian–Ciceronian political morality', the last three books presented 'reason of state–oriented prudence'.[117] This order of presentation might suggest that prudence wins over traditional morality, but the picture is more complex. As Waszink puts it:

> The *Politica* as a whole advocates a submission of *Iustitia* and *Virtus* to *Prudentia* (probably best translated here as statesmanship), though this must be a *Prudentia* ruled by a Virtue, that is a *Virtus* at a higher level, which consists in ruling realistically, rather than in accordance with the strict unadulterated moral goodness and the details of custom and law.[118]

If that is the big picture, let us examine the text and take a look at Lipsius's description of the virtue of prudence itself. In the first book of the *Politica*, he seems to start out from an Aristotelian principle, but in fact defines civil life in a utilitarian way ('the life that we enjoy in community with other people, to the mutual benefit or profit [*ad mutua commoda sive usum*]').[119] At the same time, he adds that civil life is based on virtue, consisting of (Christian) faith and goodness. This move is again counterbalanced when he adds that the other leader of civil life is prudence, which leads virtue as well. Lipsius defines prudence as 'the understanding and choosing (*intellectum et dilectum*) of what is to be sought or avoided, both in private and in public'.[120] With this distinction, Lipsius makes it obvious that prudence has a say both in private morality (ethics) and in public affairs, that is, in politics. In accordance with the teaching of the classical tradition, including Plato, Aristotle and Cicero, he claims that 'Prudence is the skill of living (*Artem vivendi esse Prudentiam*)',[121] this way assuring its power over the whole life of the individual, both in his or her private and public function, including the realm of human happiness (*eudaimonia*). Analysing prudence, he highlights the role of experience (*usus*) and remembrance (*memoria*). While the first category refers to one's individually acquired bits of practical knowledge, the second turns out to be nothing more than an acquaintance with history. At the end of the first book, he adds one final concept: erudition, which he describes as a contributor to both virtue and prudence.

So far, nothing astonishing. As we have already mentioned, Lipsius starts out from the traditional doctrines of a virtuous understanding of politics. The second book of *Politica* is about the ideal form of government and monarchy, and about the main virtues of the prince in particular. There is no direct discussion here of prudence, but there is a point which directly touches upon our theme. Lipsius wants to refute 'the new teachers from Tuscany' (2.15). Obviously, his target here must be Machiavelli and possibly Guicciardini, who do not honour faithfulness and preach to break promises. He asks with his own words: 'So where are now those new teachers?' and then quotes from Aristophanes, 'To whom no altar, no faith, nor any pact is sacred.'[122] In this first encounter with Machiavellianism, he seems to take the side of classical and Christian moral teaching.

The third book is directly about prudence, understood as a cardinal virtue in accordance with the classical tradition. It is claimed to be even more important than force and wealth in the dealings of government. In connection with public prudence, Lipsius specifically discusses the role of counsellors and ministers. He is reaching the discourse of reason of state, even if his counsellors need to display goodness besides experience, as well as giving beneficial advice. Yet, by the end of the chapter, we arrive at the pessimistic conclusion that 'all power at the court is insecure'.[123]

With that we open the second half of the book, which is more sceptical and much closer to Machiavellianism than was expected after reading the first half of the book.

First of all, the prudence of the prince is 'hard to bind down to rules', as it 'is fluctuating and veiled', therefore, no 'full instruction on this topic' is possible.[124] We do not deal here with one of the most important aspects of prudence discussed by Lipsius in connection with the prince: that his religious prudence teaches him 'that he must preserve unity of religion'.[125] Nor can we elaborate here on his views of force (*vis*), a key stabilizer of the realm when cooperating with virtue, while a disturbing element when combined with vice (4.7). Perhaps a less obvious topic of Lipsius's analysis of reason of state prudence is authority (*auctoritas*), which he strongly defends, defined as 'a reverent opinion of the king and his government'.[126] If we add to it his discussion of the relevance 'to obtain the goodwill of the people', and his reflections on *maiestas*, the outlines of his arguments take shape: politics is not simply about the sheer use of force. Lipsius wants to show that politics is more than proving one's power: it requires winning the support of the citizens together with the ancient and Christian moral standards – although for neither of these should the ruler risk civil unrest or external peace.

For us, Lipsius's key discussion is his presentation of mixed prudence. This is a concept Lipsius introduces to talk of the virtue of prudence when it is mixed with 'a bit of the sediment of deceit'.[127] The argument is simple and intriguing: if your enemies behave like foxes, are you not allowed to defend your cause and your standing (status) playing the fox? Quoting Cicero, who made it the obligation of the statesman to act 'in the interest of the people and the community',[128] Lipsius also refers to Tacitus who ensured that 'it belongs to educated behaviour to mix the honourable and the useful (*utilia*)'.[129] He seems to be worried about misinterpretation and wants to exclude any misconception, making it clear that he does not want to aim at anything else but virtue; however, if the winds are not optimal, sometimes you have to zigzag with your ship to arrive to the harbour where you want to sail. The same way as good wine remains good wine even if you drink it mixed with a little water, prudence remains prudence even if 'it is mixed with a little drop of deceit'.[130] Lipsius might be interpreted here as giving in to Machiavelli. But what he is actually doing is arguing against both Machiavelli and those critics of Machiavelli, who are themselves cheating, pretending always to be virtuous, while committing evil deeds, representing in his eyes the other extreme. His own position is moderate: he wants to preserve the advantages of both views without falling into either extreme. Lipsius makes it obvious that it is the Machiavellian debate that he addresses by his reference to the symbols of the lion and the fox, used earlier – following ancient examples – by Machiavelli, even if he does not refer directly to Machiavelli, but takes the allegory directly from ancient sources: 'And as the Spartan king warned: Where the Lion's skin does not suffice, one is allowed to sew on a Fox's skin.'[131] In a side note at the end of the chapter in the original edition, however, he even adds: 'Some rage too much against Machiavelli.'[132] This sort of referencing was sharply criticized by the Vatican censor of *Politica*. Yet, the editor of the last English language edition explains that in the later edition 'Lipsius has removed the reference to and (mild) defence of Machiavelli, without changing the purport of the passage in any really meaningful way. In fact … the "Machiavellian" content has only been masked, and not even that very thoroughly.'[133]

Let us try to rephrase this pronouncement. It is important to recall that Lipsius has a strong argument for why and when to rely on deceit. Relying on the authority of Aristotle, he makes the following claim: in politics 'a man is needed who is not ignorant of the things that happen in this world'.[134] This claim makes it the obligation of the statesman to take reality into account when deliberating about his own behaviour. In this sense, we can call Lipsius's position a realistic view of politics. This realism, however, was not antagonistic with the traditional ancient Christian understanding of virtue politics; on the contrary, Lipsius's aim seems to be to save that tradition after the Machiavellian challenge by co-opting some elements of Machiavellism, based on the preliminary decision that this-worldly politics needs to be realistic. Realism in this sense is nothing less than an acceptance of the anthropology of Tacitus and St Augustine: of (fallen) human nature or, in short, of human imperfection.

Lipsius and Machiavelli, in this sense, are not taking opposite philosophical positions. On the contrary, Lipsius does not follow Machiavelli in the direction of a denial of

Christianity and the whole tradition of virtue politics, he takes a 'middle position' between these extremes. As Waszink puts it: 'For Lipsius Tacitus and Machiavelli were the central axis of a vision of power and morality which, supplemented with the respective endorsement or dismissal of ideas from, most importantly, Sallust, Seneca, Guicciardini, Bodin, and the Christian-Ciceronian "system", produced a theory of a morally founded Reason of State.'[135] Prudential politics, in this sense, turns out to be nothing less for him than a morally founded reason of state.

3

Late modern *prudentia*

So far, we have seen the virtue of prudence used in discourses on politics and political morality in particular from the ancients to the early seventeenth century. We have witnessed a clear continuity from the Greek philosopher through the Roman senator and the medieval Christian theologian to the early modern humanist and political counsellor. In what follows, we will find the concept in a different, non-political, philosophical context. First, it will be seen as utilized by the practical philosophy of a late modern, twentieth-century philosophical school or movement, called hermeneutics. Secondly, two present-day philosophers will be discussed (the first of whom died recently, the second is still with us), both of whom have represented the criticism of twentieth-century liberalism, and are by now usually referred to together under the label 'political realism'.

The twentieth-century philosophical rebirth of prudence: Gadamer

The early modern flourishing of the Aristotelian–Ciceronian tradition was followed by a wide intellectual movement, called the Enlightenment, with its specific understanding of reason, worked out by such path-breaking authors as Descartes at its beginning and Kant, completing the story. This movement in philosophy had strong methodological and epistemological premises, which ran against the ancient virtue ethical tradition. It was only in the twentieth century that the problem field of Aristotelian practical philosophy was reborn. This time, however, it was not in the context of ethics and political philosophy, but in the philosophical critique of metaphysics and in metaphilosophy. The criticism of metaphysics was initiated by Heidegger, as a result of his reading of Nietzsche, but also as a student of Husserl, who was the first author in a school of thought that came to be called 'phenomenology'. One of Heidegger's most talented students was Gadamer, whose influential, groundbreaking work *Truth and Method* was published in 1960, when its author was sixty years old, establishing a philosophical school or movement, called 'philosophical hermeneutics'.

Gadamer started out from what he called the interpretive (*verstehenden*) sciences.[1] But he was also inspired by what he saw as the neglected connections between art and philosophy. He concentrated on what he called 'the primordial experiences that are transmitted through art and history'.² But these experiences, he claimed, included opaque perceptions of our own selves as well, and he was interested in 'how much we ourselves are immersed in the game (im Spiele) and are the stake in this game'.³ The reflexive nature of our human understanding of the world is, to a large extent, due to the fact that it has 'a fundamental linguisticality or language-relatedness'.⁴

Now, as we know from Wittgenstein, there is no such thing as private language. Language creates a necessarily dialogical situation: the words you use are there already by the time you make use of them, and the fact that language is shared among language users creates the situation that your words will be understandable for others. Language necessarily creates a community, while the loss of language leads to the decomposition of a community, as we know from Babel's story in the Bible. In other words, an utterance creates the other, who can decipher the encoded message. In this sense, there is an inbuilt dialogical element in all human language use. This is why Gadamer's hermeneutic is 'oriented toward Socratic conversation'.⁵ Dialogicity means that no message can be regarded as a final, definitive one – it always invites a response. But language itself is not final, it is not a 'fixed given', but a 'language-at-play':⁶ you inherit it, but you transform it by the very message you encode, thus, your contribution to the linguistic universe will not leave language unchanged. In other words, neither the message nor the language used has been finalized, and therefore the knowledge obtained in the humanities by language use, including philosophy, cannot be 'objective' in the sense attributed to science in Cartesian metaphysics. Instead, the epistemology cherished by Gadamer learns more from the tradition of rhetoric, and especially from Vico and his methodological criticism of 'modern science'.⁷ Vico's rhetoric is not only a return to 'the art of speaking', but it is also relevant as a theory of rhetoric for Gadamer. After all, if you want to convince an audience of the agora, as Socrates did, you need to offer more than abstract rationality. Gadamer returns to the relevance of practical philosophy, and in particular practical or human wisdom, as it was worked out by Aristotle, but embodied by the Socrates of Plato's dialogues. He claims: 'I have been formed more by the Platonic dialogues than by the great thinkers of German idealism',⁸ which might be a rhetorical exaggeration but shows us that there is an intentional choice here carried out by Gadamer to embrace the 'Socratic legacy', or the Platonic–Aristotelian tradition of practical philosophy. Certainly, it is not Plato's substantial philosophy (for example his metaphysics) that inspires Gadamer here. It is more the way the dialogue form works in Plato's writings, where the reader can directly experience 'a Doric harmony of deed and speech, ergon and logos'. As Gadamer puts it in another phraseology, what caught him in Plato was 'the authentic law of life of the Socratic dialogue'.⁹ This Platonic art of presenting Socrates as not only an author but also the embodiment of his philosophical teaching is further developed in the Aristotelian celebration of the phronetic man and, in particular, the statesman of practical wisdom.

In what follows, we will touch upon three important chapters of Gadamer's influential volume, *Truth and Method*,¹⁰ which are all connected to our own understanding of the notion of *phronesis*/prudence as follows: 'The guiding concepts of humanism', 'The hermeneutic relevance of Aristotle' and 'The exemplary significance of legal hermeneutics'.

It is in connection with the special methodology required in the humanities that Gadamer presents what he calls the key concepts of humanism: *Bildung, sensus communis*, judgement and taste. *Bildung*, translated into English as culture, in Gadamer's description contains what he calls 'tact' – a sort of practical knowledge that directs the individual in his or her daily activity. This is how Gadamer defines tact – after Helmholtz: 'By "tact" we understand a special sensitivity and sensitiveness to situations and how to behave in them, for which knowledge from general principles does not suffice.'[11] He adds to this description that tact is tacit and unformulable.[12] But the important point is that by *Bildung*, we do not simply mean a familiarity with a wide horizon of objects, artistic and cultural phenomena – it also depends on a way of being, a question of who (and what) we are. To practice the human sciences, you need to acquire *Bildung*, that sort of tact – an embodied sense for the aesthetic and for the historical. It is only with the help of this 'persona' that you can make considered judgements, that you know 'how to make sure distinctions and evaluations in the individual case without being able to give its reasons'.[13] It does not simply mean an acquaintance with a certain vocabulary, or a particular tradition, it is not simply a question of experience and memory. Rather, it is close to a kind of openness to the unknown or the unfamiliar. In order to understand how one can become so receptive, we have to return to what Gadamer calls the 'humanistic tradition'. Gadamer relies here on Hegel, the opponent of Kant, and suggests that self-reflection helps the subject to tune himself or herself to the universality of 'the other'. As he puts it, *Bildung* is 'a sense of proportion and distance in relation to itself, and hence consists in rising above itself to universality'.[14] This sensitivity is not simply the subjectivity of art, nor the objectivity of science. Rather, it is the ability to imaginatively put oneself in the viewpoint of the other – a point that Gadamer in fact takes over from Kant's understanding of aesthetic judgement in the third Critique.

The universal ability of the educated person (*gebildet*) to feel sympathy with others leads Gadamer to the notion of *sensus communis*. He explains the term with the help of Vico, and a return to the humanistic ideal of rhetoric. For Vico, to talk in the right way, to 'talk well' means to tell the truth as well: the way of talking, what Gadamer calls the 'manners and customs',[15] leads directly to the right solution to the problem with which one is concerned. '*Tone macht die Musik*', as the German proverb tells us. This sense of the right way of addressing the other leads Gadamer to the distinction between the schoolman and the wise man, a distinction that helps him to introduce the Socratic–Aristotelian concept of *phronesis* (as opposed to *sophia*). Gadamer provides the following historical sketch to reconstruct the ancient history of the term: it gained prominence 'after the Greek ideal of *Bildung* had been fused with the self-consciousness of the leading political class of Rome. Late Roman legal science also developed against the background of an art and practice of law that is closer to the practical ideal of *phronesis* than to the theoretical ideal of *sophia*'.[16] To cut a long story short, let us see how Gadamer connects *phronesis* to an analysis of the practical philosophy of Aristotle, and to the problem of the application of the law.

The importance attributed to Aristotle by Gadamer in *Truth and Method* concerns his understanding of the relationship between the universal and the particular in Aristotle's ethics.[17] Analysing this link, Gadamer points at the role reason is destined to play in Aristotle's description of moral action. This reason, as opposed to reason in Kant's system, is not concerned with metaphysics, but is connected with moral questions. For Aristotle, practice and 'ethos' are all important. In this respect, Aristotle comes surprisingly close to a situationist theory: 'If man always encounters the good in the form of the particular practical situation in which he finds himself, the task of moral knowledge is to determine what the concrete situation asks of him – or, to put it another way, the person acting must view the concrete situation in light of what is asked of him in general'. The radical rapture between the generality of the demand of morality and the particularity of the actual situation the individual confronts seems to be unbridgeable. Put differently, there is no opportunity to give universally valid, adequate answers to problems raised by concrete situations; therefore, our knowledge of the moral world cannot be as precise as our knowledge of mathematics. The rightness of the answer depends on the concrete subject who confronts the situation; therefore, 'through education and practice he must himself already have developed a demeanor that he is constantly concerned to preserve in the concrete situations of his life and prove through right behaviour'. As both Ricoeur and MacIntyre, not independently of Gadamer, will also claim, the standard of the right choice will be the narrative unity of one's life.

A further distinction follows: that between *phronesis* as moral knowledge and *epistémé* as theoretical knowledge. The former form of knowledge is not detached from and, in fact, makes no sense without the subject who is concerned with the problem, as the only point of the knowledge is to govern the subject's action there and then.[18]

And let us not forget a further distinction he makes: that between *phronesis* and *techné*, the latter being 'the skill, the knowledge of the craftsman'.[19] Interestingly, while Gadamer distinguishes the two forms of knowledge, the distinction, he claims, 'reveals the untenability of what is called the art of politics, in which everyone involved in politics – i.e., every citizen – regards himself as an expert'.[20] The distinction makes it obvious that although it is imprecise, moral knowledge, that is *phronesis*, is 'the true knowledge that constitutes a man and a citizen'. This identification of political action and the essence of humaneness reminds one of Arendt's view, who was as deeply influenced by the early Heidegger as Gadamer himself.

After clarifying concepts connected to *phronesis*, such as 'sympathetic understanding', 'insight' and 'fellow-feeling', Gadamer attributes a final distinction to Aristotle. This is the difference between the *phronimos* and the *deinos*, or cunning, the natural counterpart of *phronesis*. As he formulates it, 'the *deinos* is "capable of anything"; he uses his skills to any purpose and is without inhibition'.[21] The point is exactly the same as what is at stake in the debate about Machiavellism. The *deinos* is a person, who 'knows' just as much as the prudent ruler about the nature of human beings and the professional activity of being a politician. However, he uses this knowledge simply for his own benefit without any scruples. In other words, an important element is missing in this case from the elements that build up *phronesis*. For Aristotle, the *phronimos* can choose the right target, and he will find the most adequate means to arrive there only after that choice, which aims at *eudaimonia*, which cannot be achieved without the other. The *deinos* has no such external, long-term end: he solves the riddle of the particular situation for his own momentary advantage without any further considerations. It is for this missing link that the acts of the *deinos* turn out to be terrible: 'Nothing is so terrible, so uncanny, so appalling, as the exercise of brilliant talents for evil.'[22]

Obviously, Gadamer's problem of moral knowledge here directly led to the theoretical dilemmas brought about by the discourse on the reception of Machiavelli's revolutionary claims. His distinction between practical knowledge and the practically skilful decisions of the amoral agent sheds light on why we can still affirm that prudence is a virtue: the element of choosing a long-term end to which the *phronimos* adapts his or her choices guarantees that it will remain moral in the ordinary sense of the word, while if someone simply uses right choice in the sense of finding what is most advantageous for him or her independently of any external criteria, he or she excludes the possibility that the actions of this person can be regarded as morally right.

Finally, let us turn to the problem of application that Gadamer investigates in connection with legal hermeneutics. His question here addresses the issue of our relationship to the past, and specifically to our own tradition. What he wants to show here is how one can relate to one's tradition externally, in other words in a non-biased way, as the modern sense of the professional historian requires it: the task of the historian is to describe a particular past phenomenon by showing the internal causal mechanisms working in it. Yet, even a historian has something to learn from the judge, who refers back to his or her own tradition, or from the theologian, who returns to the tradition of his or her particular confession, to solve a pressing problem in the present. The additional element in both the judge's and the theologian's relationship to their tradition is that they 'read' it as if it was originally conceived to answer their problems, as they exist 'here and now'. In other words, their approach is made richer by the fact that they look at past norms supposing that they are still valid. In this sense, the lawyer and the theologian regard themselves as still part of the very tradition that they have to interpret. The judge interprets the ancient legal text that he or she wants to use in his or her judgement supposing that in the relevant sense it is still 'valid'. When the judge applies the law to solve a particular legal dilemma, he or she translates it into the present conditions, while keeping its 'original meaning'.

> The judge who adapts the transmitted law to the needs of the present is undoubtedly seeking to perform a practical task, but his interpretation of the law is by no means merely for that reason an arbitrary revision. Here again, to understand and to interpret means to discover and recognize a valid meaning. The judge seeks to be in accord with the 'legal idea' in mediating it with the present.[23]

The presupposition of the act of the judge is that there is a continuity between the past and the present, and that it is therefore possible to take over a legal principle from the past without distorting its original intention, even if circumstances today radically differ. He or she is able to do so, because in a legal sense the valid norm that he or she applies belongs both to the past and to the present legal order. By this example, Gadamer wants to make the point that to understand in the sense it is used in the law – and more generally in the humanities – is quite different from the use of the term in the natural sciences. In the humanities, to understand something preserves an element from how the judge and the theologian applies her or his own tradition in answering a burning issue of the present. They are not simply subjectively reinterpreting it. They are themselves the means by which a past meaning is turned into a present sense. Gadamer sums up the meaning of application in legal and theological hermeneutics: 'Application does not mean first understanding a given universal in itself and then afterward applying it to a concrete case. It is the very understanding of the universal – the text – itself.'[24]

In Gadamer's philosophy of hermeneutics, the human sciences always preserve a moral dimension. This is the crucial point that distinguishes them from the 'natural' sciences, based on value neutrality and objectivity. Arguably, Gadamer's analysis of the moral issues of the human(e) sciences can be utilized to understand the nature of politics as well. After all, indirectly, Gadamer showed that the judgement of prudence, of practical knowledge about what to do and also the determination to do it, can be compared to the application of the law in the court. His *Truth and Method* helps us to conceive that in the decision of the prudent person, ideally there is nothing voluntaristic or purely subjective. Neither is it, however, an objective judgement: rather, it is a proper reading of what is the case and also an interpretation of what is the best (or the least destructive) possible solution to the dilemma involved in the given case for the given person. Also, in accordance with the practical syllogism of Aristotle, Gadamer makes it clear that all prudential judgements necessarily finally lead to action. Their value is closely connected to the act that results from the judgement.

From the hermeneutics of action to *phronesis*: Ricoeur

Heidegger's early discussion of Aristotle's classification of forms of human knowledge and his lectures on Aristotle's practical philosophy, itself based on the ideas of Socrates and Plato, inspired the mature Gadamer to build up his own philosophical hermeneutics. Gadamer's philosophy is based on the traditional teachings of the hermeneutics of legal, sacred and literary texts. Ricoeur, almost a generation younger than Gadamer, was also inspired by Heidegger in a number of ways, more exactly by the philosophical hermeneutics initiated by Gadamer. For our present discussion, two aspects of his oeuvre are worth further consideration: first of all what is labelled as Ricoeur's hermeneutics of action, and second, his late theory of the just, and the role *phronesis* plays in this analysis.

Starting out from a Christian philosophical anthropology in the tradition of French reflexive philosophy, Ricoeur soon recognized the crucial importance of Gadamer's hermeneutics for his own way of thinking. His hermeneutic turn consisted of working out his own 'little ethics', which translated Gadamer's textual hermeneutics (itself stressing the phronetic connection between speech and deed) into a hermeneutics of action. According to the basic insight of Ricoeur's phenomenological hermeneutics, human beings make sense of the world, including each other's actions as if these were texts – reading them and interpreting them the same way as they read and interpret a text. They regard both physical objects and human acts as utterances and look for the message in the utterance.

That human beings can make sense of each other's actions this way is made possible by an awareness of their own being. Ricoeur's description of this awareness of the self and the other is a rather fine philosophical analysis, presented in his *Gifford Lectures* from 1986, published in English as *Oneself as Another* (1992). Ricoeur distinguished different layers of the self.[25] First, a distinction was made between things and persons, or selves, with the help of human language, as a distinguishing mark. The human person is an agent, in the sense that we can attribute actions to him or her, both in the sense that he or she can express himself or herself by language and that he or she can also communicate by deeds – both of them require an interpretation of the one by the other, which gives birth to interaction, or interpersonal communication. The sequence of such actions of self-expression and interpretation of others builds up one's temporal awareness of oneself – one's narrative identity. This linear order of actions and their perceptions is not conceptualized as aimless. On the contrary, narrative identity provides the grounds for what is called in an Aristotelian–Hegelian fashion the ethical aim of human life. But even with this ethical aim, one's life only makes sense in the context or (to use another metaphor) in the mirror of other selves, through the testimony of others. This way, selfhood necessarily concludes in a discourse with others.

The dialectical nature of Ricoeur's practical philosophy is revealed by a further conceptual distinction: that between what he calls the *idem* and the *ipse* identity. The distinction reveals both the unchanging core of the person and the dynamically changing part of the person. Like the hero of a story: the individual passes through the different phases of his or her life, changing in certain respects but remaining the same in others, in order to attribute the changes to the transformation of his or her core identity.

By introducing the notion of narrative identity, it becomes possible for Ricoeur to establish 'the primacy of ethics over morality – that is, of the aim over the norm'.[26] Ricoeur, at this point, relies on both MacIntyre[27] and Gadamer.[28] From MacIntyre, Ricoeur takes over the idea of the narrative unity of one's life, his notions of practice and the 'standards of excellence', while Gadamer helps him to reconstruct the Aristotelian notion of *phronesis*.[29] But how does the Aristotelian tradition relate in Ricoeur's thought to the Kantian heritage? Ethics and morality represent two different levels for him: the first, the Aristotelian element stabilizes the aim of the narrative of one's life, while (Kantian) morality provides the norms, which will help to find the right actions. However, the norm itself needs to be applied practically in particular situations – and that is safeguarded once again by an Aristotelian tool: by *phronesis*. In this way, three layers are built together: the ethical, the moral and the *phronetic* dimension represent different distances between the universality of one's system of values, as it unfolds along the temporal vector, and the particularity of singular acts of the moment. The self is in constant motion between these layers of abstraction, in order to find the right choices in difficult situations, and to make sure that the moments fit into the life plan they are realizing, or to modify that very plan as a result of experiences. Ricoeur formulates the dynamic of this hermeneutic work of interpreting one's individual actions and the totality of them in the following way:

> It is in unending work of interpretation applied to action and to oneself that we pursue the search for adequation between what seems to us to be best with regard

to our life as a whole and the preferential choices that govern our practices ... between our aim of a 'good life' and our particular choices a sort of hermeneutic circle is traced by virtue of the back-and-forth motion between the idea of the 'good life' and the most important decisions of our existence (career, loves, leisure, etc.).

Here, he joins Charles Taylor, and makes use of his term 'the self-interpreting animal': 'For the agent, interpreting the text of an action is interpreting himself or herself.'[30]

The hermeneutics of action, presented in the last part of *Oneself as Another*, reintroduces Aristotelian *phronesis* in the context of what Ricoeur and MacIntyre call the 'narrative identity'. As Ricoeur admitted, this combination is inspired by a number of contemporary authors, from Gadamer to Nussbaum and Charles Taylor. The arguments put forward here are developed later in his series of lectures published under the title *The Just*.[31] Here, Ricoeur makes an excursion into the field of legal philosophy, without giving up thinkink about the social and moral issues involved in the questions he confronts. Most of the criticisms he formulates here confront what he calls 'the purely procedural theory' of – the early – John Rawls. That is not surprising if we recall his views on the teleology of one's life. As we have seen in *Oneself as Another*, and as it is repeated in *The Just*, Ricoeur accepts the Aristotelian starting point of moral thinking, according to which the human agent needs a certain conception of what would count as a good life for him or her, without this choice no conception of the formal criteria of justice would hold.

Ricoeur completes the deontology of Kantian–Rawlsian political philosophy with an Aristotelian element of the good life for humans in both *Oneself as Another* and *The Just*. He also repeats in *The Just* the reference to *phronesis* as the practical translation of the first two higher, more theoretical levels (that of teleology and deontology) to the down to earth layer of actual human behaviour. In the introductory essay of *The Just*, entitled 'Preface', which provides a framework for the rather diverging essays that follow, Ricoeur talks about two axes: a horizontal and a vertical one. The horizontal axis is that of the 'dialogical constitution of the self',[32] and it consists of two distinct senses attributed to the notion of the other. The immediate relationship to the other is the interpersonal relationship, of which the emblematic virtue is friendship. In this relationship, the other is present – bodily, through his or her face or in his or her voice. The parallel virtue of justice is embedded into a different notion of the other 'based on a relation of distance' from the agent.[33] To negotiate the distance, the other here is mediated by institutions, which is why this part of the vertical axis can be called an institutional concept of justice, opposed to the unmediated presence of the personalized other in friendship.

Along the vertical axis, as mentioned, on the highest level, the good is the control over one's action, and the good here 'designates the telos of an entire life in quest of what human agents can consider as an accomplishment, a crowning achievement'. In Ricoeur's sense, this is the level of ethics understood 'as the wish for a full life'.[34] Ascending from that level of universality, we arrive at that of the obligatory, the deontological level. 'This is the level of the norm, of duty, of interdiction.'[35] With obligation, however, comes coercion, power and violence. In order to make it acceptable, the deontological norm needs to have universal validity, and a formal status attached to it. This is the level of the legal. Ricoeur, however, cautions us that the deontological is not autonomous. With it, we have not yet arrived at the just. On the one hand, its formality makes it dependent on the teleological. On the other hand, its universality leads us to the level of practical wisdom, the third level along the vertical axis.

It is practical reason, operating on this third level, which liberates Ricoeur's theory from a binary opposition between the teleological and the deontological. As he already made it explicit in the title of an essay in 1991, the just is to be found between the legal and the good.[36] From Ricoeur's point of view, this level becomes all important, because 'the confrontation with those situations I place globally under the heading of *the tragic dimension of action*'[37] takes place here. And this tragic dimension of action is all important for Ricoeur, a witness and a victim of the twentieth century. On this level, a 'climate of incertitude and of serious conflicts' rules.[38] Among such unstable and hostile circumstances the only thing one can rely on is 'the Aristotelian virtue of *phronesis*, reinterpreted by Heidegger and Gadamer'.[39] This virtue, which translates into the language of phenomenology elaborated by Ricoeur as 'heartfelt conviction',[40] however, is not left alone even in this climate: both the long-term life plan of the subject and the procedural formalism of the institutions of justice made obligatory by the deontological level circumscribe it.

Ricoeur explains the mechanism of the *phronetic* decision as a *via media* not only between the legal and the good but also as a judgement 'between proof, defined by the constraints of logic, and sophism'.[41] In other words, it is a middle zone between what can be known for sure and a *doxa*, a pure opinion. This zone can be identified with the traditional discipline of rhetoric, which, Ricoeur recalls, Aristotle characterizes as 'giving a rejoinder to dialectic, itself understood as a doctrine of probable reasoning'.[42] However, he associates two more adjectives with this activity of the human intellect: first, hermeneutic – as it is based on the operation of application, and secondly poetic – since 'the invention of an appropriate solution to the unique situation stems from what, since Kant, we have called the productive imagination'.[43] In other words, Ricoeur associates *phronesis* with the Aristotelian understanding of rhetoric, with Gadamer's notion of the hermeneutic and with Kant's sense of the productive imagination.

To sum up Ricoeur's message: *phronesis* works in the middle zone of rhetoric (and dialectic), of hermeneutic and of the productive imagination, to complement the levels of the good (understood in terms of a whole human life) and of the legal (understood as universally valid obligatory legal norms and the institutional structure of justice).

In a significant essay, Ricoeur returns to Hannah Arendt's experiment to reinterpret Kantian political philosophy on the basis of the central notion of the third Kritik, *Urteilskraft*, translatable both as judgement and as taste. For Ricoeur, the main point here is the affirmation of the act of judging itself – that is why he (re)constructs the unfinished last part of Arendt's trilogy, *Thinking, Willing, Judging*. For Ricoeur, the act of judging is a momentary human act, which might however have long-term effects, and which therefore needs to be accomplished with a reflective awareness and a responsibility that is characteristic of the Kantian view of human dignity, shared by Ricoeur as well, in spite of the much more tragic overtones he attributes to the human condition than his Prussian precursor. With this touch of the spontaneous, Ricoeur completes his view of the moral realm, where the good and the legal are joined by the third category of the *phronetic*, identified as the equitable in the classical legal terminology.

The twentieth-century rebirth of political realism: Williams

While Gadamer and Ricoeur confined their researches into prudence to the moral realm of practical philosophy, without directly considering the political, a recent philosophical direction is engaged to return to the phenomenon of the purely political with the help of practical philosophy. In this chapter, we have two heroes: Bernard Williams and Raymond Geuss, two philosophers from Cambridge with rather different interests, but often mentioned together, under the label of 'political realism' understood as a philosophical movement. In this chapter, we look at their respective views on politics, which in many ways resemble the early modern reflections on the dark sides of politics.

The interesting thing about Bernard Williams is that he starts out from assumptions not so distant from what is called 'virtue ethics', which is philosophically much less sceptical than political realism, but which is neither directly interested in nor interesting for the political philosophy of prudence.[44] The fact that Bernard Williams had a rather unorthodox take on political philosophy must have had its roots in his special (rather traditional) philosophical training: he started his studies in classics, with the so-called Greats Course in Oxford. This old-fashioned disciplinary preparation enabled him to look at himself as part of what is usually referred to as the great tradition of European philosophy and political thought.[45] As he saw it, 'the ideas of the ancient world fill a reservoir from which moderns and postmoderns may slake their philosophical thirst', or in even stronger form: 'Contemporary self-understanding depends upon understanding the Greeks.'[46] He held the radical belief: 'We have much more in common with the Greeks than we believe.'[47] His philosophical track was determined by this early interest in the classics: he deals with the Greeks from his very first books up until his posthumous writings. Perhaps the most relevant in this respect are his books entitled *Moral Luck* (1981), *Ethics and the Limits of Philosophy* (1985) and *Shame and Necessity* (1993). Of these works, let us look at the most influential one, *Ethics and the Limits of Philosophy*, in which he presents, in a rather elaborate manner, his criticism of contemporary Kantian, as well as analytic moral philosophy. In the very first sentence of the book, he returns to Socrates and to the central claim that what we are talking about (in philosophy) is how one should live. Williams's book is a denial of the hope of Socrates and Plato that philosophy can indeed answer such a demanding question. These Greek philosophers trusted philosophy's 'power to develop the virtues', and the virtues, they thought, led humans to well-being. Williams was closer to 'Aristotle's outlook', which he regarded as 'less ambitious' and had 'much greater psychological and social elaboration'.[48] He claimed that as opposed to the idealist view of the Socratic tradition, which identified the human being with a soul, Aristotle, as he understood it, argued that the human being is 'essentially embodied and essentially lives a social life'. It was also crucial to him that Aristotle strictly separated practical reason from theoretical reason. The significance attributed to practical reason comes from the Aristotelian claim that 'the exercise of practical reason in a personal and civic life' is in fact crucial for human well-being.[49]

Compared to the Aristotelian conviction cherished by him in *Ethics and the Limits of Philosophy*, Williams arrived at political philosophy too late. Although he had a permanent interest in moral philosophy and ethics, his influential *In the Beginning Was the Deed*,[50] which was a characteristic move in political philosophy with a major impact on the profession, was published posthumously in 2005, two years after his early death.

As for contemporary philosophy, Williams had serious reservations about certain elements of the mainstream Western liberalism of his day. No doubt, both his being a late-comer as well as his disregard for the accepted ways of the day contributed to his fully fledged attack on two well-established ways of English-speaking political philosophy, the 'enactment model' of utilitarianism and 'the structural model' of Rawls and company. As he saw them, 'they both represent the priority of the moral over the political',[51] and both were a dead end, labelled by Williams as 'versions of political moralism'.[52] It is in contrast with these versions that he offers his own version, which he labels as 'political realism'. He admits: 'My view is in part a reaction to the intense moralism of much American political and indeed legal theory'.[53] His version of political realism is embedded in what he claims is a European tradition of political realism, and in particular in the thoughts of his great hero, Hobbes.[54] In what follows, I will sketch this theory, and then I will show how it is embedded in Williams's reinterpretation of certain Greek authors.

In political realism, his point of departure is 'the securing of order, protection, safety, trust, and the conditions of cooperation' as the primary tasks in political life.[55] These preconditions turn his interest towards 'historical circumstances' which determine how the securing of the foregoing list might be possible in a given state of affairs. A further condition for the preceding target is what he calls the basic legitimation demand, or, put differently, a non-coercive way to justify the state monopoly of power – along Weber's lines – as 'might does not imply right'.[56] Legitimation means that a given historical structure makes sense to us as a structure, which exemplifies the human capacity to live under an intelligible order of authority. The test whether something makes sense belongs to what Williams calls historical understanding, it is in fact – with another of his concepts – a 'hermeneutical category'.[57] In his view, in the present context, mainstream American discussions of liberalism lack a vital component: they are overmoralized, and therefore the distinguishing mark of 'the political' (*das Politische*) falls out of their focus. Present-day moralizing political essays address 'utopian magistrates or founding fathers',[58] while they should address the historically conditioned audience of a political pamphlet. Departing even from Habermas, he claims that we should not think about our own task as to 'argue with those who disagree', but we should treat these persons as political opponents. With this gesture, we recognize them as independent political actors, which is to show more respect than if we only looked on them as participants in a discussion. Similarly, Williams suggests that we should understand a political decision not as a conclusion to a political debate, but as an announcement that the representatives of the opposite view have lost politically. This emphasis on the theory of the political as a description of actual decisions in a historically contingent set of circumstances as opposed to a prescriptively normative account of 'what is platitudinously politics'[59] distinguishes the theory of Williams from mainstream Rawlsian or Dworkinian theory. With this, we can turn to another crucial aspect of Williams's political realism.

In his essay 'In the Beginning Was the Deed',[60] the target of his criticism is referred to as rights-talk. He claims that in contemporary political theory there is a line (or rather a circle) of arguments connecting 'rights–principles–moral discourse–person–autonomy–rights' which has no contact with reality. Williams suggests that 'we do need to identify a place in the world, a practice, which will give the set of concepts a grounding in reality'.[61] He wants to bring this touch of reality with his reference to the famous line in Goethe's Faust: '*Im Anfang war die Tat*' (In the beginning was the deed). We cannot explain here the specific authorial intention with the famous line, or the 'truth' of the poem as a work of art. Let it suffice for the moment that the word 'deed' for Goethe was the alternative to the Bible's original, which was the term Word (*logos*), while further versions of the concept in the same verse include *Sinn* (reason) and *Kraft* (power). But for Williams, as we saw, the biblical paraphrase in the epic poem by the classical German poet functions to wake up the political theory of the world of imagination, and connect it back to reality. Relying also on Wittgenstein's philosophical appropriation of Goethe's line, Williams uses it as a reminder that 'political projects are essentially conditioned, not just in their background intellectual conditions but as a matter of empirical realism, by their historical circumstances'.[62] This recognition of the relevance of the historical occurs, of course, after what he calls his historicist turn.[63] After that turn, which recapitulated history as relevant for philosophy, he was ready to affirm that a 'historical situation cannot fully be theorized or captured in reflection'.[64] Therefore, Williams concludes: 'There is no way in which theory can get all the way ahead of practice.'[65] In the context of a Rawlsian analytical Kantianism, these statements represent quite a break. Here, Williams comes much closer to strands of Continental philosophy – his references here are Hegel, Marx and, perhaps most significantly, Nietzsche.

I am of the opinion that Williams did not trace down all the consequences of his confirmation of the primacy of practice in comparison with theory – although he comes to the surprising insight, for example, that, in fact, philosophical good sense sometimes cannot be separated from political good sense. After the historicist turn, he became much more open to the particular. But relying on his ideas, as I would like to explain in the Chapter 4, people such as Raymond Geuss could push his questions further, and also draw some conclusions, which he was not yet ready to draw. The originality of Williams's approach in a twentieth-century Anglo-Saxon context is quite remarkable, something that earns him a stable position in the ranks of those thinking philosophically about politics in the late 20th century in English.

Let us finally see how his political realism suits his interest in Greek philosophy, literature and theatre. In particular, let us see whether Williams's political realism is deepened by his reliance on some of the argumentations of the ancient Greek philosophers and playwrights.

His relationship to the Greeks is, as we saw, first of all a relationship to Aristotle. This relationship, however, is a rather ambiguous matter. He appreciates Aristotle on the grounds that as far as he can see, he was 'the only colourable attempt to provide a foundation for ethics',[66] and also because of the connection between his ethical views and his views of nature (*cosmos*). Nevertheless, he is dissatisfied with Aristotle's views on the grounds of a threefold criticism. First, he doubts if it is possible to establish a theory of human nature based on rationality as its distinguishing mark. Secondly, he doubts that Aristotle's account of human virtues would definitely lead to the one and only *telos* of human life that Aristotle supposes, including the duality of that very *telos* (a political life versus a speculative life) in different parts of *Nicomachean Ethics* (book VI and book X, respectively). Thirdly, he doubts that we can determine 'a distinctive set of ethical dispositions based on that distinctive conception of human flourishing'.[67] It is at this point that he finds Aristotle's effort to harmonize the internal world of the agent and its natural environment fruitless. He straightforwardly claims: 'We must admit that the Aristotelian assumptions which fitted together the agent's perspective and the outside view have collapsed.'[68] Williams is too sceptical a thinker to accept the cohesion of the Aristotelian epistemological, metaphysical and ethical universe. He finds Aristotle's grand theory no more than 'an astonishing piece of cultural wish-fulfilment'.[69] Yet, this harsh criticism of the Aristotelian position does not lead to a final break with the ancients. On the contrary, his late writings are full of the spirit of the ancient Greek – only this time not so much with the ideas of the philosophers, but more with the scepticism of history writers, such as Thucydides, or with the tragic air of the tragedy writers. If his basic problem is with Aristotle's naïve effort to reconcile the different aspirations of individuals, as well as the norms of social life with the laws of nature, he finds similar doubts about the possibility of constructing the vision of a harmonic social and natural universe in the great theatrical achievements of the tragedy writers, as well as in the naturalism of the historians. He is impressed by the gloomy, often dark picture of human nature provided by writers such as Thucydides. But perhaps even more important for his own view of the human world is the conclusion he draws from classic Greek tragedy. This is the insight that we moderns overestimate the freedom of choice of the human agent – as the tragic fall of the heroes of classic Greek drama show, humans are often unable to exercise full control over the events and acts of their lives, including those that are supposed to belong to the terrain of their responsibility by society and the Gods. On the two sides of free choice, Williams keeps emphasizing, we find both chance and necessity, neither of which offers opportunities for the free exercise of human will. In this respect, the tragic hero Ajax gives the clue to Williams that Greek drama had very similar sceptical doubts about human responsibility as he himself. What is more, through the lessons he learns from Greek drama and Greek historical writing, he is able to formulate his own view of human potentials. Referring to Thucydides and Sophocles, he writes: 'Each of them represents human beings as dealing sensibly, foolishly, sometimes catastrophically, sometimes nobly, with a world that is only partially intelligible to human agency and in itself is not well adjusted to ethical aspirations.'[70] He expresses the same view in the following quote about human will: 'If you just take the will in an everyday sense, the world is only very imperfectly under its control.'[71] This is obviously a very strong criticism of the Kantian position, where will is free, subordinated only to human duty and responsibility. But Williams's main point of criticism is that 'the degree of self-understanding of post-Enlightenment ethics is rather poor'.[72] In his view, this period has no serious doubts of the 'truth-conditions' of its theories. This naivety led to the hubris of theorizing in the post-Enlightenment era, which discounted the reality check. Williams is much more sensitive to what is already existing, the status quo, than most of the post-Enlightenment authors, including Habermas. He finds it necessary to underline that in actual proposals of reform, as in the committee he participated in about pornography, one has to start out from the content of the law in force. He knows this might be labelled as a conservative starting point, which is distant from his own political preferences, yet he does not hesitate to go for it, as he demands from any theory, including his own one, truthfulness, and that means by definition a heavy reliance on reality. If you want to give advice on such ethical issues as pornography (Williams was member of that specific parliamentary committee), you need to see how far the practice in question is embedded in 'existing institutions and practices', after all this is what you need to judge in your advice.[73] As he saw it, the committee had to take into account the actual legal regulations and their specific approach to the problem, even if, in his own view 'it's better to think about pornography as a cultural phenomenon'.[74]

This historically reductionist approach to politics opens up a window on the tragic dimension of reality, which was not visible from the universalist–normative stance of Kantianism and certain other mainstream analytical approaches. For Williams, in this respect the Greek tragedies are much more revealing than philosophical treatises – presumably because they are much more in tune with his own historical and practical political experiences. Sophocles's *Oedipus* reveals, for example, the extent to which a commitment to truth might lead to tragedy: 'The further question is of course whether our commitment to truthfulness leads to strategy or to everybody being happier.'[75] Further tragedies that play a major role in his pessimistic reappraisal of the human condition along Greek lines are Sophocles's *Ajax* and his *Women of Trachis*. As he reads it – in a markedly different mode than, for example Nussbaum – they represent a world that is beyond human control.

Interestingly enough, this view, however, did not lead him to considerations of divine control, as was the case in ancient Athens. He himself remained at least an agnostic, and more probably a self-conscious non-believer, who excluded the traditional answer to this vision of human importance in any of the historical religions. This choice is, of course, non-negotiable, but this exclusion is the more surprising because the pessimistic line of Christian thought as far as human nature is concerned, from Augustine through Luther to Pascal, is closely linked to a Christian type of conservative thought. Williams seems to remain sceptical through and through – he does not find divine grace a trustworthy solution to the problem. Instead, he remains an atheistic sceptic with strong views of a politically realistic nature. In one of the interviews conducted with him, Williams refers to his late book *Truth and Truthfulness*, where his last reference is to Joseph Konrad's *Heart of Darkness*, with 'the appalling face of a glimpsed truth'.[76]

Political realism in a radical gear: Geuss

The special flavour of Raymond Geuss's philosophy is perhaps largely due to his wide and deep knowledge of Continental philosophy, especially of its German branches. Although brought up and educated in the United States, according to Alasdair MacIntyre, he is an inheritor of German philosophy, especially of the Frankfurt School, and there, too, of Adorno.[77] Geuss's criticism of mainstream liberalism, and especially of Kant, or Kantians, such as Rawls, comes from that direction. However, it is not only this criticism that relates his work to that of Williams. The two of them have some common heroes, including Thucydides and his late admirer, Nietzsche. Geuss himself explicitly and in a well-articulated manner refers to the analogies in their respective works in one of the essays of *Outside Ethics*, in which he mentions the following names: Thucydides, Nietzsche and Bernard Williams. The innovative element of his presentation is that he connects Nietzsche and Thucydides in a more philologically documented way as did Williams: he refers to the notes of Nietzsche in the 1870s and 1880s on Thucydides. Guess claims that as a result of his systematic readings, Nietzsche 'became increasingly aware of the importance of the strand of realist and empiricist thinking that Thucydides represents, and of seeing the demise of tragedy and of Thucydidean "inquiry" synoptically'.[78] MacIntyre points at the crucial claim made by Geuss about the line leading from Thucydides to Nietzsche and further, to Williams and presumably himself: he invites his readers 'to reflect on a possible historical path not taken, one from ancient shame, tragedy, and Thucydidean "inquiry", rather than from Plato, Christianity, and guilt'.[79] As MacIntyre stresses, this alternative route of intellectual heritage is offered because Geuss has serious doubts about the use of some of the key concepts of the established historical line, including such central categories as responsibility. Not surprisingly, MacIntyre not only questions whether Williams is indeed so much outside ethics as the others are, according to Geuss's narrative, but also questions the central claim according to which these concepts cannot be treated with some more historical accuracy.

The book, however, which turned out to be conducive to presenting Geuss on the central stage of the booming industry of political realism, together with Bernard Williams, is his *Philosophy and Real Politics* (2008). This volume is an extended version of a lecture Geuss gave in Athens in 2007 with the title '(Lenin), Rawls, and Political Philosophy'. Geuss's title reveals an evident political agenda in the midst of the Greek financial crisis. Once again, this book is arguing against the acclaimed 'strong "Kantian" strand... visible in much contemporary political theory'.[80] Against the self-disciplined, wholly moral agent of Kantian theory, Geuss presents a human being who is 'most of the time... weak, easily distracted, deeply conflicted, and confused'.[81] The community of such beings is also rather weak: 'People often have no determinate beliefs at all about a variety of subjects; they often don't know what they want or why they did something.'[82]

A further problem beyond this moral–epistemological scepticism is the fact that when human agents want to translate their ideas and aspirations and strive for practical terms, their values will be re-evaluated as soon as they are put into practice. In other words, there is an unavoidable tension between what is imagined and what is actually done. If the life circumstances and the interior motivational resources of human beings are like that, it is understandable that Geuss objects 'to the claim that politics is applied ethics'.[83] It is because of this acclaimed discrepancy between the imagined and the real that Geuss looks for a political philosophy, which is more interested in the specific distinguishing marks of politics as a distinct field of practical human activity. He seems to share Williams's suspicions of a political theory simply built on the foundations of ethics.

Geuss's proposal for an autonomous political philosophy is along the following lines. He writes, 'First, political philosophy must be realist.'[84] His distinction between politics as applied ethics and realism follows the Kantian 'ought-is' distinction, which can be explained in a nutshell: 'Don't look just at what they say, think, believe, but at what they actually do, and what *actually happens* as a result.'[85] This explanation is already hinting at the second point, which is that political philosophy is not about 'mere beliefs or propositions', but 'in the first instance about action and the contexts of action'.[86] If so, the third point comes logically: 'Politics is historically located' and therefore political philosophy needs to be historically informed. Finally, the fourth assumption is that 'politics is more like the exercise of a craft or art', and less like applied theory.[87] He finishes this introductory part of his proposal with the claim that his own view of politics is 'orthogonal to the mainstream of contemporary analytic political philosophy'. In other words, he seems to push the issue even further than where Williams stands. After all, MacIntyre is right, that Williams never renounced his own analytical training, even if he, too, heavily criticized the ahistorical practice of analytical philosophy.

The second part of Geuss's book starts with an excavation of the sources of the tradition that the author wants to join. Geuss admits that '"the realist approach to political philosophy" develops... (a) basically Hobbesian insight'.[88] Later on, he presents three further names of that tradition: Lenin, Nietzsche and Max Weber. Of the three, Lenin is obvious and Nietzsche is by now not a surprise. However, Weber is not an obvious choice – after all, his reputation in mainstream sociological theory is not challenged these days. The members of the group are hard to reconcile. Lenin does not have real credit among intellectuals after 1990, except for a relatively minor group of leftist radicals and fundamentalists. Yet, if we look at the particular point attributed to Lenin, it is not so iconoclastic; in fact, it is not much more than an emphasis put on the agency aspect of politics: 'To think politically is to think about agency, power, and interests, and the relations among these.'[89] Sharpening Lenin's thesis, Geuss adds that agency is crucial even within the reflective sphere of politics: 'Entertaining, developing, and propounding a theory are actions.'[90] In other words, thoughts are deeds.

The second point that Geuss attributes to Nietzsche is about priorities and timing. Here, Geuss, too, returns to the Greeks – after all, Nietzsche was a classical philologist. He concentrates on the term *kairos*, which means the proper moment for action. Finally, he discusses the issue of legitimacy with Max Weber. As Geuss interprets Weber, to find an action legitimate is to find reasons for it. Legitimacy is also time and place bound, what works in one scenario may prove impotent in another scenario. And certainly, opposed to Weber's trust of a rational way of legitimating action, Geuss holds that our beliefs that provide legitimacy are often 'confused, potentially contradictory, incomplete and pliable as anything else, and they can in principle be manipulated'.[91]

The next question for Geuss is: If we take human nature to be like that (human agents are not the rational agents of rational choice theory, to put it mildly), and if the image of politics in a realist key is like that (agent centred, dependent on a sense of timing and in need of legitimation), what should political philosophy look like? He answers his own question under five headings. First of all, through political philosophy one needs to understand coordinated common action. This understanding needs to be historically informed. Next, one needs to be able to evaluate political issues through this understanding; after all, as Nietzsche famously put it: 'Der Mensch ist ein abschätzendes Tier.'[92] What is more, and this is already a third point, we have to interpret and evaluate political affairs with looking at what makes a meaningful life, in other words, in accordance with ancient Greek *eudaimonia*. But perhaps more importantly, fourthly, political philosophy might make 'a constructive contribution to politics by conceptual invention or innovation'. His example is, once again, Hobbes, to whom he attributes the invention of the concept of the state. The claim is that once the concept is established, it starts to behave as a natural kind, i.e. as a living organism, not as something linguistically invented. Finally, political philosophy might participate in fostering or, for that matter, in deconstructing ideologies.

But the real novelty of Geuss is not his new proposals about the potentials of political philosophy. Rather, it is his sharp criticism of mainline liberal political philosophy, with its moralizing melodrama and irresponsible relationship to politics, in other words, with its fully apolitical attitude. Geuss refers to the common-sense assumption that you cannot practice political philosophy in any relevant way without taking into serious consideration the nature of that very phenomenon. In the second, reflexive part of his book, Geuss's sharp critical voice dissects such fashionable notions of liberal political philosophy, as rights, justice, equality, fairness, ignorance, impartiality. He convincingly shows the illogical nature of the efforts of mainstream Western political philosophy to present these categories as the real foundations of a desirable framework for politics. Geuss presumably does not question the achievements of Western political philosophy as far as its contribution to the birth of contemporary constitutional democracy is concerned, even if he seems to have an uncovered sympathy for the way of thinking of such subversive figures as Marx and Lenin. Yet, by reintroducing figures such as Marx and Lenin, he seems to underestimate the dangers of brave utopian ideas, attributed to his heroes, and the destruction of human life on the level of mass murder committed with reference to them. One should also be critical about his defence of a rather shallow view of political neo-Leninism. Geuss seems to have forgotten to provide his reader with an explanation, which might calm down historically underpinned worries.[93]

For our present purposes, it is his final gesture that is relevant – where he presents the concept of power as his conceptual alternative to Rawlsian justice. What is more, he declares that he is not talking about his own ideals but about the realities of politics. He argues that power is the ultimate guiding principle of politics, and justice as equality is an ideal, which as such is too wide and too general to be operationalized. 'If you want to think about politics, think first about power.'[94] This is his first advice to newcomers to politics, without which they would easily be misguided. This is why he criticizes Rawls: 'The topic of power, in particular, is simply one he never explicitly discusses at all.'[95]

It is because of the apolitical nature of Rawls's theory, including his inability to confront the issue of power, that Geuss draws the conclusion: 'In real politics, theories like that of Rawls are nonstarters.'[96]

And yet, this is not the final point he wants to make. It is in the conclusion where he deals with the ideas of justice and power once again, and where he refers to the notion of political judgement. This is not a term he used too often earlier, and it is somewhat surprising that in the conclusion this concept is so central. Yet, I am of the opinion that he indeed attributes real significance to this concept. It is introduced in a manner that reminds one of the ancient Greek discourse about it: he defines politics as a 'craft or skill'.[97] Although apparently this redefinition of politics seems to simplify it to a handicraft, Geuss is careful: he also adds that a part of this art is 'being able to choose skilfully which models of reality to use in a certain context'.[98] In other words, practical judgement is not independent of our intellectual capacities to interpret our impressions of reality, even if it is basically part of political practice.

The main point of the 'practical turn' of Geuss is to put political judgement on the stage, into the centre of his thoughts on politics. Politics is a handicraft, he puts forward in his strongest thesis, which consists of not much more than political judgement.[99] No system-building, no theoretical considerations can take the place of it: 'No further theory will help you avoid the need to judge.'[100]

Conclusion of Part One

To conclude the historical part, let us return once again to Aristotle. To understand the art of politics as the need to judge properly is nothing less within the framework of the present venture than a chance to reintroduce into the discourse on politics the Aristotelian notion of *phronetic* knowledge and the *phronimos* as the desirable agent of politics. It requires giving up the highbrow notions of contemporary political philosophy, including 'considerations of fairness, equality, justice', and instead returning to the down-to-earth reality of the practice of politics, by flesh and blood human beings, in the context of the daily business of human communities to deliberate, decide, speak and act for the common good. As the short historical overview suggested, there exists a continuous tradition in European political thought, which worked out the details of this way of thinking. It started in the ancient Greek *polis* of Athens with Aristotle, and was continued by such diverse authors as Cicero and Augustine in ancient Rome, Aquinas in medieval Europe, Florentine humanists and Italian Jesuits, by Lipsius and Montaigne in the post-Reformation era, by twentieth-century Continental philosophers interested in ancient Greek practical philosophy as Gadamer and Ricouer, and ending with political realists such as Bernard Williams and Raymond Geuss. All of them shared a belief that to act properly in politics requires the guidance of the virtue of (political) prudence, which means practical wisdom enabling us to decide what is proper in a given situation for us, individual human agents. Practical wisdom (*phronesis*) in this context is contrasted with speculative reason (*sophia* or *episteme*), which abstracts from the here and now. If humans are motivated by the latter, they tend to be driven by speculation, which can do more harm than good in the practical life world of politics. The Aristotelian–Ciceronian tradition rather suggests relying on practical experience, both in its individual and communal form. While the former also requires the control mechanism of the virtue of moderation, the latter is available by institutions as well as by formal and informal traditions. This understanding of a constrained form of politics is based on a rather pessimistic note of human nature, and yet regards politics as crucial for a fully developed human life. The fact that what is regarded here as the Aristotelian–Ciceronian tradition has survived more regimes seems to be proof of its survival capacity.

Part Two provides an analysis of the main challenges for a politics of prudence. It introduces the individual and communal resources available to political agents and presents a description of how this politics of prudence can work smoothly in a rather hectic and uncontrollable social world and in a manner that is not always friendly to human beings and their communities. It also explains in what sense this politics of prudence leads to a grand political philosophy of conservatism, based on the idea of tradition as the communal reservoir of practical political wisdom.

Part Two

Prudence in conservative philosophy

Preliminary remarks

Part One provided a historical overview of some of the most important phases of what is called here the prudential paradigm in Western political thought. This was, of course, not an exhaustive account. We had to select some of the most relevant representatives of this paradigm, ranging from Aristotle through Cicero to Aquinas, to certain authors of the early modern Christian humanist tradition and only two authors each of the twentieth-century philosophical directions of hermeneutics and political realism. The aim of the overview was to show that in spite of the sharp differences in these phases, as far as both the sociopolitical environment and the *Weltanschauung* of the representatives of these directions are concerned, there are important returning themes and even concepts in their writings, including returning basic convictions about human nature and the nature of politics.

Yet, at this point, the reader might pose the question: Does this historical overview have any contemporary relevance, or is it simply a historicist exercise purely to satisfy the antiquarian curiosity? The answer is a definitive yes to its contemporary relevance: the historical overview serves to be helpful to a political philosophy of conservatism, which makes sense of politics in the context of the political uncertainty which has become a permanent feature of the modern European scene in the twenty-first century.

The end of the millennium and the beginning of a new one witnessed an especially risky, sometimes even scary period with the fall of the Berlin Wall, 9/11, a world financial crisis, the migration shock, Brexit and Trump's presidential victory, not to mention the rebirth of a capitalist and communist China, the awakening of an imperialist Russia, newcomers in the geopolitical arena, from India to Brazil and a serious internal schism within the European Union. Climate change also causes disconformity on a global level. Also, a major development is the global rise of authoritarian political regimes that challenge the positions of both constitutional democracy and the rule of law, as they were known in the Anglo-Saxon world, or the *Rechtsstaat* model of Continental Europe. No doubt, the fall of the Iron Curtain liberated political forces, with unknown intentions and characterized by unfamiliar political cultures, and certainly by the removal of the rigid rules of a bipolar system, new perspectives opened up for new players who could widen their sphere of influence on a global scale. Predator mentality was, however, not a new experience internationally after the block structure of global politics was deconstructed, as international relations has always been characterized by the Hobbesian mentality of all against all. Yet, with the rise of new political risks, the unpredictability of politics became even more manifest. Although this is perhaps not a totally new experience, not even an unparalleled political moment, to realize the new risks helps us to remind ourselves of the fact that politics on all levels is and remains for the foreseeable future a realm of uncertainty and a delicate balance. If we accept this standard, we can easily see the relevance of working out a conservative philosophical account of political prudence. In an environment of unpredictable challenges, prudence is all-important as a guide for the human political agent to remain on the surface in novel political situations.

However, here a further note of caution is required. The last canonical figure of our historical overview was Raymond Geuss, a representative of the direction usually labelled political realism. His view of politics starts out from the darkest possible assumptions of human nature and of the political aspirations of the human agent. On the cover of his book, we see a war scene, with the dead body of a young man among the building rubble, as well as a gunman on the reverse side, with a distorted face, looking at him. In his review of the book, the critic of the *London Review of Books* describes the scene the following way:

> The new book's jacket image, a striking black and white photo by John Sadovy, shows a young man almost literally biting the dust. Only after turning the book over to look at the back does one notice his presumed killer, reloading his rifle. This example already poses questions beyond the ken of liberal orthodoxy. The dead man, a member of the AVH, the Hungarian secret police, was among those put to death by anti-Soviet partisans in the 1956 uprising.[1]

The intention behind the decision to put the photo on the cover is obvious. Geuss wants to destabilize our basic convictions of the moral and political evaluation of killing by providing an example that can be claimed as justified killing – after all, the guerrilla fighter of the 1956 revolution was fighting for a just cause, namely liberty, while the dead man was a member of the secret police of a totalitarian regime. However, there is a – perhaps unintended – consequence of putting on the cover an image of an exceptional moment of an armed revolution. It suggests that after all, or – to put it another way – ultimately, politics can be translated simply as the (legitimate?) use of violence. In other words, Geuss's book relies on the assumption that one should interpret politics as if it was not much more than the successful use of violence. Certainly, in a minority of cases this assumption is quite legitimate: Carl Schmitt showed that the sovereign is he who decides on the state of exception.[2] Yet, it would provide only a simplified view of political life, if we generalize on the assumption that to interpret politics we only need to determine who holds the potential to use violence finally against the other. Although we accept that politics is an underdetermined field of crossing or coordinated individual and communal human actions and intentions, we would like to keep in mind the presumption that in the normal case all human societies rely on a list of taboos, in other words, of written or customary, external or internalized norms of prohibitions, which narrow down the occasions for using pure and uncontrolled violence to solve problems. In other words, in the normal case – and we will decidedly concentrate on the state of normality – prudence should prevail against the use of sheer violence. In this context, prudence should be looked at as the art of individual and communal decision-making and execution in the world of politics, where these decisions and actions have very well defined control mechanisms and external barriers. In this sense, the concept of prudence relied on here will be unlike the barefooted rationale of the gunman on the jacket of Geuss's book. Rather, it will be a composite of Machiavellian insights into the witch's brew of efficient real politics and a tradition-based account of their rapport with a rich social matrix of mores, prescriptions and interdicts moderating human will. This is based on the firm foundation that only a collateral description of these two sides of the coin (freedom to act and control over human acts) can give us a faithful view of the true nature of the human intercourse called politics.

In other words, the political philosophy presented here can be characterized as a *via media* between the ideal world of the Rawlsian utopia of a rather deep moral intrusion into the world of politics, and the amoral attitude of political realism, from Machiavelli and Hobbes to Carl Schmitt and Raymond Geuss. Its key notion, prudence, is both one of the key (cardinal) virtues within the ancient and the Christian understanding of morally charged interpersonal relationships and a reminder of the specific demands within the realm of politics. Although in what follows, this theory does not directly confront these two rivals, the reader is advised to consider it in comparison with these two, the Rawlsian and the Machiavellian alternatives.

Prudence before justice

This book is based on the assumption that a new and fruitful account of politics can be gained by relying on the virtue of prudence instead of that of justice as the first guiding principle of our political philosophy. Justice certainly remains a key notion for the present endeavour as well, as was the case in the European tradition, from Socrates, Plato and Aristotle, through the Christian doctrines of the ideal political regime up to the modern liberal authors from Locke to Rawls. The offer of the present approach is that justice will be replaced as the central virtue of political philosophy by another of the four cardinal virtues, namely prudence.

To explain this replacement, first a redescription of the political philosophy of justice is required, in order to show how the present theory differs from the earlier theory. The political philosophy of justice – more or less already in its scholastic form and in full swing in its Rawlsian version – is based on a view of politics that focuses on the right preconditions and the acceptable or desirable consequences of political decisions and actions, instead of those very decisions and actions. In order to avoid any possible forms of social injustice, it presents the ideal principles, which should guide the distribution of goods in society, institutions that would channel political operations and boundary conditions such as individual rights that should be honoured regardless of the particular political aims and challenges of a political regime. In other words, it offers an order or a constitutional arrangement, which would guarantee that our values will prevail: that equality will be honoured and injustice avoided. It also yields arguments how a just institutional system could make society better. All these aspects make justice a good starting point. Unfortunately, in most of the cases it fails the reality test, and consciously disregards particularities. In order to fight utilitarian and intuitionist arguments, which were his main theoretical opponents, Rawls's aim was not to solve an individual state of affairs but to present arguments that were meant to 'lead to an original agreement on principles of justice'.[3]

His set of methodological devices, including the original position and the veil of ignorance, had the function to create social agreement in a generalized, apolitical way. As Geuss critically interpreted it, 'the "original position" was supposed to be disjoined from real politics, an ideal standpoint from which to survey the human world disinterestedly and impartially'.[4] Geuss, however, wants to plant decision and action in the centre of political thought. As he sees it, a realist political philosophy 'must start from and be concerned in the first instance not with how people ought ideally (or ought "rationally") to act, what they ought to desire or value, the kind of people they ought to be, etc., but, rather, with the way the social, economic, political etc., institutions actually operate in some society at some given time'.[5]

From a rather different perspective, Ricoeur, too, attacks Rawls's methodological device. He wants to show that without a substantial, politically informed account of the good, Rawls's arguments in favour of the procedural principles of social justice he defends, would hardly be convincing. In his view, Rawls starts out from a wrong hypothesis, from the assumption that 'a purely procedural conception of justice can make sense without any presupposition concerning the good'.[6] Ricoeur thinks that without the cultural baggage of our 'long *Bildung*' and without the conceptual apparatus it provides us – including the Golden Rule – Rawls's 'maximin rule would remain a purely prudential argument'.[7]

Although when he mentions prudential argument, Ricoeur surely did not think here of the virtue of prudence, let us take him at his word, and see how far we can go with the help of building our political philosophy exactly on the virtue of prudence. Instead of a normative account of an ideal social setting, here the reader will find reflections on the experience of individual and communal agents of the political field, and only on this basis will efforts be made to find out how and where the limits to purely power considerations can be found. In other words, this is going to be a conservative account of the virtue of prudence, practice and experience based, relying on human nature as its foundation, and on the nature of the sphere of politics, as a specific form of interpersonal relationships. In this respect, it accepts the Machiavellian, realist criticism of Rawlsian forms of theorizing the apolitical construction of political justice. Conversely, the virtue of prudence is not the prudence of pure self-interest. Rather, it is embedded into a traditional discursive framework, which allows a conservative political philosophy of prudence to describe the normative dimension of politics, without getting dogmatic and scholastic. Political prudence in Aristotle is an embodied knowledge as exemplified by Pericles, and therefore its criteria cannot be given in a taxative form. But conservatism as a political philosophy never aimed to pin down its founding principles. Rather, what it finds necessary is a narrative about politics, which is able to describe both the challenges of finding the proper act in a delicate political situation and the resources, which the political agent can mobilize. In what follows, this conservative methodology will be followed to delineate the main outlines of a conservative political philosophy based on the virtue of prudence.

4

Agency-constraint

'The political' in the decisions of individuals and communities

When searching for the distinguishing mark of politics, realists tend to return to Carl Schmitt's views on the political (*'das politische'*), as presented in his 1932 book, *The Concept of the Political*. According to Carl Schmitt, the criteria of the political should be compared[1] and contrasted with such fields of human thought and action as the moral, the aesthetic or the economical. All these fields are defined by counter-concepts like the good and the bad in the moral realm, or the ugly and the beautiful in the aesthetic realm. The political is defined by the contrast between the friend and the enemy. The friend–enemy test shows where the frontline in politics is drawn, where unification is possible and where dissociation is required. The enemy is existentially distinguished from the friend, and one's proper relationship with the enemy can only be characterized as a political conflict. Those who fall within the camp of the enemy will unite into one, hostile group, while the other group, those of the friend, will unite into another, allied group separated from the other by a demarcation line, threatening with the potential of an articulated conflict.

However, from our aspect, this is not the most important point of Schmitt. The most important point of his theory of the political is the significance of making the decision about who the enemy is. 'To the state as an essentially political entity belongs the *jus belli*, i.e. the real possibility of deciding in a concrete situation upon the enemy and the ability to fight him with the power emanating from the entity.'[2] This point is important for political realism as it draws attention to the exceptional significance of agency in political matters. A given state of political affairs, from this perspective, is not an objective set of criteria, existing externally to the political agent, who is in a position to decide in a neutral, distanced manner, but something on which he or she has to decide. The outstanding interest in the moment of the decision makes Schmitt's theory a par excellence theory of decisionism. It is here that his work on the political coincides with his other major work, *Political Theology: Four Chapters on the Concept of Sovereignty* (1934). In this last piece, Schmitt's question concerns how to define the sovereign in a given political field. The importance he attributes to the sovereign decision is not dependent on the fact that it is made by the highest constitutionally authorized authority, for decision in this strong sense of the word is not simply a decision, which applies the law to a concrete situation. On the contrary, it is a decision that decides on its own right, without relying on external factors, institutional or provisional. It depends on the authority of the particular person who makes the decision. The decision in a state of exception is made within a political order, but the agent needs to get rid of the normative legal content of that order, to solve the exceptional case in a free and therefore sovereign manner.

Political realism takes over this significance attributed to the sovereign agent's decision from the decisionism of Schmitt. But the present theory of the political philosophy of prudence finds Schmitt's theory too voluntaristic, and therefore proposes the following modifications to Schmitt's theory. It argues for the significance of the particular decisions of each and every political agent, individual or communal, disregarding their sovereignty or the lack of it. Politics in this sense is nothing more than decisions of agents, and the actions resulting from those decisions, not depending on whether the one who decided was a natural or a legal person or entity. Any choice that is political in the sense accepted here (i.e. a decision and the action resulting from it to solve a political situation) is necessarily made within a political and legal order, in other words, within the scope provided by the existing legal norms and the standing political customs of the given political community. The political philosophy of prudence denies the strong sense attributed by Schmitt to the notion of the exceptional case in the decision. Following Gadamer's and Ricoeur's interpretation of *phronesis*, a socially provided legal framework is seen here as a prerequisite for the individual's actual decision – it is not an obstacle to a free decision, but a precondition of it. On the contrary, without supposing an agent, and without the agent making a decision (and denying the decision is also a decision), politics is logically not possible. This understanding of politics as the decision of a constrained agent leaves him or her a responsible agent in the political, legal and moral sense of the word, without claiming autonomy or sovereignty in the full sense of the word. Yet, as we will see, the virtue of prudence consists of understanding that your responsibility does not ensure that you can make a good decision in a given situation – how you make use of your agency does not fully depend on you – you are responsible morally, but you are not fully free in the sense of political sovereignty.

The conservative political philosophy of prudence differs from Schmittian decisionism in one more respect. It does not stop at the intellectual act of the decision but wants to understand the realm of political actions, as the realization of the decisions made and the significance of political actions for us, humans. In this respect, inspiration comes directly from Arendt and indirectly from Aristotle. Both the modern and the ancient thinker keep emphasizing that human life has an essentially political character, in the sense that acting in community in favour of the common good is not only essential for the survival of the individual and the good of the community but also helps the individual fulfil the potential he (and for Arendt she, too) has by his or her very nature. In other words, politics is not understood by them as an abstract structure of systems of dependences, or put differently, an institutional order, but rather as processes of decisions and actions within a certain institutional environment that have outcomes which will create the preconditions for further decisions and actions. Both the decisions and the concluding actions are surrounded and limited by the institutional frameworks of laws and *mores*, but the continuous line of these actions will be preserved in different forms of public memory, including political narratives and traditions.

Interestingly, while realists keep criticizing the *naivité* of the supporters of Aristotelian virtue politics, Aristotelians and realists find common ground as far as the centrality of decisions and actions is concerned in politics. This common ground enables us to appreciate the realist component of virtue politics. Also, both camps keep emphasizing that politics is an unpredictable affair, and this hazardous nature directs our attention to the instability of the realm of politics, especially in a democratic regime. This fact leads to the temporal dimension of politics: decisions and actions build up longer chains of causal links, which make politics not as easily readable as analytical philosophers would wish, that is in the present moment, because you have to acquaint yourself with a prehistory and a certain mindset to understand a given state of political affairs. Also, political agents and commentators must reconcile themselves to the fact that the success of a particular political decision and action will only be clear in the future.

Political action, of course, differs, depending on the nature of the political agent concerned. First of all, it depends on whether the agent is an individual player or a community or an association of agents. Obviously, the depth of individual memory is not as far-reaching as that of a political community. In other words, a community's decisions and actions are much more determined than those of an individual player. From this perspective, we can assert that the historicity of a communal agent is much more pervasive, or at least it is much more centred on *longue durée* than that of an individual agent. However, as a result of the decisions and their concluding actions, both acquire a narrative political identity, an identity formed by the memory of the line of these decisions and actions, reconstructed by their memory as a narrative. Therefore, each and every decision and action has a long-term effect besides its practical consequences. But even more importantly, the fact that politics is determined by human agents' actions and decisions about human affairs makes human agency in the Aristotelian–Arendtian paradigm central to politics. In fact, agency is much more central than institutions or norms and values. But this agent-centred nature of politics is, in fact, a constraint on politics: political success will always finally depend on individuals, including individual agents who decide and act and individuals who suffer the consequences of these decisions and actions. This is why politics remains a human affair, and why the first constraint on politics is agency-constraint.

Human sociability

If politics is a human, interpersonal affair, primarily dependent on human agents, one needs to realize that there are two opposing sides to an individual human being's nature. One is the unquestionable sociable leanings of the human being, the other the self-centred, egoistic side of him or her. The present philosophy of prudence takes human nature as a combination of these two sides, which makes human cooperation a hard, but not evidently impossible task. In what follows, let us briefly summarize these two sides of the same coin, human nature as it supports human cooperation, and the way it deconstructs it. The vector of these two opposing anthropological motivations has been called 'unsocial sociability' by the tradition, going back to the Scottish Enlightenment and Immanuel Kant.³

Let us recall two different approaches to this complex of human sociability. The first was worked out by Cicero, reintroduced by Shaftesbury, critically rephrased by Kant and once again reappropriated by Oakeshott. The other is the category of the person in the social teaching of the Catholic Church, worked out mostly in the twentieth century. As for human asociability, it is regarded as a basically Augustinian theme, reappropriated by the Reformation, but also present in theories of human conflict from Hobbes to Schmitt.

The issue is, of course, the old-fashioned one: who is right? On the one side, there are those who believed that human nature is fallen from the very beginning and society should be managed accordingly, and on the other side those who think that human beings are born sociable, and envy is something that develops later in one's life, perhaps it is learnt from others, and when receiving the right sort of humane *Bildung*, it is socially avoidable. Although one would think that this is a debate between two rival directions of Christian philosophy, the issue can certainly be traced back to the Greek philosophical scene, continuing after the decline of European Christian religiosity. There is no opportunity to clear up the mess of that huge debate here, and there is no need to either: this theory takes the side of a mitigated interpretation of human sociability. It suggests that we need to look at the arguments of the philosophers of sociability in order to show that there are good reasons to argue that politics should not simply be seen as a field of eternal conflicts, as is by now generally claimed among theorists of political realism within the Schmittian paradigm.

It was Cicero who, in his *De Officiis*, used the term *societas*. What he meant by that was not much more (even if not much less, either) than the potential for fellowship, an openness to join efforts in a common venture.⁴ The fact that the recent English translation renders the term 'fellowship', as well as the fact that Cicero's fellowship is based on what he calls natural sociability, coupled with its use in a global context, connects the Ciceronian concept of sociability to the Christian teaching of the love of fellow man or benevolence. Already the Ten Commandments define the Christian believer as one who loves one's neighbour as oneself. Certainly, we all might have questions whether or not that sort of openness is possible for the fallen human being, but even the potential of it clears up our view of human nature, darkened by the tradition from the Greek sceptics to Augustine and Pascal. Certainly, the religious commandment to love your neighbour is based on a more optimistic view of human nature than that obtained by Augustine. In its centre, we find a programme of human perfectibility, based on the assumption that God has created man in his own image and likeness. The traditions of early church fathers such as Irenaeus lead to Aquinas, and from him up through the mystical writers such as St Francis or St Theresa, to Rahner and neo-Thomists such as Maritain or Réginald Garrigou-Lagrange. All of them shared a view according to which even if humans were open to commit sins, they also had a natural inclination towards each other and the good.

Trust in the human propensity helps believers to find a way towards each other. This trust is encouraged in Christian teaching by the fact that it is through the other that human beings can reach God, according to the Ten Commandments. In other words, as opposed to the individualist ethics of modern atheism, as well as of some of the Greek moral schools, in Christian thought moral perfection and a community with one's fellow human beings are logically connected. It is at this point that the teaching of the third Earl of Shaftesbury about a common moral sense and the role of benevolent emotions to lead human beings to cooperate, resonates with Christianity. However, his main reference point is, of course, ancient Greco–Roman philosophy. And while he shares the Christian view of a human nature directed towards the others, he keeps criticizing religious strife fuelled by superstition or enthusiasm, as it creates civil war and internal crisis. Attacking the immoderate, subversive and, in that sense, anti-communal and self-centred morality of the fundamentalists of the religious and civil wars, his teaching is an optimistic and liberating teaching of sociability, dependent on the notion of *sensus communis* and the moderation of overwhelming passions. Being widely read in the ancients, Shaftesbury tended towards the teachings of the Stoics, and yet his main message as far as interpersonal relationships were concerned, was an idea of natural sociability.

Shaftesbury's most important philosophical opponent was Hobbes, because of Hobbes's emphasis on the egoistic tendencies in human nature, determining eternal conflicts in interpersonal relationships. Certainly, their different views are, to a large extent, explained by their different experiences of the two: while Hobbes was a child of the long-standing struggles of the English Civil War, the third earl must have had rather different experiences in the post-1688 compromise. Shaftesbury is much more optimistic not only about the existence of a sociable (moral) sense within the human mental make-up but also about the possibility of negotiating between sociable virtue and asocial self-interest. As he puts it, '*Virtue* and *Interest* may be found at last to agree.'[5] Although there are interpreters who claim that Shaftesbury, too, admitted certain egoistic tendencies in human nature, the important point about him was that he based his practical philosophy on the idea of a natural sociability available to us. In addition to Hobbesian egoism, he criticized the idea of a strictly passion-ridden human being, which was defended by his eager reader, David Hume.

The egoistic account of human nature

While the supposition of sociability promised to be a reliable basis for a politics of cooperation, the obviously egoistic traits of human nature produced an agonistic account of politics. This view of human nature was the result of a sort of scepticism, which returned convincingly in the political philosophy of both classical liberalism and British-style conservatism. The confrontation of these two perspectives of the human being took place in the eighteenth century.

The Scottish Enlightenment, a very powerful cultural movement in the eighteenth century, was heavily influenced by Shaftesbury, even if its most powerful philosophical voice, David Hume, while admiring Shaftesbury's style and manners, criticized the philosophical naivety of the earl, being himself influenced by the extremely pessimistic Mandeville as well.

It was Mandeville who represented the polar opposite of Shaftesbury's optimistic sociability thesis of the age. He claimed that, in fact, human beings tend to be motivated by egoistic impulses. In his *Fable of the Bees* (1705, 1714), he argued that public benefits are often the result of individual (or private) vices. In other words, he was among the first to show that the common good and individual self-interest do not necessarily contradict each other. Although this is a modern paraphrase of the well-known Augustinian criticism of our human condition, the interesting point in the story is that even if the individual human agent can be morally condemned, this fact does not exclude the possibility of the smooth operation of the social-economic machinery, as competition and rivalry are quite helpful, and also because through egoistic gratifications of desires a new impetus of market demand can be awakened, while cooperation and consensus might slow down the circle of supply and demand, in other words, market equilibrium.

Asocial sociability

Inspired by both Shaftesbury and Mandeville, David Hume's more elaborate and philosophically more sophisticated and therefore more defendable philosophical position on sociability preserved the point of the innate natural sociability of humans, although he claimed that instead of reason, passions are the main motivating force of human agency, while also admitting inborn selfish tendencies in human beings.

Interestingly, Hume's own complex answer to the Mandevillean challenge is that although human beings are, to a large extent, interest-ridden, they are less rationalistic than the Dutch doctor thought. This is Hume's special sort of moderated scepticism, which is also sceptical of the potential of human rationality to move one's actions towards one's self-interest. In this sense, he is not less, but more sceptical than Mandeville was before him. Interestingly, Hume still really believed in the force of a natural sociability born with (or within) us. A key example of this is his description of his own philosophical crisis, during the writing process of his *Treatise*, when at a given moment he left his room in despair, not being certain of the meaning of even the most obvious concepts of human nature.

> Most fortunately it happens, that since reason is incapable of dispelling these clouds, nature herself suffices to that purpose, and cures me of this philosophical melancholy and delirium ... I dine, I play a game of back-gammon, I converse, and am merry with my friends; and when after three or four hour's amusement, I would return to these speculations, they appear so cold, and strain'd, and ridiculous, that I cannot find in my heart to enter into them any farther.[6]

This is the famous climax of Hume's description of his own philosophical sojourn in the first book of the *Treatise*, where he gives up his hopes to metaphysically pinpoint his philosophical convictions, and where he turns his investigations towards human passions and morals. This description of the climax is itself part of the narrative, and can be interpreted as a very strong thesis about a philosophical naturalism overwriting metaphysical dilemmas and denying the hegemony of the rational activity of the mind.

Interestingly, Hume, in fact, opposes here the Cartesian heritage, and rather comes close to the spiritual exercises of the church fathers or even to the sort of embodied philosophy, or philosophy as a *Lebensart*, described by Pierre Hadot's reconstructions of ancient Greek and early Christian philosophy.[7]

It is, however, Immanuel Kant, with admittedly Humean inspirations, who went as far as to bridge the gap between emotionalism and rationalism as well as that of sociability and egoism. His concept of asocial sociability (*ungesellige Geselligkeit*) seems to be an oxymoron, or paradox, but it is a philosophically – and even metaphysically – quite useful concept of how a political community or simply a non-political social bond is possible if human beings turn out to be rather selfish by nature. Although the present-day secondary literature rarely refers to this fact, Kant was a Protestant thinker with a Pietist Lutheran family background, who partly relied on the Augustinian tradition in his view of human nature. Conversely, he seemed to trust the social potential of human beings not so much against their egoistic tendencies, but rather more because of them. As he puts it in his essay *Idea for a Universal History from a Cosmopolitan Point of View* (1784):

> Man has an inclination to associate with others ... But he also has a strong propensity to isolate himself from others, ... he expects opposition on all sides because, in knowing himself, he knows that he, on his own part, is inclined to oppose others. This opposition awakens all his powers, brings him to conquer his inclination to laziness and, propelled by vainglory, lust for power, and avarice, to achieve a rank among his fellows whom he cannot tolerate but from whom he cannot withdraw.[8]

Kant's point is about competition for honour and glory, a theme also embarked on by Montesquieu, who found those aims the most important motivating force behind French culture and politics. But Kant is not talking here about national glory, but about the universal propensity of human nature: this is an issue that Hegel discusses in his analysis of the master–slave relationship under the concept of a struggle for recognition. The point made here is that besides natural sociability, humans have a motivation to excel. This is because society rewards excellence in the form of social recognition. For this, members of society are ready to invest. Competition has, however, no disruptive consequences as long as it is kept under social control – on the contrary, it can lead to an overflow of human products, which would have never been born without this impetus to excel. The overflow of creative energies caused by the motivation to excel is behind the innovative potential of modern commercial society, according to the moral economists of the Scottish Enlightenment. In Kant's view, this desire to be recognized by others directly leads to the birth of culture and morality. According to his narrative, through the paradoxical motives of asocial sociability human beings can develop together to achieve the levels of culture, taste and morality.[9]

The Christian concept of the person

No doubt, this analysis has a very realistic overtone, which makes it legitimate even in the eyes of disillusioned twenty-first-century readers. However, I would like to introduce another theory of human sociability to show that one can reach a realistic account from the opposite direction, too. While Kant starts out from what is later called 'methodological individualism',[10] the theory of the person in Christian social teaching starts out from a rather different notion. According to its self-definition, the social teaching of the church is 'neither a bundle of practical instructions for the solution of social questions nor a skilful selection of certain findings of modern sociology useful for Christian social training, but "an integral component of the Christian doctrine of man" (Mater et magistra)'.[11] Although, according to this very teaching, it 'was proclaimed by the Church "from the very first centuries"',[12] it became pertinent in the age of industrialization, with a line of social encyclicals, including *Rerum novarum* (1891), *Quadragesimo anno* (1931), *Mater et magistra* (1961), *Pacem in terris* (1963), *Gaudium et spes* (1965), *Populorum progressio* (1976), *Laborem exercens* (1981), *Solicitudo rei socialis* (1987) and *Centesimus annus* (1991).

The centre of the Catholic doctrine on man is the idea of the person, as described by the catechism of the Catholic Church: 'Being in the image of God the human individual possesses the dignity of a person. The human individual is capable of self-knowledge, of self-possession and of freely giving himself and entering into communion with other persons.'[13] This positive account of the human being is important as the foundation upon which the legitimation of human rights can be built. However, it has another relevance for our discussion here.

The idea of the person as conceived in the Catholic social teaching suggests that a reconciliation between two radical views is possible: the individualism of the liberal view and the idea of the community of communitarian theories can complement each other in this scheme. This is made possible by the fact that the Catholic philosophy of personhood preserves and reconciles the valuable elements of both the individualist and the communal perspective. What is more, it shows the internal logical connection between the two views. The key novelty of the approach of Catholic social teaching is, as pointed out by Joseph Höffner, the insight that there is a mutual interdependence between personhood and sociability. An individual becomes a person through his or her social connections, while there are no social connections without the individual having a hard core of identity. 'He is a person, and it is only in terms of personhood that his social nature can be comprehended.'[14] This duality of selfhood and sociability is expressed by the assertion that personhood means self-sufficiency and uniqueness, as well as freedom and social responsibility, operated by a lively conscience. However, 'in grounding the essentially social nature of man, it seems obvious to emphasize first of all his dependence on others and on society in the bodily-material, spiritual-cultural, and moral realms'.[15]

It is important to realize that the teaching on sociability in the age of Enlightenment, from Shaftesbury to Kant, differs in important respects from the Christian social teaching. As we saw, Shaftesbury's source of inspiration was partly ancient philosophy, partly his own innovative theory of moral sense and natural sociability, based on his 'intellectual roots in the latitudinarian divinity of the Restoration'.[16] Kant had puritan leanings, but his metaphysics was original, and his practical philosophy was based on this metaphysical foundation. However, neither Shaftesbury nor Kant tried to talk about this issue in a theological perspective; in particular, neither of them understood the human condition in the framework of social and moral theology and theological anthropology.[17]

The novelty of the Christian social teaching (compared to the Enlightenment and Kant) is that instead of defending the sociable nature of man on either utilitarian or philosophically substantiated metaphysical grounds, it returns to the Christian understanding of human nature. Although it wants to show that sociability is part of the metaphysically determined nature of man, this metaphysics is based on the Catholic teaching of the human being's relationship to God: 'The social nature of man is most deeply grounded, not in a utilitarian way in external dependence on others, but metaphysically in the essence of man, which means wealth, not poverty.'[18] The metaphysical notion of sociability that is in play here, is connected with the idea of *imago Dei*, of the human being's resemblance to his creator. If man resembles his creator, and God is essentially benevolent, man will necessarily turn out to be inherently social, too. In connection with this line of thought, Höffner refers to H. de Lubac, who claims: 'The sociality of God is reflected in human sociality.'[19] It is this parallelism between man and his creator which gives the view of human nature in the Christian social teaching its philosophical depth.

Yet, there are new elements in this description of the human being. Catholic social teaching strongly emphasizes the human inclination to build community despite its claims of human being's autonomy. Besides biological instincts, a special emphasis is laid on an Aristotelian–Christian motivating force: 'Two spiritual powers are especially effective in community-building: the readiness to imitate and to love.'[20] The readiness to imitate is famously present in Aristotle's *Poetics* while love is, of course, taken from the Bible including the Ten Commandments of the Old Testament, and Christ's teaching in the New Testament, as expressed in his Sermon on the Mount. This teaching has a Christian Aristotelian foundation, in other words, it is more or less in the Aristotelian–Thomistic framework, which we have seen in the historical part of this book.

But there are some more contemporary elements in it. A reflection on the linguistic turn of contemporary philosophy is shining through the claim that language creates community, even if it certainly has its biblical textual source as well. In a crucial pronouncement of the scripture, God is identified with the word (*logos*): 'In the beginning was the Word, and the Word was with God, and the Word was God.'[21] Also, the Bible itself illustrates the relationship between language and community, in a negative way in the Old Testament's story of Babel, which is about the impossibility of cooperating without a common language, and in a positive way in the New Testament story of the Pentecost, where the Spirit descends on the Apostles, and they start to speak 'languages'. The connection between human linguistic abilities and sociability needs no further arguments, since the linguistic turn, and Wittgenstein's denial of the private language argument, it can be taken as obvious.

For our present purposes, one of the most important elements from the Christian teaching is the principle of solidarity. As Höffner explains it, solidarity as understood in social teaching unites the two aspects of human nature discussed previously, the responsible personal and the social aspect of solidarity, and excludes their immoderate versions, individualism and collectivism. 'From the characteristically dual direction of this tie, which constitutes the metaphysical essence of society, it follows that persons "are tied to the whole from an inner fullness of value", "but in such a way that the whole only has its own fullness of value in its dependence on the personal fullness of value of the members".[22] Importantly, Höffner points out that the same principle that we find in social teaching returns in a 1954 decision of the *Bundesverfassungsgericht*, which proves that the principle of solidarity is taken over by other discourses as well, besides the Christian social teaching. Thanks to the German Constitutional Court, the concept of solidarity is included in the secular understanding of twentieth-century Western political communities, along the lines of the constitutional principles provided by the court.[23]

All these aspects of Catholic social teaching (including the concept of the person, sociability as part of human nature substantiated by the *imago Dei* argument, imitation and love, sociability as proven by linguistic competencies and solidarity) support a view of human nature that finds sociability a natural, inborn attribute of human beings, even in the state of fallenness. In other words, the enlightened view and Catholic teaching coincide in this respect, both directions affirming human sociability even if human beings are fragile and morally corruptible. The role of prudence in this context is to help human agents realize that it is in their interest to let their sociable part prevail. While there is no doubt that prudence has the potential to achieve this aim, prudence itself is not infallible, and therefore agency-constraint remains a crucial boundary on political creativity. The more so that agency-constraint is closely connected to temporal and knowledge-constraint, too.

5

Time-constraint

The temporality of prudence

The political philosophy of prudence, as we saw in Chapter 4, takes as its basis the fact that politics consists of decisions made by agents in particular moments in particular contexts. The primary temporal dimension of the political phenomenon is, therefore, necessarily the present. In other words, politics is not atemporal. On the contrary, we know already from the ancient historians that to make the right decision we have to make it in the right moment. Which means that a sense of tempo and rhythm is required, as well as an overview of the process of which it will be a part. But this present tense needs to be open on what happened earlier as well as on the prospects for the future. Good decisions in this sense require a temporal embeddedness.

This temporally determined awareness of prudence is made explicit in Titian's painting entitled *Allegory of Prudence* (c. 1550–65) (Figure 5.1).[1] The painting portrays three male faces, one turning towards the viewer, the other two in profile, with their backs to each other. Their position in the space depicted by the painting suggests that they coalesce, as if they were representations of three separate postures or poses of the same person. The central face, however, is that of a middle-aged person, while on his left side we see an old man's left profile, and on his right side a youngster's right profile. One can discover reminiscences or, as Wittgenstein put it, family resemblances on the individual faces, suggesting either that they are phases from the visual life narrative of one single individual (i.e. presenting side by side the young, the middle-aged and the old man phase of the same person's life narrative) or that they represent different generations, perhaps within the same family. There are allusions to the possibility that perhaps it is a self-portrait of the painter himself, painted in his old age – Titian was born around 1490, so if the date of the painting is correct, he must have been about 60–75 years old by the time the painting was executed. If we accept the family story and the self-portrait as the genre, we can suspect that the old man is Titian himself, the middle-aged man could be his son, Orazio, while the youngster is his cousin and heir, Marco Vecellio. However, for us it is much more important than simply identifying the sitters, that traditionally there is one further dimension to the meaning attributed to the picture, which is expressed by its title.

Figure 5.1 Titian's *Allegory of Prudence*, c. 1550–65, Wikimedia Commons.

Its title suggests that the picture is a symbolic (or rather allegoric) rendering of the virtue of prudence. This dimension of the interpretation is based on the traditional meaning of the three animal heads that are below the three human faces: from left to right a wolf, a lion and a dog.² This interpretation also makes good use of the inscription of the picture: *ex praete/rito* above the old man, *praesens prvden/ter agit* above the middle-aged man and *ni fvtvra/actione de/tvrpet* above the youngster. If we put together the three parts, the message is: 'From the/experience of the/past, the present acts prudently,/lest it spoil future action.'³ The old man seems to be associated with the past, the middle-aged man is confronting the present, while the future is embodied by the young man. Panofsky decodes the temporal meaning of this triad in the following way, relying on Macrobius's *Saturnalia*:

> The lion's head thus denotes the present, the condition of which, between the past and the future, is strong and fervent by virtue of present action; the past is designated by the wolf's head because the memory of things that belong to the past is devoured and carried away; and the image of the dog, trying to please, signifies the outcome of the future, of which hope, though uncertain, always gives us a pleasing picture.⁴

He also claims to have found a direct influence of this tradition on Titian, namely the *Hieroglyphica* (1556) by Pierio Valeriano. Panofsky even quotes what that author had to say under the heading *Prudentia*: prudence 'not only investigates the present but also reflects about the past and the future, examining it as in a mirror, in imitation of the physician who, as Hippocrates says, "knows all that is, that was and that will be"'.⁵ After this quote, Panofsky also adds another one: the 'three modes or forms of time' 'are *hieroglyphice* expressed by a triple-head (*tricipitum*) combining the head of a dog with those of a wolf and a lion'.⁶

The interesting thing in Titian's composition is to bring together the three phases of a man's life with the three temporal dimensions of prudence in the tradition. In this way, the temporal dimensions are seen as matching the three 'psychological faculties in the combined exercise of which this virtue consists: memory, which remembers and learns from, the past; intelligence, which judges of, and acts in, the present; and foresight, which anticipates, and provides for or against, the future'.⁷

Panofsky's interpretation of Titian's mysterious work is helpful for us, as it sheds light on the temporal dimension of political prudence. Titian could provide a visible form to the cautious deliberative process of the prudent person: he looks back, faces the situation as it is given in the moment of action and looks at the future consequences of it. There is even an opportunity to find a political meaning in the picture: after all, the lion was the emblematic animal of the Venetian republic and, in this sense, the picture can be read as the political programme of the city in its prime time, the middle of the sixteenth century, the heyday of the Renaissance. Even the temporal dimension of the picture might have a direct political meaning: we know that the myth of Venice was that due to the wisdom of its constitutional machinery, its political system could survive the centuries unchanged. The figures of the past, the present and the future could turn into each other smoothly, without the need for a generational revolution, due to the prudence attributed to the leadership of the city.⁸

In what follows, we will rely on another helpful source, Joseph Pieper's analysis of the virtue of prudence in his *The Four Cardinal Virtues*, originally published in German in 1964.⁹ Before actually embarking on a reconstruction of some of the relevant points of the neo-Thomist thinker's work, one should stress that the part on prudence was already published in 1937, after the first part on fortitude (1934) and the second part on hope (1935). The part on Klugheit was followed by another part on temperance, still before the Second World War. Only justice could not be addressed before the fall of the Nazi regime. What Pieper showed through his publications was nothing less than his own struggle with Hitler's Nazi regime.

It is not by chance that Pieper's analysis of justice could only be published in 1953. This well-educated German Catholic was devoted to classical learning, meaning a combination of the ancient Greek philosophers and the medieval doctors. He was led in this direction by his teacher (a priest) in the Gymnasium Paulinum, and by a lecture on Goethe and Aquinas by Romano Guardini in 1924. In his autobiography of these years, Pieper recalls the event, and even more the effect of the talk ('that totally unexpected "significant assistance"') on him. The connection between the two authors was their classical status, meaning they both shared 'what Goethe calls the "objective orientation" and the respect for reality; not, of course, merely factual reality, but what is genuinely real'. And through the inspiration of that moment, the young Pieper found the message on which he was going to build his philosophical life: 'Every ought is grounded in an is; the good is what corresponds to reality. If anyone wants to know and do the good, he must direct his gaze to the objective world of being.'[10] This message is also translated into his analysis of prudence.

The priority of prudence and Pieper's reality principle

The starting point of Pieper's story is dramatic: 'The virtue of prudence is the mold and "mother" of all the other cardinal virtues, of justice, fortitude, and temperance.'[11] He also adds the metaphysical underpinning of the dramatic claim: 'Being precedes Truth, and ... Truth precedes the Good.' We cannot deal here with the theological basis of the underpinning, but let us repeat it the way Pieper suggests: 'The Father begets the Eternal Word, and ... the Holy Spirit proceeds out of the Father and the Word.'[12] If we view together the moral, the metaphysical and the theological points, we see the method used by Pieper: he follows the meticulous methodology of the Thomists, but combines that method with a specific creativity characteristic of his own philosophy. The relevant point of Pieper's starting statement is that the Christian–Thomist view of the virtues is determinedly realistic: it is based on the right appreciation of reality: '"Reason perfected in the cognition of truth" shall inwardly shape and imprint his (i.e. man's) volition and action.' When using Aquinas's term of reason, in order to avoid a basic misunderstanding, Pieper promptly adds: '"Reason" means to him (i.e. to Aquinas) nothing other than "regard for and openness to reality", and "acceptance of reality"'.[13] This reality principle – that human behaviour cannot get rid of the externally given – is the key to why the Thomistic ethical doctrine is so crucial to the present analysis of political prudence. For as in ethics, in political philosophy too, we think it vital that 'prudence is the standard of volition and action; but the standard of prudence, on the other hand, is the *ipsa res*, the "thing itself"' – or in short form: 'The good is prudent beforehand; but that is prudent which is in keeping with reality.'[14]

The reality principle in politics is nothing less than the demand for a reality check; 'good intention' and 'meaning well' is not enough, not even an excuse here. You cannot be politically good without first conforming your behaviour to the inherent standards of the particular circumstances in which you have to act or restrain from acting. 'Realization of the good presupposes that our actions are appropriate to the real situation that is to the concrete realities which form the "environment" of a concrete human action; and that we therefore take this concrete reality seriously, with clear-eyed objectivity.'[15] The terms used by Pieper when describing the concerns of prudence are 'the realm of "ways and means" and down-to-earth realities'.[16] This is the language that a conservative political philosophy of prudence has to take on board.

It is also important that Pieper connects this reality principle to what he calls 'situation conscience'.[17] This principle is, as it were, a counterbalance of *synderesis*, or innate, natural conscience, which defines the general principles of ethical conduct. Situation conscience has the role of applying the general principles to the specific situations of the here and now of the decision.

Taking all these elements into account, identifying the priority of prudence with the reality principle, as it is revealed by the 'situation conscience', is the most important lesson the political philosophy of prudence needs to learn from the Thomistic approach as Pieper applies it.

Three phases of prudence: From deliberation to judgement to decision

Pieper's reconstruction of the traditional account of the virtue of prudence distinguishes three different phases within the procedure, how this virtue exercises its influence on the individual's action. While deliberation and judgement belong to the part of the procedure that is epistemic, or in more general terms, cognitive, in its nature, the last phase, decision, has an imperative and practical character. This distinction is based on the assumption that prudence has two aspects: it requires both a reliable cognition of the external word, and the power of volition, which helps adapt the individual's action to the objective conditions of external reality. While deliberation and judgement add up to what Pieper calls the '"silent" contemplation of reality',[18] decision is proactive: it leads directly to action. This is the moment of the middle-aged man in Titian's painting: he turns towards us, glancing into the 'external' space of reality.

According to Pieper, silent cognition is further divided into the following three elements: *memoria, docilitas, solertia*. Memory certainly can remind us of the profile of the old man in Titian's painting. The past, however, can take its part in the deliberation of the prudent man only as soon as it is reconstructed. Here, the main point is the trustworthiness of this mimesis: it is required to be 'true-to-being' memory.[19] This sentence sounds rather pathetic, and it has a certain Heideggerean stylistic overtone. Yet, its relevance is clear for political prudence as well. 'The true-to-being character of memory means simply that it "contains" in itself real things and events as they really are and were.'[20] This precaution against false memory is necessary because the self is so easily ready to be taken in by seemingly realistic illusions of the past. 'There is no more insidious way for error to establish itself than by this falsification of memory through slight retouches, displacements, discolorations, missions, shifts of accent.'[21] *Docilitas* is interpreted by Pieper as 'open-mindedness', and the 'ability to take advice', in other words, a readiness to learn from others and generally to change views as a result of rational argumentation or in accordance with the changes in one's experience. And finally, *solertia* is the virtue of 'objectivity in unexpected situations', without which no perfect prudence is possible.[22] But, as prudence is not simply the cunning cleverness that our ordinary language would imply, so *solertia* is not simply 'fickleness' – it is rather 'nimbleness' in response to new situations. The difference is that this second type 'serves the *finis totius vitae*, the genuine end of human life', while the former is a pure technique of survival in unexperienced new situations.[23]

We have seen how the detailed dogmatics of prudence worked out by Pieper includes a reference to memory, and what is meant in that context by this term. But where does the future dimension play its role in this complex?

The future is brought up in connection with foresight. While deliberation and judgement, as the cognitive components of prudence, rely on past experience, decision concerns what needs to be done in the future. 'The first prerequisite for the perfection of "prudence as imperative" is, therefore, *providentia*, foresight.'[24] Pieper identifies foresight with the capacity instinctually, but surely to find out, if a certain action will lead to the result we hope for. As the terms used (instinctually, hope for) illustrate, by introducing this dimension, Pieper opens a window on the uncertain, the risky. It is a reaction on his part to the fact that the political issues that prudence has to tackle are 'concrete, contingent' and reside in the future. Aristotle calls our attention to the fact that the realm of politics is a realm of constant and unavoidable uncertainty. The prudent politician takes precautions, as far as it is possible for him or her to narrow down the realm of uncertainty, but he or she should not strive to eliminate uncertainty, as the nature of the matter, politics, does not allow that to happen. Rather, he or she relies on what he or she has learnt from experience, together with the help received of communal wisdom. But neither will these components do the job. He or she will also have to rely on grace. What matters is that he or she should not lose his or her sangfroid or composure. Virtue is, in fact, an acquired second nature that works in a more reliable way without formal reflection on what is being done, and therefore political decision-making works instinctually, without the aid of a constant second-order, reflective reasoning. Although there are no guarantees or safeguards, 'the decisions of prudence and the "intuitions" of providentia' 'receive "practical" assurance and reinforcement'.[25]

Rigid casuistry versus ethical realism

As we saw, there is no way to exclude risks or chance from human affairs, in particular from moral considerations, even less so from political considerations. Already Aristotle forewarns his audience that there is no hope of achieving security in the affairs of the *polis*. Yet, the virtue of prudence refers to something more radical: it tempts us to think in terms of relativism. In this sense, it is dangerously close to situationist ethics. In what follows, we have to consider how it is possible for prudence to avoid the trap of relativism. In other words, the task is to distinguish between a situation-based realist ethics and situationalism, in the sense of moral relativism.

Pieper helps us in this respect, too. What he calls classical Christian teaching obviously excludes all sorts of irrationalism and voluntarism. Unlike modern natural law, which was heard as an important voice in discussions of political and legal philosophy in the early modern period, the teaching of prudence is not dealing with universals. Pieper quotes Aquinas, who claims: 'But the means to the end, in human concerns, far from being fixed, are of manifold variety according to the variety of persons and affairs.'[26] To the modern reader, this sounds close to the relativism associated with Machiavelli, who is charged with introducing an immoral relativism into the discussion of human affairs, even if he did not admit it. However, certainly, Aquinas is not an anticipation of Machiavelli. On the contrary, he certainly held the view that prudence does not choose freely and spontaneously the aim of the individual agent: 'The goals of human action do not change, nor do man's basic directions.'[27] This is an obvious sign that Aquinas's emphasis on the variety of human means does not concern the end of the action, which is fixed, but only suggests that to achieve it, different circumstances demand different strategies.

Pieper is ready to step even closer to the problem of relativism in his account of prudence, in order to explain the protean nature of prudential norms. He describes casuistry as a form of ossification of ethical standards, as they showed themselves in individual cases. Let us see the definition he constructs: casuistry is the result of 'man's efforts to "order" the limitless variety of modes for achieving the good, to render it surveyable by the longitudes and latitudes of abstract rational measurement'.[28] While most of its critics – including Pascal – attacked the casuistry of early modern Jesuits as a form of relativism, which may have the unintended consequence of making exceptions the norm, Pieper, in fact, criticizes it for the opposite reason: 'The string for certainty and security can gravitate, by virtue of its own direction and its natural inclination, into the degenerate, anti-natural state of nonhuman rigidity.'[29]

In order to avoid that sort of moral rigidity, Pieper is ready to go into details in defence of the right understanding of the Catholic tradition of case-centred ethics. His solution to the temporal gap between the creation of an abstract norm and its application in the future is prudence. 'This standard cannot be abstractly construed or even calculated in advance.' And he immediately adds: 'Abstractly here means: outside the particular situation.'[30] Pieper proves to be sensitive to reality once again: in the prudential paradigm of ethics, the future is even more vague than the past. Of the past, we have at least some remnants or recollections, but that is not the case with the future. We cannot overcome vagueness, however, by stepping back and relying on abstraction, a specific form of rationality, in connection with politics. The realist approach does not regard abstraction as a valid operation here, as abstraction requires a full account of what is the case, and a decision is only possible after the assessment is finished. Further on, realism requires deliberation and action to be in tune with the basic circumstances of the case, rather than a harmony with any overt rationalization of acclaimed general rules. For these reasons, realism requires humble attention to the specific.

> The strict specificity of ethical action is perceptible only to the living experience of the person required to decide. He alone has access to the totality of *singularia circa sunt* operations, that is to say, to the totality of concrete realities which surround the concrete action, to the 'state' of the person himself and the condition of the here and now.[31]

Interestingly, Pieper does not find it necessary to explain how this decision will avoid being subjective. As a firm believer in the human capacity to get acquainted with the world by attention, Pieper relies on Aquinas, and his conviction that it is possible to make the right judgement by closely examining our external circumstances. The position of the observer demands objectivity from the agent, and Aquinas's programme expresses a trust in the adultness of the human being. Prudence, for Pieper, after all, means the 'objective estimation of the concrete situation of concrete activity' and 'the ability to transform this cognition of reality into concrete decision'.[32] The prudent person's maturity of character leads him or her to the concept of 'ethical maturity', which is the first prerequisite not only of prudence but also of all four cardinal virtues.

We only need to add in connection with it the requirement of a 'political maturity', as the normative dimension of political prudence. Accordingly, a mature prudent person will be able to judge the case in question correctly, and this will help him or her to act accordingly. As opposed to abstraction, this realist assessment of the circumstances does not require extra time – the whole perception and decision can be processed within the available time frames of the particular political situation.

Kairos: Timing in politics

If maturity and an attention to reality is a necessary condition for acquiring the virtue of prudence, a further reference to it is helpful to underline the claim that prudence has a very obvious temporal dimension. Human beings are bound by their temporality in a number of ways, which might be relevant from the perspective of finding the right action in politics. This is so because political circumstances, as we have explained, dynamically change their outlines. To act properly, you have to meet certain preconditions, and these preconditions have a certain temporal order, as we have seen. But there is a further aspect to temporality that turns out to be crucial for practical philosophy, which is to find the right moment to intervene in politics. The claim that there are certain moments when a window will open is based on the assumption that it is only under certain circumstances that a particular action can prove to be successful: to make a judgement whether these circumstances obtain here and now is therefore crucial. The fitting moment (when our action fits the circumstances) is the moment of occasion (*occasio*) in the life of the agent and also of his or her political environment.

If it sounds convincing that one should accept the relevance of the temporal dimension in human decisions to act, and in carrying out the actions, let us focus on the concept that was classically used for the temporal dimension of human decision-making in practical affairs: *kairos*.[33]

Let us, once again, start out from Aristotle, who picks up the notion of *kairos* (translated into English as opportune moment by Reeve) more than once. I would like to recall two Aristotelian loci in his *Nicomachean Ethics*. First, it is in connection with war, where he claims that generalship is needed to find the opportune moment, just as in the case of disease, when the right medicine is required at the right moment.[34] The second locus is even more telling, perhaps. In relation to the proper action, Aristotle stresses the impossibility to state it in advance in an exact way, partly because 'things in the sphere of action ... have no fixed identity', therefore 'the account dealing with particular cases is still less exact' than those in other spheres.[35] Instead of relying on professional standards or precepts, 'the agents themselves always have to inquire to find out what is opportune to do, just as in the case of medicine and navigation'.[36] By now, it is no surprise that *kairos* is closely connected to *phronesis*, practical wisdom, in Aristotle's *Nicomachean Ethics*, instead of being connected to *episteme* or *sophia*. And it is also very telling that the timing of the proper action in politics is compared to that in medicine – it shows that in both activities you need to identify the symptoms and deliberate about the right treatment for the particular case defined by these symptoms.

To use another metaphor, in both medicine and in politics, you need your ear to 'hear' whether your act fits harmoniously into the music of the situation.

Let us take another ancient example, this time from the Bible. In the Old Testament book, Ecclesiastes, we read: 'For everything there is a season, and a time for every purpose under heaven; a time to be born and a time to die; a time to plant and a time to pluck up that which is planted; a time to kill and a time to heal ... a time to weep and a time to laugh.'[37] As pointed out by John E. Smith, the expressions '"a time to" are translations of the term *kairos*, the right or opportune time to do something often called "right timing"'.[38] While there is an eschatological dimension to the temporal perspective of the Bible, which is connected to the narrative of Christ's coming, the biblical narrative also introduces a new linear perception of time. Continuity only makes sense in contrast with discontinuity: *kairos* seems to play a major role in the context of the biblical narrative as well. Think about the right time coming for Christ to act.

Finally, the third context for classical *kairos* is certainly the Roman world. It is most particularly Cicero, and his rhetorical theory, which translates the Greek concept of *kairos* into the Latin language and Roman republican culture. As one of the experts on the intellectual history of the term summarizes: 'In Stoicism, particularly Latin Stoicism, the concept of *kairos* merged with that of *prepon* (propriety or fitness). ... In this guise, *kairos* is the dominating concept in both Cicero's rhetoric and his ethics.'[39]

If we regard these examples, we can certainly claim that in both the classic Greco–Roman and the Hebrew–Christian tradition there is a notion of qualitative time, which is connected in its perspective to the ancient Greek philosophical concept of *kairos*.

Conversely, if we want to see the distinguishing mark of the concept of *kairos*, let us first separate it from *chronos*, which is a monotonous, apersonal concept of time, and from *aion*, which refers to eternity, the non-human, non-mortal aspect of time. For us, in the context of politics, it is the relationship of *kairos* to *chronos* that is perhaps the more important.

It is in connection with the temporal perspective of Renaissance humanism that Douglas L. Peterson notes: 'There is a twofold conception of time that is new in the Renaissance: time as duration and time as occasion.'[40] As we saw, this duality is not new: the first one is close to *chronos*, while the second one to *kairos*. He also quotes an early modern exposition of the distinction, the one found in John Foxe's *Time and the End of Time* (1664), which indeed very convincingly proves that Christian humanists made this distinction very clear: 'Time and opportunity differ, time is the duration or succession of so many minutes, hours, days ... Opportunity is the time apted and fitted in order to this or that work of business, namely, a meeting of time and means together, to effect the end.'[41] One should also recall in this connection a biblical locus in the book of Job, with the question: 'Is there not an appointed time for a man upon the earth?'[42]

The common point of these quotes implies that the *kairotic* perception of time depends on the perspective of the individual agent: it is his or her time for action. In connection with art, Frank Kermode defines the term in the following way: *kairos* is 'a point in time filled with significance, charged with a meaning derived from its relation to the end'.[43] The difference between *kairos* and *chronos* is that while the second is agent-neutral, the first is agent-specific: it is the time for a certain person to execute a certain action. No one else can execute it at the given moment, and no other moment is available even for the specific agent to execute it. It is the time rendered for the agent for the specific action he or she can and should execute.

The same difference is expressed visually in the emblem in Jan David's *Occasio Arrepta, neglecta* (1605). Here, the classical notion of *kairos* is embodied by the figure of Occasion, who is kept back in a crowd of people by her hair, while Time in the sense of *chronos* successfully flies away. According to the author's explanation: 'While Time passes onward, men keep Occasion prudently back by the hair on her forehead.'[44] The meaning of the emblem is obvious: men cannot stop time in the sense of the objective flow which determines human life, but they have the chance to make use of the opportunity or occasion opening up in the midst of that flow, when certain acts might take place if the actor is alert and ready to grasp it and translate will to act, in other words to perform it.

It is this meaning of *kairos*, referring to the moment when action is possible here and now for the political agent, that is relevant for political prudence, as well. The political agent can never gain full control over the temporal dimension, it cannot be conquered or invaded the same way as a spatial unit can be covered. To win in politics, you need to have that sense of timing that allows you to hit upon the moments when to commit a certain action and when to abstain from action.

Of the group of concepts related to *kairos*, not all are temporal, but each refers to order and to the human ability to sense temporal order and the right proportion even where it is not directly available to human agency. This group of concepts related to *kairos* includes 'symmetry, propriety, occasion, due measure, fitness, tact, decorum, convenience, proportion, fruit, profit, wise moderation'.[45] Most of them seem to have an aesthetic overtone, while they are regarded as terms of rhetoric, in other words, the right way of addressing others. This Latinized vocabulary of *kairos* is also connected to our central concept of decorum.

A key connection between rhetoric and politics is obviously the interpersonal dimension: in both, there is an exchange between people, between speaker and audience in the one case and between actor and recipient of action in the other. Both the speaker and the political agent need to find the right tone – after all '*Ton macht die Musik*' – in order to achieve the desired audio effect. The right tone in this context requires toning up one's message or action in order to let it sound/look/feel harmonious with its (musical, rhetorical, political) environment. Politics in this sense is a coordination problem: you want to join an orchestra, which is already playing – you have to feel the rhythm, surf the melody, find out the tonality of the music, if you want to step in. An alternative metaphor refers to jazz music, where musicians need to listen to each other in order to solve a rather complex artistic coordination problem involved in real-time improvisations. Or let us take the role of the conductor in classical music – he or she is responsible for the balance of individual musicians, and to realize the intentions of the composer through negotiating individual performances.

None of these musical examples is, of course, fully similar to the case of the temporal demands of political prudence. Most importantly, in the political arena you do not have a fully perfected score to rely on – and you are lost even compared to jazz musicians, as you do not even know the musical genre that the other members of the group are performing, or even the melody, not even the musical key – all of that is underdetermined in politics, and therefore fully improvised. And yet, political improvisation is not creation ex nihilo, either. Only those musicians who not only know each other's (and their own) musical abilities very well but also know (and feel?) the musical tradition they are part of, can improvise successfully even if in an unreflective manner. The individual musical talents, the sheer abilities of the artists are not enough to achieve success in an orchestra – what you need is experience of playing together with others, for which you are required to learn and become part of your own tradition. This is a sort of knowledge that is, to some extent, reflective, but most of the time it is a kind of personal, tacit, practical knowledge, like a child riding a bike or a sleepwalker balancing on a rooftop: if you ask them to reflect on what they do, they would most certainly crash down. The sense of timing, the ability to grasp the right moment and perform the right action, playing together with others, the *kairotic* virtue remains to a large extent unreflected, and in fact, even if cognitive, not rational in the sense of abstract, conceptual reasoning. To make sense of this sort of political sense, we turn to Chapter 6 on knowledge-constraint in the political field.

6

Knowledge-constraint

Pieter Bruegel the Elder's famous painting, entitled *The Blind Leading the Blind* or *The Parable of the Blind* (1568), is kept in a collection in Naples. The theme of the painting is the parable from the Bible, presented by Matthew as: 'Let them alone: they be blind leaders of the blind. And if the blind lead the blind, both shall fall into the ditch'[1] and by Luke as: 'And he spake a parable unto them, Can the blind lead the blind? shall they not both fall into the ditch?'[2] The proverbial status of the parable shows that it had become quite popular by the time of Bruegel – his painting has been preceded by a number of drawings, among others, by Bosch. Due to its biblical source, however, it served for a long time as a Christian parable – even if a similar saying can be traced back to the Upanishads.[3] As the same theme appeared in Bruegel's *Netherlandish Proverbs* (1559) – see the three men in the background clinching, moving forward slowly without any recognizable aim – one can argue that the painter wanted to show the sort of folly that is described by the parable of the blind as a universal characteristic of human nature. In fact, we can easily connect the picture's meaning with Erasmus's famous book, *The Praise of Folly* (1511). Published in Latin, the book soon became very influential in Europe. Enveloped as a general criticism of human nature, the main thrust of the criticism of Erasmus's book is, of course, the corruption and misdeeds of the church. It is, for example, a criticism of priests who lead non-thinking believers in the wrong direction: 'Almost all Christians being wretchedly enslaved to blindness and ignorance, which the priests are so far from preventing or removing, that they blacken the darkness, and promote the delusion.'[4] This criticism of church leaders can easily be transferred to the political realm, describing the blindness of political leaders and their subjects who accept their blind decision without reflecting upon them.

Besides religious or literary influences, Bruegel might have had a more direct motive to paint the picture. It was painted one year before his death, and its dark satire and sarcasm might be connected with his overall psychic depression in those years. But even more particularly, he was driven to despair because of the political situation of the age: living in that time in Brussels, the centre of the Spanish Netherlands, he was a close witness to the brutality of Spanish rule. Especially brutal was the establishment of the Council of Troubles in 1567, which had the function to punish non-Christians and rebelling inhabitants, causing arrests and executions on a massive scale. While the painting makes no explicit reference to the political situation of the day, the date of the painting and its political relevance allow us to use the painting as a rather sceptical general comment on human misery and the sheer lack of clear-sightedness in seventeenth-century political leadership, being deeply involved in sharp theological conflicts as well.

By now, we have seen two constraints on the prevalence of rationality in human political participation: obviously, both agency-constraint and temporal-constraint have a negative effect on the prospect of the success of rational calculation in politics. If political decision and action finally depend on the agent who is going to perform it, the agent's abilities will surely have a direct effect on the decision itself – and the fragility of human nature makes the birth of perfectly rational decisions less than probable. And even if we suppose a decision maker who has the best possible human capacities to decide, the available time frame both to make and execute the decision hardly ever makes the process a thorough enough deliberation and thus an informed judgement is very rarely probable. Yet, this chapter has the function to concentrate on the particular obstacles before the rule of rationality in the political field.[5] We will focus on three aspects, namely, perspectival distortion, situational mutability and value dependence.

Three constraints on political knowledge

Perspectival distortion

The first constraint follows from the simple fact that there is no Archimedean point in politics. To explain the term, the *'punctum Archimedis'* is the claim attributed to Archimedes that if he had a solid point under his feet, and a long enough lever, he could move the earth off its foundation. This claim is all the more interesting for us as such an important figure in the history of philosophy as Descartes referred to the Archimedean point when he said: 'Archimedes used to demand just one firm and immovable point in order to shift the entire earth; so I too can hope for great things if I manage to find just one thing, however slight, that is certain and unshakeable.'[6] Obviously, in the political field there is no such solid ground, as there are no certain and unshakeable things. This is not to deny the universal validity of moral principles, only to remind ourselves that as soon as they enter the field of politics, their solidity, certainty and unshakeability is endangered. Think about the cautionary remark of Burke in connection with the natural rights of men – as soon as we want to defend them in the political realm, their clarity will be lost: 'These metaphysic rights entering into common life, like rays of light which pierce into a dense medium, are by the laws of nature refracted from their straight line ... it becomes absurd to talk of them as if they continued in the simplicity of their original direction.'[7] This is because of the particular passions and interests that are attached to them in public life, and because of the fact that the government, which is expected to defend them, 'is a contrivance of human wisdom to provide for human wants', and therefore cannot be as unshakeable as an Archimedean point. What is more, even if we had the best possible constitutional arrangements, 'as the liberties and the restrictions vary with times and circumstances and admit to infinite modifications, they cannot be settled upon any abstract rule'.[8] The Archimedean point of Descartes was an abstract, *a priori* truth, and the existence of such an abstract truth is denied in the realm of politics.

The interesting difference in this respect is between conservatives who want to establish this denial of an abstract truth as their political foundation, and all other political convictions, which have a certain well-founded ideology, or principled doctrine. A typical example of that principled account of politics might be that of John Rawls and his *Theory of Justice* (1971). His idea of the original position serves as a way out from the intricacies of historical particularities previously mentioned by Burke. In the revised edition, Rawls directly admits: 'I used a more general and abstract rendering of the idea of the social contract by means of the idea of the original position' to 'provide a satisfactory account of the basic rights and liberties of citizens as free and equal persons'.[9] In other words, in his theory the original position provides an Archimedean point. At one point, he explicitly uses this term when speaking about his own conception of justice, posing the question: 'How, then, can this doctrine determine an Archimedean point from which the basic structure itself can be appraised?'[10] And he even answers the question frankly: 'Justice as fairness is not at the mercy, so to speak, of existing wants and interests. It sets up an Archimedean point for assessing the social system without invoking *a priori* considerations.'[11]

Instead of going into the details of assessing Rawls's system, let us be content with the claim that as opposed to doctrinaire liberalism like that of Rawls, conservatism does not believe in the possibility of finding or for that matter of creating such an Archimedean point. To illustrate the point which excludes that possibility, let us take another example, this time from art history. In his *On painting* (original Italian version in 1435, the more refined Latin version a few years later), Alberti worked out a theory of pictorial perspective. His main invention was to suggest geometrical procedures to project the view of a three-dimensional object onto the two-dimensional surface of a canvas. The problem, of course, is foreshortening. No matter where you choose to view the object you want to depict, your representation of it will necessarily distort the original proportions of the object, because of the specificities of your viewpoint. This problem is, to a certain extent, less pertinent in the case of frontal representation (think about the façade of a building or the face of a human being). Yet even in those cases, to translate a three-dimensional body to a two-dimensional representation according to a naturalistic–realistic standard would require a proportional distortion of the original.

Certainly, to apply this art theoretical example to the case of the political agent's view of the complexity of the political situation is itself imprecise, but hopefully the point of the comparison of the two cases is not too difficult to grasp. It is meant to show that there is no such unique viewpoint from where a three-dimensional body and all of its parts could be visually embraced by one single glance. Even the best possible scenario cannot offer more than a partial (and distorted) segment of the subtotal of the views of the object, or an idealized (but contrafactual) 'overview' of the object. In the same way, due to the nature of the matter, a political situation cannot be fully understood by any of its participants or observers.

Situational mutability

In addition to perspectival distortion, there is a further dimension of the agent's knowledge-constraint in political affairs. This concerns the inborn instability of a political situation. To keep with the earlier metaphor, paintings are depictions of natural settings (landscapes, portraits, still life) where the stability of the object allows scrutiny of it by the artist. Most of the time, these objects can also be double-checked by the viewers themselves. The same way that researchers in most scientific research can deal with their topic with the presumption that their object has a certain solidity, which allows for its close observance required for an objective description. And here, too, experiments can be double-checked. There are, of course, exceptions to this general rule: certain topics, such as the movement of a horse in gallop, were not reachable by the eye of the artist (or members of an audience) for a long time because the human eye was not able to adequately differentiate the different phases of the movement due to its very fast transformations. The same way that certain physical experiments (such as the research on atomic particles) were not successful, because the research equipment was not adequate to catch the movements concerned. Even when that obstacle was tackled, a further problem remained: the equipment used to grasp the phenomenon distorted the internal structure of the object itself.

Politics is particularly prone to such mutability. Because a political situation has a great number of variables, and by far the greatest number of them are of human origin, which depend on incalculable subjective sources of motivation, political situations have the general character of instability and mutability. Certainly, crisis situations by definition belong to this category of incalculably mutable situations. But the point to be made here is that political situations as such are to be understood as situationally mutable.

Let us take an example. The result of the Brexit vote depended on the actual decisions of the 30 million voters participating in the vote. While many of the opinion polls forecasted the victory of the no vote, the opposite result came out as the sum total of the different voters' decision-making procedures. That the 'Leave!' votes won with a narrow margin (52 per cent vs 48 per cent) was hardly imaginable only a few days earlier. Yet, the difference was hundreds of thousands of voters' decision, made in front of the polling box. And this difference in favour of the 'leave' votes launched an avalanche in British politics, starting with the stepping down of the prime minister and the initiation of a long process of political bargaining and wrangling between the UK and its European partners. It also had some further 'unintended consequences', a term used by the historians of the Scottish Enlightenment, among them Adam Smith, for historical results of political decisions which were unforeseen and even unpredictable, but which were – as it turned out – logical conclusions of the decisions made. Such (although not historical) unintended consequences of the Brexit vote were the fall of the exchange rate of the British pound, a decline in the economic growth of the country and a radical reshuffle of the UK government. The most obtrusive result, however, was the uncertainty that took control over the political landscape, causing disorientation, social and generational conflict and a feeling of loss and despair in many. During the whole protracted process of the unprecedented Brexit negotiations, an intense experience of the mutability of the political situation was easily discernible. And still today, while I work on this chapter (end of 2018), we do not yet know if it will turn out to be a soft or a hard Brexit, and what exactly the decisions will be.[12] The political see-saw descends and ascends in an unforeseeable way, and brokers of the negotiations as well as observers or those who will suffer the worst consequences of it, do not yet know what to expect from the final result of the internal and external negotiations.

Value dependence

In addition to the aforementioned elements, namely perspectival distortion and situational mutability, there is a third major cause of knowledge-constraint in politics, an even more pertinent obstacle to obtain reliable knowledge of the political situation by observer and participant alike. This is what we will call the 'value dependence' of knowledge claims in politics. By value dependence, the following consideration is meant here: whenever something is stated to be known in the political sphere, it is necessarily implied that it is also known as something which has (a negative or positive) value for the agent/observer and the community to which the agent/observer belongs. Thus, to successfully transmit a reliable piece of information in politics most often supposes a shared value horizon between sender and receiver, otherwise the factual content of the message might suffer distortion.

The distinction between the factual content of a political statement and the values on which it is built is parallel with the distinction between descriptive and normative knowledge, or that between facts and values. When we (no matter as participants or as observers) claim to know a political situation descriptively, it means that we can give a full account of the stakes of the political situation, deciphering the most important protagonists, their aims and vested interests in the situation, as well as the expected outcomes of the possible patterns of actions in the particular situation. The description necessarily turns into a complex of normative claims, as soon as we explicitly relate it to value judgements concerning the given situation.

Earlier, we claimed that the difficulty in fully knowing and therefore in fully sharing one's account of a political situation with someone lies in the fact of perspectival distortion and situational mutability. Now, we take one further step: the claim is now that we are in fact unable to fully detach our factual political observations from our relevant implicit values. The procedure is made more difficult by the fact that our political values are embedded in the perceived political facts, and therefore the interconnections between a political fact and the value attributed to it are mutual and impossible – even conceptually – to distinguish.

Let us, once again, take our example of the aforementioned Brexit vote. First, let us look at our description of it. When the narrative mentioned the 'launch' of an 'avalanche' as a result of the unexpected outcome, it attributed a certain value to the stability of the political situation, perhaps exaggerating the potentially risky consequences of the surprising (shocking?) result. The words we used to describe the situation implied, therefore, certain values attributed to the potential consequences of the decision. In other words, already the concepts we use, including the conceptual reservoir just as much as the rhetorical tropes we apply, are value laden. Although, arguably, we have to suppose a shared horizon of value among language users, after all linguists assert that a language both presupposes common values and helps to homogenize alternative values as well, still it is the case that there is no direct or logically necessary connection between external facts, their individual perceptions and their public linguistic display.

Add to this problem complex that a political situation certainly does not exist until an observer identifies it as such, the observer's perception of it will be determined by his or her own political and non-political experiences and prejudices, and the way the perception will be shared with others cannot be done in a politically neutral way.

Certainly, the foregoing line of thought about the internal connection between political facts and values grossly simplifies the issues involved in the by now quite nuanced discourse on the fact–value dichotomy in practical philosophy. It cannot pay due tribute to the relevant views of Hume, Kant or the logical positivists. It is based only on some Weberian insights,[13] but it refers to them in a critical manner – like to the strict separation itself, which it wants to deny, or the radical objectivity of facts, which it again opposes. The interpretation offered here (of the coalescence between facts and values, and therefore the fatal dependence of factual knowledge on – conscious and unconscious – background value choices, which are themselves determined by facts) is inspired by Weber, even if it is opposing his main claims. Starting out from Weber, it reaches those theories of political knowledge where a strict separation of facts and norms is out of question.

In addition, but not independent from the fact–value dichotomy, we need to refer to the realist–idealist divide when introducing the political axiology of a conservative political theory. The claim that knowledge of fact is imbued by value judgement might seem to be the antechamber of radical relativism. After all, if one cannot make value-independent factual claims, this sounds like a denial of objectivism. It makes it urgent to underline that although facts are not presented here as value-neutral, neither are they regarded as simply human constructions. Quite the contrary: this is a naturalist theory, in the Aristotelian and Thomist sense that there are hard facts in particular political situations, even if their descriptions and/or interpretations (Weber's *Verstehen*) vary according to the value preferences of the observer-interpreter-agent. The sometimes remarkable differences among rival descriptions of the same political states of affairs do not say much about the actual situation concerned: rather, they prove the limits of human epistemic capacities to make sense of it. Which makes it all the more urgent to try to do one's best to learn the hard facts of a case as they happen to be, and to try to rely on that knowledge when making one's decision and performing one's action. But the possibility of shooting in the air remains, of course, relatively high.

Three explanations of why political knowledge is possible

If we consider the above-mentioned three causes of knowledge-constraint in politics – perspectival distortion, situational mutability and value dependence – we might be inclined to think that the political philosophy of prudence is a radically sceptical theory, which grossly underestimates the epistemic conditions of politics. It needs to be affirmed, therefore, that this is not the case – in spite of the severe constraints on knowledge in politics, this theory is not to deny the possibility of learning in politics. It argues for a specific kind of knowledge in this field – one which could be reached from the perspective of personal, tacit knowledge as worked out by Michael Polanyi, or from Hayek and Oakeshott's views of practical knowledge.

Polanyi's notion of personal knowledge

The starting point of Michael Polanyi's 'reconsideration of scientific knowledge', as presented after his Gifford Lectures in 1951–2 in his masterwork, *Personal Knowledge* (1958, 1962), is purely scientific. He claims a misunderstanding in the 'ideal of scientific detachment'. What he wants to show is that even in the natural sciences, research activities which lead to new discoveries include and require

> knowing as an active comprehension of the things known, an action that requires skill. Skillful knowing and doing is performed by subordinating a set of particulars, as clues or tools, to the shaping of a skilful achievement ... Clues and tools are things used as such and not observed in themselves. They are made to function as extensions of our bodily equipment and this involves a certain change of our own being. Acts of comprehension are to this extent irreversible, and also non-critical.[14]

Polanyi's description of this sort of apprehension resembles what Merleau-Ponty calls 'embodied knowledge'. The French existentialist philosopher's book presents the activity of typing as an example of the sort of knowledge to be labelled as embodied. The following is his often quoted formulation:

> To know how to touch type is not, then, to know the place of each letter among the keys, nor even to have acquired a conditioned reflex for each one, which is set in motion by the letter as it comes before our eye. If habit is neither a form of knowledge nor an involuntary action, what then is it? It is knowledge in the hands, which is forthcoming only when bodily effort is made, and cannot be formulated in detachment from that effort.[15]

As we see, Merleau-Ponty's embodied knowledge and Polanyi's personal knowledge are not far from each other, even if their philosophical backgrounds and therefore the register of philosophy they rely on might be quite different. They agree that in performing their activities, human agents rely on an unreflected form of knowledge, what Polanyi calls 'skilful knowing and doing' and Merleau-Ponty calls 'knowledge in the hands'.

Importantly, Polanyi keeps emphasizing that this is not a subjective, but an objective form of knowledge, as it is 'a responsible act claiming universal validity', 'establishing contact with a hidden reality'.[16] As he puts it, it is a 'fusion of the personal and the objective'.[17]

Polanyi's description of this personalized form of knowledge not only covers scientific investigation but he also discovers it within what could be labelled as 'ordinary human activity'. For example, he refers to swimming, riding a bicycle or even the 'touch' of piano players (i.e. the way they depress the keys of their musical instruments). For all of them, he regards as true that the successful performance of the activity requires 'the observance of a set of rules which are not known as such to the person following them'.[18] The interesting thing is that even if we try to explicate the (say physical or physiological) principle, which is the main drive behind a certain activity's success, it still cannot tell exactly how to perform the given activity. The practical knowledge, that is the knowledge that makes the successful performance possible, includes an indeterminate set of 'factors to be taken into account in practice which are left out in the formulation of this rule'.[19] These factors remain tacit during the process, as 'we can know more than we can tell',[20] and they will build up that tacit dimension which is so important behind our practical activities, that without it we could not execute them.

After explaining its meaning, we can connect Polanyi's concept of personal knowledge to the conservative theme of the uncertainty of knowledge in the political field, a point already made by Aristotle. To be sure, in most cases, a political act does not necessarily involve physical movement as in riding a bike or swimming, or this is not the distinguishing mark of it. But to make political judgements and then to execute them presupposes a mechanism which is surprisingly close to Polanyi's personal knowledge or Merleau-Ponty's embodied knowledge. We will take a look at the sort of practical knowledge necessary in politics as delineated by Hayek and Oakeshott in opposition to the sort of rationality that is expressed in the central planning of totalitarian regimes, which is not only undemocratic, but killing the logic of the market also has a disastrous economic effect. From free trade it is not difficult to get to freedom in politics, an issue, which, as we will see, has an epistemological significance, too.

Hayek on spontaneous order

Friedrich Hayek attacked the voluntarist form of rationality exemplified in the military administration of Britain during the Second World War in his first famous book, *The Road to Serfdom* (1944). A parallel to Orwell's *1984*, it offers a sweeping criticism of the interfering, hyper activist ideal of the state in his age. Addressing 'the totalitarians in our midst',[21] Hayek built his stunning criticism of large-scale government intervention on the earlier work of nineteenth-century Tory critics of state control over the economy and civil society, among them on the views of Benjamin Disraeli. A note by the editor of the recent edition quotes the following attack of the then popular utilitarian movement by Disraeli: Utilitarians 'form political institutions on abstract principles of theoretic science, instead of permitting them to spring from the natural course of events, and to be naturally created by the necessities of nations'.[22] The criticism of establishing political institutions on abstract principles famously goes back to the very first critic of the mechanical '*raison*' of French philosophers, which Edmund Burke claimed to be directly responsible for the outbreak of the French Revolution. The founder of British-type conservatism was just as much crucial for Hayek, even if he criticized him on certain points, as were his compatriots, the theorist of the *bonmot* private vices, public benefits, Bernard Mandeville and the critic of social contract theories, David Hume. Famously, all three of them were antagonists of French-type social constructivism, as was Hayek. His criticism of the false form of rationality is a criticism of Cartesian rationalism:

> Since for Descartes reason was defined as logical deduction from explicit premises, rational action also came to mean only such action as was determined entirely by known and demonstrable truth. ... Institution and practice which have not been designed in this manner can be beneficial only by accident. Such became the

characteristic attitude of Cartesian constructivism. ... Man's reason alone should enable him to construct society anew.[23]

It is in contrast with this explicit, abstract and deductive notion of knowledge, attributed by Hayek to Descartes, that Hayek presents the sort of knowledge he claims is crucial in actual politics. The first chapter of his opus magnum bears the title 'Reason and Evolution'. There he refers to the sort of knowledge that he thinks is necessary in society: 'The success of action in society depends on more particular facts than anyone can possibly know.'[24] How is action in society possible, if the conditions for successful action are not available to the individual on his or her own? It requires 'adaptation to the general circumstances that surround him', 'observance of rules which he has not designed and often does not even know explicitly, although he is able to honour them in action'. This is the sort of practical knowledge we are looking for: paying special attention to 'circumstances which we are not aware of and which yet determine the pattern of our successful actions'.[25]

The best-known example of what is called 'circumstantial knowledge' in society, which Hayek refers to, is, of course, the market. One of his commentators sums up his position on the sort of knowledge that runs markets in our societies in the following way: 'Hayek argued that the knowledge which was characteristic of a modern market economy was local, dispersed, and fragmented, and much of it was tacit – it could not be articulated.'[26]

The key to the possibility of such an inarticulate, local knowledge is the human potential to make sense of the other's acts. As Hayek put it: 'We all constantly act on the assumption that we can interpret other people's actions on the analogy of our own mind.'[27] This human potential was already acclaimed by the eighteenth-century British heroes of Hayek: they called this hypothetical figure in moral philosophy the 'impartial spectator'. The figure was originally used as a methodological device: it served as a test of one's sentiments and actions. If the impartial spectator could feel sympathy with them, they would pass the test. The novelty of the device was that the theory did not require the full list of moral laws, as was the case in most instances of the natural law tradition. Instead, the impartial spectator embodied the laws and *mores*. When correctly applied, it could represent the manners and *moeurs* of the society in question. In fact, the terms 'manners' and '*mores*', *moeurs* refer to that grey zone, can be identified as that soft form of social control, which is not initiated from an intellectual centre, but which pervades nevertheless the whole realm of the everyday life of the community.

It was J. G. A. Pocock who did most to recapitulate the Scottish discourse on manners, which – although using a somewhat different terminology – was also important for Hayek, too.[28] Pocock explained the phenomenon in the following way: in eighteenth-century Britain, 'Virtue was redefined ... with the aid of a concept of "manners"'. This was the innovation of members of the sociable middle classes, the main protagonists in the new practices of commerce, as he puts it, in 'the increasingly transactional universe of "commerce and the arts"'.[29] 'For Hume and other Scottish enlightened thinkers, manners denoted active conduct, which was the result of experience and social interaction through conversation.'[30] In the same way, Burke, who in many ways was an Irish British parallel of the idea of the cultured gentleman of the Scottish Hume, also concentrated on the term, comparing it to explicit laws: 'Manners are more important than laws ... they aid morals, they supply them, or they totally destroy them.'[31] While in this sentence Burke is criticizing the French revolutionaries, he had a debate even with his Scottish friends, for he thought, as Pocock pointed out, that 'manners must precede commerce, rather than the other way round'.[32] Hayek declares to be an Old Whig, a term which points back to Burke's close circle which left the Whig party led by Fox, after Fox denounced his *Reflections* on the French Revolution. Hayek seems to share more with Hume and Smith than with Burke as far as the soft control of, or rather coordination within society is concerned.[33] Hayek claimed not to have been conservative, as far as his political allegiance was concerned, which means that he probably would not share Burke's more militant conservative position as far as the substance of his politics was concerned. Yet, the following description by Pocock of Burke's conservatism seems to cover much of Hayek's own position as far as political knowledge is concerned: 'If "manners" were *moeurs*, refined and enriched by the progress of society, they were also *consuetudines*, disciplined and reinforced by the memory of society; and presumption, prescription and prejudice were signs and means of society's determination to keep its memory alive.'[34]

Hayek's political position was, of course, shifting during the years in a radically changing political climate. However, we, too, as readers of Hayek, are also interested in different sides of his theory according to our different aims and circumstances. One of his most famous distinctions between spontaneous order (*kosmos*) and planned order (*taxis*) is itself open to competing interpretations. From our specific viewpoint, this idea is still relevant because it leads him to the famous claim that 'there exist orderly structures which are the product of the action of many men but are not the result of human design'.[35] This is important for us as far as it concerns the main issue of the present chapter: how to account for high-level human cooperation if we suppose the powerful constraints on human knowledge in the political realm. His claim is that there are highly coordinated (although not perfect) social institutions, such as language, the market and the law, which grew naturally without intention or plan. Speaking about the development of law, for example, he distinguishes between *nomos* and *thesis*.[36] *Nomos* 'evolves, a "grown" law which is a spontaneous order'. *Thesis*, however, is 'the law of legislation', in other words, 'made by design'. As the conceptual distinction shows, Hayek seems to share the views of British common jurists who prefer the law that has grown in a trial-and-error process compared to the law that has been created by the lawful assembly's legislative act. Hayek, too, prefers grown laws 'which merely articulate already observed practices', and when reforms are needed, he again prefers to complement existing rules step by step to let them 'operate smoothly and efficiently'.[37] In other words, he suggests that, condemned to be performed in a situation of the aforementioned knowledge-constraint, political action should always be cautious and self-disciplined, otherwise it risks too high social costs in the form of the destruction of the existing, albeit never perfect social fabric – once again a Burkean warning in Hayek's thought.

Oakeshott's concept of practical knowledge

If there is anywhere that Oakeshott and Hayek are close to each other, it is indeed in connection with their scepticism of political knowledge and conclusively with their criticism of what is labelled 'political rationalism'. In spite of their philosophical differences, they can strengthen each other's position only as long as we keep track of their specific accounts of the knowledge-constraint problem in politics. Although the leading essay of Oakeshott's breakthrough volume of essays, *Rationalism in Politics*, which had the same title as the volume itself, was already published in 1947–8, in the newly established *Cambridge Journal*, edited by Oakeshott, his real entry into political philosophy was somewhat delayed until the appearance of his collected volume of essays, which entry itself illustrates Oakeshott's more cautionary way of progress in academic life.

It is not by chance that Oakeshott takes a maxim by the short-lived, eighteenth-century French moralist, the Marquis de Vauvenargues, as the motto of his ice-breaking essay. It runs like this: 'Great men, by teaching weak minds to think, have put them in the way of error.'[38] The marquis, a close friend of Voltaire, a the primary example of an enlightened intellectual who actually tried to make politics, hit on an important point: by criticizing the intrusion of philosophy into the realm of politics, he prepares the ground for later writers, such as Burke, who attacked French intellectuals for having played a major role in the process that led to the outbreak of the revolution. For us, the main point of the marquis is the background supposition of the maxim: that by inducing (formalized) knowledge into the political realm where people traditionally did not have it, one can cause more problems than one can solve. This is not simply a reference to *arcana imperii*, the secrets of the state, but seems to reveal the practical (non-reflective, non-conceptual) foundation of ordinary political activity (common sense or *bon sens*), which can in fact be thrown off balance as soon as a more reflective sort of activity is performed.

When Oakeshott attacks doctrinaire rationalism for representing an ideology-driven politics, he has in mind this cautionary remark of the marquis. He warns his readers of a typically modern misunderstanding of the nature of politics: when rationalism wants to take control over the political field. Writing after the Second World War, Oakeshott no doubt had similar worries of the totalitarian tendencies of the age as had Hayek, Popper and Berlin, for that matter. All of them had good reasons to criticize the phenomenon. Oakeshott made all efforts to distance himself and his readers from political rationalism. In this respect, he relied on the distinction between technical knowledge and practical knowledge, or traditional knowledge, as he also calls the second one.

The conceptual distinction had the original function to show in what sense political rationalism is a false 'doctrine about human knowledge'.[39] To be sure, every practical human activity, writes Oakeshott, which requires skill, is in need of knowledge. It requires first of all technical knowledge, in Aristotelian terms, the knowledge of *techné* or art.[40] Oakeshott introduces it the following way: 'In every art and science, and in every practical activity, a technique is involved.'[41] The distinguishing marks of the expression of this sort of knowledge is that one can translate it into rules, which means that the substance of the knowledge can be taught, learnt and remembered. Oakeshott's first example is the Highway Code, which presents the technique of driving a car on English roads, and the cookery book, which contains the technical knowledge of cooking.[42] One would not be able to drive, however, by simply reading the Highway Code, and no cook can simply rely on the explicit precepts of the cookery book.

There is, therefore, a further dimension of knowledge present in skilful practical activity. Oakeshott calls it 'practical knowledge', sometimes labelling it as 'traditional knowledge'. There is no doubt, however, that it is close to the Aristotelian concept of *phronesis*, usually translated as practical wisdom – or to what in his famous essay 'On being Conservative' he labels as 'rational prudence'.[43] Oakeshott defines practical knowledge the following way: 'It exists only in use, is not reflective and (unlike technique) cannot be formulated in rules.'[44] When describing it, Oakeshott admits his indebtedness to Polanyi.[45] But more importantly, besides talking of cookery, painting, natural science and religion, he admits that in politics, too, practical knowledge has its role. In other words, he attributes a specific function in politics to the 'customary or traditional way of doing things', which he, in fact, identifies with the concept of practice.

When Oakeshott wants to define the specificity of practice, interestingly enough he uses concepts taken from the discourse on aesthetic qualities. The words he uses include 'taste', 'connoisseurship', 'apprenticeship to a master', 'artistry', 'style', 'sort of judgement'. These are terms used to describe human behaviour from an aesthetic perspective, disregarding its substantial or utilitarian concerns, and focusing simply on its effects on the viewer. In fact, most of the terms come from the immediate semantic field of Roman *decorum*, a Ciceronian term characterizing the behaviour of the well-bred Roman citizen, who is able to rule himself in a self-constrained way. Once again, practical knowledge serves as a form of social control over the behaviour of the human being, directing him or her without determined, explicit rules, simply relying on his or her own capacity to judge the merits of different actions. Admittedly, to arrive at this level of discrimination, what is required is 'a certain kind of society' with its 'large unrecognized inheritance'.[46] And even this kind of society cannot educate the next generation without undertaking to transfer the implicit knowledge in the form of bodily presence and 'exemplum' – relying on pedagogical *eros* mentioned by Plato and some other Greek thinkers. Practical knowledge for Oakeshott can 'be acquired only by continuous contact with one who is perpetually practising it'.[47] Obviously, the Aristotelian notion of *mimesis* is at work here once again – the view of education based on imitating a master. It also recalls the Spartan and Roman way of educating citizen soldiers by allowing the children to follow their fathers in their military campaigns on the battlefields.

When put together, the two forms of knowledge in activity (technical knowledge versus practical/traditional knowledge) show us the main missing link in the rationalist view of politics. 'Rationalism is the assertion that what I have called practical knowledge is not knowledge at all.'[48] It simplifies political action to the sphere of technical knowledge, disregarding the elements of risk and uncertainty. This is done because it trusts only absolute and perfect knowledge, a perfectly controlled form of knowledge, with its illusion of certainty, too. In politics, in the realm of human actions and human passions, this sort of knowledge is not available, except in the illusory world of ideology, while the shaky, vague and risky notion of practical knowledge builds up tradition in the political field. Oakeshott is ready to point out that the birth of a belief in (or ideology of) rationalism was connected to that level of uncertainty and fear, which is the result of a period of intense political and religious conflict and even civil wars. Oakeshott associates the period, following Renaissance humanism (think about the narrative of the post-Machiavellian world in Chapter 2 on early modern prudence), with a higher level of uncertainty, which explains the birth of *Rationalism in Politics*, as an alternative to avoid civil unrest and the disruption order and peace. Yet, in the long run, rationalism reaffirms the conditions it was meant to heal – think about the historical fact that rationalism serves as a demarcation line (or, to present the case in affirmative language, as a bridge) between humanist and enlightened ideas of widespread social control built up by a centralized power. Rationalism, on the whole, is an automation of human social order, which destroys the nice little details of the fabric of society while it only wants to solidify it. This problem was addressed by the short gnome of Vauvenargues, quoted by Oakeshott as the motto in his *Rationalism in Politics*.

7

The prudent individual's resources: Virtues and character

So far, we have considered three major obstacles before informed decision-making and finding and executing the right action in politics. These are the constraints of agency, time and knowledge. The conclusion one can draw from such momentous barriers before informed decision-making and action is that one should have very modest expectations as far as social order and a flourishing human community are concerned. Look at the twentieth century: a period of long steps forward in what could be labelled the 'democratization' of society, and yet it proved to be a period of national and international social disaster, when human brutality was raised to unprecedented levels.

However, beside obstacles there are sources of hope, as far as the practically wise (prudential) activity of agents in politics is concerned. In what follows, we take a look at two major factors that provide resources to help individuals arrive at the right decisions in politics. What is more, these factors play a major role in determining the relationship between the individual and the different types of groups of which she or he is a member, and more generally, the way individual agents and their communities relate to each other. First, therefore, we look at the individual agent's resources and, more particularly, at what is called virtue on the personal level. This is followed by a short overview of the communal support of individual agent's judgement and action, of the individual preconditions of what is going to be called here 'conservative republicanism'.

Personal resources: Virtue and character

Annas and Aristotle: The skill analogy of virtue

Although virtue ethics is a fashionable topic since Anscombe's famous paper on moral theory, it is still not obvious what exactly is meant by the term 'virtue'.[1] As there are competing approaches to the concept itself, one has to make decisions before embarking on a discussion of it. In what follows, I will rely on a single author, Julia Annas, and her approach to virtue in her slim volume *Intelligent Virtue* (2011).[2]

Virtue was a key notion in ancient, medieval and early modern ethics. The present volume has only recalled this history as far as views on prudence are concerned.

But how should we proceed to make sense of the more general term, virtue? Our presentation of the virtue ethical position will focus on the relationship between two major concepts: virtue and character. This choice is made on the assumption that the two concepts together provide the substance of individual resources of political agents in their political activity – a claim that is not based on Annas, who only talks about the moral dimension of virtue, disregarding the communal, political aspects of it. Relying, however, on her elaboration of the two notions, I will venture to take one further step and talk about virtue politics – with the help of another guide, this time Catherine Zuckert.[3] Finally, this part of the chapter will conclude with a look at the virtue politics of the Italian Renaissance, as presented in the writings of James Hankins. Through Annas, Zuckert and Hankins, I hope to provide the reader with a somewhat loosely connected story about the prime mover of a moral and political actor, the relationships between her virtue and character, the relationship of moral virtue to political action and the connection between the individual political agent and his or her political community as exemplified by the Italian Renaissance city.

Annas builds her interpretation of virtue on a simple idea: she relies on what is called the skill analogy in the secondary literature.[4] The skill analogy is the assumption that 'the practical reasoning of the virtuous person is analogous, in important ways ... to the practical reasoning of someone who is exercising a practical skill'.[5] But what is the relationship between virtue and practical reason? According to Annas, 'A virtue is a lasting feature of a person, a tendency for the person to be a certain way'.[6] Yet, this is not a full definition – not even a simple one. Annas develops this first approach to virtue by adding further dimensions to this description. For example, she adds activity: virtue is not an undisturbed, lasting feature, but importantly an active element in a person's moral profile: 'To have it is to be disposed to act in certain ways'.[7] It is also developing: not given in a fully fledged form at once, the person has to strive to perfect it. Annas calls virtue a developing, active feature of a person.

Next, she regards virtue as a reliable disposition. If we take someone to have a certain feature, we also suppose that he or she will remain so, in other words, we rely on the supposition that he or she will consistently respond to certain things in certain ways. Also, Annas emphasizes that a virtue is a characteristic, deep feature of the person concerned. It belongs to his or her identity, one could say. 'A virtue is a disposition which is central to the person.'[8] So Annas introduces the link which connects virtue to character at this point, without offering further explanations. But without further explanations, Annas stresses the link between virtue and character.

A further connection established by Annas connects routine, habituation and virtue. If virtue is only built up by constant repetition, or habit, and turns activity into routine, it would not mean too much for character. The point Annas wants to make is rather that virtue is a form of habituation exactly unlike the ones which lead to routine. Annas takes two examples: learning to drive from A to B and learning to play the piano. According to Annas, the second can be called habituation that does not lead to routine – it is a practical skill.[9] During the process that leads a piano player to perform a sonata, for example, the first phase is a form of habituation: 'Fingers pick out the right notes in the right relation to one another at the right speed, without anything like a decision or conscious thought before each action of striking the keys.'[10] This habituation is, of course, a necessary but not a sufficient condition of the performance. It is a prerequisite for any further artistic progress to come. But the most important thing is to ask how far is the result of this habituation a performance in the form of a mindless routine activity, and not one that is in direct connection with the agent's consciousness. The point Annas wants to make is that the activity of the fingers of the piano player is a go-between: it is neither conscious nor unconscious: 'The ability, though a habituated one, is constantly informed by the way the person is thinking. ...The practical mastery is at the service of conscious thought, not at odds with it.'[11] In other words, unlike habits and routines, complex skills such as the performance of musical pieces require a consciousness which follows or even, as in the case of performing a sonata, directly leads the activity, without making an explicit judgement before each and every move. What is more, unlike habituated routine activity, the repeated performance of a sonata might help to improve the quality of its artistic achievement, although playing it too many times, too frequently might kill the same quality, and might turn the performance into a routine exercise.

No musical performance would be successful if the audience could not attribute certain sound effects to the will of the player. In other word, the consciousness of performing it has a further dimension – the activity is adapted to the intention, or to use a more general term, to the character of the player. Each piano player has a style, a particular way of performing, which is characteristic of his or her artistically, and which identifies his or her performance when it is distinguished from others. Character makes the artist. One of them is more dynamic while the other is more lyric, this one has an intellectual style, the other one a more robustly passionate style. As a skill, in other words, the performance is the result of a disposition requiring habituation, which is closely connected to a frame of mind, eventually, to a character through style. If the skill and the character of the player are connected like that, a specific way of improving the quality of that connection could be to work on the character of the player. To facilitate character development, artistic performances demand self-knowledge and a certain form of self-discipline. To develop one's character seems hard – most of the time, it requires the support of a master. It is through learning from someone else that you can find yourself as an artist. Artists learn by example, where the important point is not to acquire the technique, but to draw conclusions from the connection between the actual performance and the character of the player.

Imitating masters during the learning process, young artists are heavily influenced by them. To become original, they have to accommodate themselves to their environment. Here, we depart from Annas, who cannot accept the argument that this contextual dependence does not make the skill – or virtue – by definition conservative. Her claim is that the would-be artist's wish to become an original interpreter of a musical piece guarantees that the performance will be able to keep a critical distance from the context. As the reader will see, the present account of the role of virtue holds a different view in this respect: it will argue that indeed individual virtue is conservative in the sense that it remains closely related to its context.

Annas pushes the skill analogy as far as to claim that skills and virtues are analogues also in the sense that both require congruence between feeling and reason, for example in both cases you need to enjoy what you chose to do, to do it properly.

Preparing the ground for the next step, which is finally a distinction between virtue and skills, Annas talks about an important condition of Aristotelian virtue: that one type of virtue requires the presence of the others in the character of the agent. This is what is called in Aristotelian theory 'the reciprocity of the virtues' or 'the unity of virtue'. According to Aristotle, the practical intelligence that is required to perform a certain virtue will enable the person to develop the other virtues – in other words, it prepares the ground within the character for the reception of other virtues.[12] To have the virtues, Aristotle argues, demands, together with the process of habituation, developing one's character, to have practical intelligence to help to acquire and practice the virtues. As Annas summarizes it, to acquire a virtue we need the formation and guidance of practical intelligence, 'which functions holistically over the person's life, integrating lessons from the mixed and complex situations that we are standardly faced with, and developing a unified disposition to think, act, and feel, one which gets things right in action, thought and feeling'.[13] This is a very suitable summary for us, as it connects the practical dimension of virtue with the feedback mechanism, through which experiences can be built into one's character. Character is the powerhouse that prepares the person for later challenges.

It is only at this point in Annas's Aristotelian story that skills and virtues depart from each other. She offers two points for the conceptual distinction. First, virtues are valued – once again in accordance with the Aristotelian tradition – for their own sake, and regarded as ideals themselves. In other words, in the behaviour of a virtuous agent no instrumentality is present: if something is chosen for some further, external good, it is not virtue in this classical sense, but a skill.

Secondly, Annas points out that there is one single standard for virtue – it needs to be committed to value, or, as Annas puts it at other times, to goodness. While skills are value-neutral activities, or they simply have a practical, instrumental relevance, the practical activity involved in the virtues is only committed to goodness – the concept, which covers the teleological dimension of Aristotelian moral theory. This side of virtue ethics will present some problems for our paradigm – to answer the question how to combine the pragmatic, realistic approach of political virtue and a commitment to ideal goodness may cause some problems for our own interpretation. On the contrary, if our reader is convinced that political virtue shares this distinguishing mark of the virtues, that it also requires a commitment to goodness, it will help to distinguish action driven by political prudence from that directed by Machiavellian *virtù*, or the political judgement of contemporary realists. However, it will make it harder to argue against the abstract, apolitical, moralistic normativity of Rawlsian theory.

Annas also addresses the issue of human flourishing in connection with virtue. This is a point that means something different in ethics than in politics, but there are certain aspects of the question that seem to be relevant for the present discussion, too. Politics, too, has a more far-reaching level, beyond the practical, pragmatic issues to be solved and deeds to be done. When we think about the success of a political leader or a political regime, we can test whether he/she/it has made his/her/its political community flourish. But once again, it is rather difficult to weigh human flourishing (*eudaimonia*) here – even more so when the happiness of a whole community is at stake. Individual and communal well-being needs to be distinguished – you cannot theorize a community's well-being without first taking into account the individual's personal happiness. But the second step is not much easier, either. There is hardly an easy solution to the question of how to cumulate all the existing forms of individual happiness in a community to get the political *summum bonum*. After all, we can surely give examples of great statesmen who were not successful in certain respects (including social satisfaction), and successful heroes who were not virtuous (not even politically). In other words, it is hard to decide whether political virtues are simply necessary, or necessary and sufficient to have a flourishing community. But Annas's reminder of the longer perspective is quite useful to leave the question of the link between virtue and communal flourishing alive and open, because – as we will see – virtue theory serves to prepare the ground for communal wisdom as well.

These last points – the 'for-its-own-sake' value of virtue, its commitment to goodness and its relationship with *eudaimonia* – show us that to be able to give a more direct account of political virtue, we need to see the difference between moral and political virtue, and how one relates to the other. To answer these questions, let us rely on Catherine Zuckert's account of Aristotelian virtue ethics and virtue politics.

Zuckert and Aristotle: From virtue ethics to virtue politics

Zuckert's paper came out in a collection of historical reconstructions and analytical interpretations of Aristotle's *Politics*.[14] It is part of and, at the same time, provides an overview of the neo-Aristotelian renaissance in moral and political philosophy, which has unfolded since Anscombe's famous essay. This is obvious from her starting point, which is the famous Aristotelian dictum that *ethiké* belongs and is subordinate to *politiké*.[15] In other words, a virtuous life has certain political conditions: at least a correct upbringing is required to enable human beings to 'acquire the habits needed to make them virtuous'. This upbringing, however, needs correct legislation, to explicitly honour virtues and punish vice.[16] This would, however, contradict the basic convictions of liberal democracies, which is that they do not want to determine the paths their citizens follow in their lives, except for discouraging them from breaking the law. Zuckert takes three late twentieth-century examples of neo-Aristotelian thinking: Nussbaum, MacIntyre and the pair of authors, Den Uyl and Rasmussen, and provides a critical analysis of their not fully satisfactory answers to the question of this connection, in order to prepare the ground for her own solution to it.[17]

Nussbaum's reasoning, argues Zuckert, for example, 'shifts from the "ethical question" to the "political question"' concerning the just distribution of goods necessary to provide all human beings with the capacity to choose to live as they think best. Nussbaum disclaims Aristotle's understanding of human nature, and relies on his 'famous claim that human beings are by nature political for two reasons'.[18] First, because it provides her with a global perspective, and second, because the emphasis on the political in human life 'highlights the importance of developing one's practical reason and affiliation or association with others'.[19] Interestingly, this parallel emphasis on the political and on association with others does not lead her to work out a cooperative alternative to the agonistic theory of the political provided by Carl Schmitt – rather, she focuses more on intimate relationships, including friends and family, and less on civic political participation. Zuckert criticizes Nussbaum for not providing arguments for why and how a global community would hold together.

Zuckert's second example is Alasdair MacIntyre. MacIntyre shares with Nussbaum the view that both ethics and politics are better understood 'in terms of the good rather than rights'.[20] For MacIntyre, the common nature of human beings finds its expression in specific traditions, which might have rather divergent views of the good in human life. MacIntyre's approach to human communities is historical, and he keeps emphasizing that even within a given tradition conflicting views about the good are possible, and therefore the meaning of the common good is controversial, historically contingent and open-ended. If it is necessary to mediate among them, MacIntyre stresses the importance of authority, the force of law as well as the role of religion to tackle these conflicts. His point is that 'the place, time, and people among whom we are born shape our lives in irrevocable ways'.[21] While MacIntyre looks at practices (the activity to use certain skills) 'in terms of their particular ends', says Zuckert, these practices will finally be 'evaluated in terms of their contribution to the common good'.[22]

The local, practice-bound nature of particular virtues, however, goes hand in hand with MacIntyre's view of the human potential to cooperate – even if the basis of human relationships is the Aristotelian notion of friendship, which, in his view, in direct opposition to Nussbaum's cosmopolitan premise, 'cannot be extended over great distances'.[23] MacIntyre remains communitarian in the sense that his Aristotelian agenda allows only small, self-sufficient communities to thrive – avoiding the risks and dangers of huge inequalities persistent in the interplay of free-market capitalist economies. MacIntyre has to accept the existence of modern nation states (basically for security reasons), but he thinks that small communities formed as participatory associations should keep vigilance over the transgressions of their own borders by those nation states. Although some critics such as Coleman question the accuracy of MacIntyre's reconstruction of Aquinas, when he focuses on the internal dependencies of communities instead of the external standard provided by the teleology of human nature so characteristic of the Aristotelian–Thomistic teaching,[24] MacIntyre remains an influential voice in appropriating the communitarian (and as I will argue, in certain senses republican) agenda of that very tradition.

Finally, Zuckert refers to a third understanding of the Aristotelian view of political virtue. The pronouncedly neo-Aristotelian (in this sense non-Aristotelian) view of Rasmussen and Den Uyl is[25] that not only Aristotle but also his modern interpreters such as Nussbaum and MacIntyre miss the actual nature of virtue, if they connect it to the political dimension of human action or even simply to the common good. Instead, they propose, the state should leave individuals alone to realize their potential and act virtuously.[26] They associate their allegedly Aristotelian understanding of ethics with a Lockean political philosophy, restricting the playing ground of the state. Relying on common-sense views of human life, they share with Nussbaum and MacIntyre the conviction that practical reason needs to be developed by individuals, and that with help they will be able to freely exercise virtue. Rasmussen's and Den Uyl's view of virtue, however, is far away from that of Nussbaum and MacIntyre, due to their insistence on human flourishing as 'self-directed'.[27] The former authors claim: 'Only by imitating and maintaining the effort to gain the knowledge, to cultivate the proper habits of character, to exercise correct choices, and to perform the right actions can someone achieve moral excellence.'[28] 'They do not deny that *philia* (friendship) is one of the constituents of human flourishing.'[29] They accept that humans are born into communities, but they assume more freedom for the individual to dissociate himself or herself from the group he or she is born into, and also 'to refashion a community's values'.[30] They trust humans' intellectual capacities to obtain a general and theoretically underpinned knowledge of human nature, and also that this abstract knowledge can lead them to create new communities and refashion their own personality. Yet, here again, they remind their readers of a conceptual distinction: 'We should not confuse speculative with practical reason.'[31]

Zuckert draws the following conclusions from her critical reconstructions of Nussbaum and MacIntyre and Rassmussen and Den Uyl. She accepts the Aristotelian point that humans are by nature political, and refers to language, a social product, as proof of a certain form of social determinism. Yet, she finds the individual responsible, which was stressed by Rassmussen and Den Uyl as well. In fact, she finds that 'defining morality simply in terms of an opposition between self-interest and the common interest is not sufficient',[32] which is a view quite close to the one presented in the final part of Chapter 4 on agency-constraint, and even closer to the concept of the person in the Catholic social teaching, also introduced in Chapter 4. Yet, what she lacks in all three examples is adequate care for education when talking about the political dimension of ethics – a point that is indeed relevant for Aristotle, a teacher of young Athenian gentlemen. Unlike skills, she emphasizes, virtue is a complex capacity based on practical wisdom – the English equivalent of the Greek *phronesis* and the Latin *prudentia* – and on developing a good character. This educational dimension of virtue politics is something that was already crucial for Renaissance humanists, as James Hankins keeps emphasizing in his works on the intellectual and political elites of Renaissance Florence. Let us take a look at the meaning of the term in that historical context in order to see its actual political philosophical content.

Hankins and Aristotle: Renaissance virtue politics

James Hankins approaches the problem of virtue in politics not as a political philosopher or as a theorist, but as a historian of political thought. He is specifically interested in the discourse on the relevance of virtue in politics in a Renaissance humanist context. His historical reconstruction, however, is crucial for our present concern because what he provides is a description of the term 'virtue politics' as it was exercised by intellectuals and actual political agents. Let us focus on two main points of his description of virtue ethics in his introductory essay of Renaissance virtue politics.[33] The first is a political, but non-Machiavellian, classical account of virtue in politics, which keeps emphasizing the fact that in Italian Renaissance political communities virtue was referred to as a norm that was widely used to control the behaviour of political actors. The second is a critical point: Hankins narrows down the discourse of Renaissance virtue politics perhaps too radically, when he stresses that it is idealistic, non-pragmatic, non-realistic. A number of Renaissance humanists took political jobs, for example becoming members of urban magistracies or accepting court positions or positions as advisers to individual political leaders or to full communities. These humanists were, it will be argued, not idealists but political practitioners, and their use of the concept of virtue politics was not simply the use of an abstract concept, it actually served the strategic goal of limiting aggressive princely or elite rule, which was lost by Machiavelli's disregard of virtue as a traditional expression of human excellence.

The introductory note of Hankins's paper is that it is a misunderstanding that liberty would be the key term for Renaissance humanists. He suggests that 'the central theme of humanist political writing' was 'the theme of Virtue',[34] which explains why he refers to this discourse as virtue politics, and to virtue as its 'master value'. Hankins reminds us that virtue is not only present in the discourse on politics but also 'in its literature, philosophy, art and even music'. Hankins defines virtue politics in a rather loose way, relying on the term 'virtue ethics', in the rivalry of three 'languages' or 'ways of thinking' (these are not Hankins's own terms, but ones used in the methodological literature of the early modern history of political thought) in contemporary moral theory. This is how he lists the main elements of it: virtue politics

> focuses on improving the character and wisdom of the ruling class with a view to bringing about a happy and flourishing commonwealth. It sees the political legitimacy of the state as tightly linked with the virtue of rulers and especially their sense of justice, defined as a preference for the common good over their own private goods – their 'other-directedness' as a modern might put it.

The Aristotelian point of the description is quite obvious. Virtue politics looks at political rule not as of divine origin, or coming from hereditary right. Rather, for them it is 'qualities of character and intellect that win trust and obedience from the ruled'. The right character traits are those that help the magistrate to properly manage the affairs of the community. It selects what is called by humanists a 'true nobility', a term which connects virtuous character and the ability to participate in ruling. The idea is backed by Aristotle's *Politics* and Cicero's *De legibus*, as Hankins reminds us.[35] Hankins quotes Leonardo of Chios: 'Whoever has this nobility, endowed as he is with wisdom and virtue, is better suited to govern the republic or to perform significant individual deeds.'[36] Unfortunately, it is not clear what the Latin original is for the English word 'wisdom' in this quote, and therefore it is not clear whether he means practical reason or wisdom in the sense of *sophia/sapientia*. But obviously this true nobility means intellectual as well as practical excellence, and it enables the agent to govern. This is a meritocratic view of political agency, elitist, but relying on a notion of the elite which is 'open to the industry and virtue of all citizens'.[37]

Although this is a nobility that is 'natural', the humanists were keen to emphasize the importance of education to fully realize one's potential for virtue. The qualities which they saw as indispensable for governing, namely 'noble *mores, ingenui mores*, and practical wisdom, *prudentia*', were to be acquired by what they called liberal education – the so-called *studia humanitatis*. These Renaissance theorists were idealists. They thought that training in the classics, which meant for them 'the language arts of grammar and rhetoric, plus poetry, history, moral philosophy, and other humane studies' would provide not only 'precept and example' but also the rhetorical skill required to prevail in politics. Hankins rightly reminds us that Aristotle had a much more complex view of how to acquire virtue, including practice and habit, besides philosophical reflection, as well as such objective criteria as 'good birth, wealth, good upbringing and good friends'. But there is no doubt that a society needs a proper educational track to perfect the intellectual and practical abilities of the next generation of the political elite. Schooling is all important for Renaissance theorists because it develops in students such virtues as 'justice, goodness, prudence and modesty', as described by the great educator of the age, Guarino of Verona. It is in this sense that the Muses who inspire practitioners in the arts and the sciences govern, in an indirect fashion, 'also republics'.[38] Even if this strong influence of the Muses on political affairs is not fully explained, one should note that, in fact, Renaissance theorists reconceptualized the role and function of education in the ancient city state, or to put it in a more precise way, they connected education with the *vita activa* instead of keeping it within the sphere of the *vita contemplativa*. Guarino presents a number of examples of great teachers providing tuition for would-be statesmen: 'Anaxagoras taught Pericles, Platon Dion, Pythagoras the Italian Princes, Athenodorus Cato, Panaetius Scipio, Apollonius Cicero and Caesar'[39] – quite a compelling list of great political leaders having been taught by schoolmen. The idea of becoming a political leader by studying literature and philosophy, however, came from Cicero's *De Officiis*, which Hankins regards as perhaps the most important single philosophical text about politics in the Renaissance (before Machiavelli). The specificity of Cicero's account of the interplay between education and politics is that it is a typically conservative account of knowledge transfer: as he understands it, teaching is the transfer of the '*mores et instituta*' of ancient Rome – 'the native virtues that had made her great'.[40] In other words, it is the bridge between accumulated communal knowledge and the personal resources of practical wisdom, a topic to which we will return in Chapter 8. Interestingly, however, the experience of the community is transferred not in the form of principles, rules or other norms, but in the form of literature and philosophy – which makes it obvious that it is not to be learnt with the help of the abstract, rationalistic methods of the schools. The fact that literature and philosophy are better means to help develop the right character traits and attitudes in the leaders of the city than anything else, is proof that it is, after all, character formation that is at stake. It is not simply intellectual development that makes the right political leader, but the right habits of his or her mind and deeds, in other words: his or her character. And character formation is not an aim that can be achieved by conceptual knowledge – it is something you acquire by experience, by imitation, by deep emotional impact and attachment. Philosophy in the practical, Ciceronian sense, together with rhetoric and literature, as it was condensed in the Ciceronian package, is better on these fields than abstract, conceptual knowledge in the scholastic tradition or later Cartesian or Kantian rationalism.[41]

For the moment, let us imagine that through the Ciceronian educational programme the community was successful in letting the next generation develop similar moral senses as the earlier generations. Still, a major problem remains: how can the morally superior elite get recognized by a majority that has not yet obtained the necessary moral qualities? Here, too, the same mechanism is at play: the force of ethos and rhetorical eloquence might make the difference. Although Hankins finds this argument a bit naïve, it is not such nonsense after all: if the elite acquired the moral, political and, in general, practical wisdom of the forefathers by studying the humanities, why could it not be done between them and the *popolo*, even if not on the same level. Members of the *popolo* do not have to rise to the same level as those of the elite – they need only acquire such capacities to enable them to recognize and, if possible, imitate the practical wisdom of the magistrates. And this is perhaps not impossible to achieve.

Certainly, the humanists formulated an elite among themselves. However, some of their work directly addressed a wider audience within the city. They spread ideas by addressing their compatriots using an efficient rhetoric and 'a more accessible, Ciceronian form of moral philosophy'. Although they primarily targeted political and church leaders in their writings, they also tried to make ancient knowledge accessible to a wider audience: their reconstructions of the classical past and the history of their native city were designed to have an impact on a wider audience – first by rhetorical speeches and later in writing, especially after the invention of printing. Although the humanists are usually described as a network of scholars, participants of a European-wide Republic of Letters, there are good reasons to think that at least some of them were adequately embedded in the political culture of their respective city, and thus had a wider impact beyond the strictly academic field usually associated with humanism. Also, among them were courtiers, and these humanists must have been aware of the type of brutal real politics so characteristic of the Renaissance, thus their practical and ideological aim was to soften or replace it by softer inclinations through their wider educational programme.

As they saw it, writing local histories might help rulers acquire practical wisdom, or *prudentia* indirectly, without turning them into Machiavellian princes. Through reading about history, they might be led to gather proofs that – as Cicero claimed – 'Fear is a poor watchman even in the short run, but benevolence keeps faithful guard forever'[42] in politics as well. Readings in history can provide for the missing experience in one's actual capital of political knowledge. And past experiences are just as relevant as present ones. Cicero, for example, brought his readers the experience of ancient Rome, his written work was 'a repository of ancient prudence', as Hankins phrased it. By widening readers' horizon of literature, philosophy and, in general, culture, by bringing back ancient authors, humanists hoped 'to forge a wider culture that celebrated classical virtue and shamed those who fell short of its ideals'. Public orators and humanist classical philologists transmitted the communal moral standards to magistrates and other public figures. Instead of relying on envy, they relied on the thirst for recognition among statesmen: they assured them that honour and admiration are only to be achieved in a political community if you excel in a positive mode, by your erudition, and not by your cruelty. They encouraged those in public service to follow the path pointed out by Cicero and Sallust. The latter reminded them of the moral expectations of the community: 'Small states grow with concord (*Concordia*), discord causes great ones to dissolve', a gnome that was often inscribed into the walls of the halls of town councils and other public buildings. With the help of these references to classical *loci*, humanists tried to inspire magistrates to virtuous behaviour and thinking. But this effort to help political leaders become virtuous was not confined to moral rules. They expected legal regulations to help magistrates to sense how to reach human virtue and, in particular, prudence. As Hankins sums it up, the lesson they left to posterity was 'that a successful republic cannot be simply a system of procedures for adjusting interests, employing institutional means devoid of any moral orientation. We too need to find better ways to educate the young in the core values of our society and our civilization, and to persuade adult citizens to act in the public interest'.[43]

To summarize this section, we collected some recent efforts (Annas, Zuckert and Hankins) to return virtue to the forefront of early-twenty-first-century political thought. Virtue was taken in the contexts provided by these authors, achievable both in speech and in action, in ethics and in politics. They and the authors they introduced were keen to show how virtuous speech and virtuous action are connected in politics, and how virtue can be helpful to keep this connection. Also, virtue was regarded here not only as an important building block within the individual's natural resources but also as an important element in a certain political community's political culture.

The political virtue of moderation

If we look at virtue in the realm of politics, besides justice (the virtue most often associated with political philosophy; however, as we stated at the very beginning of this endeavour, excluded from our present concerns) certainly, prudence is the first cardinal virtue that might come into one's view. But as it is interpreted here, prudence is a virtue that cannot work without the virtue of moderation. In what follows, we have to consider how and in what sense political virtue (and especially prudence) is connected with the virtue of moderation. Relying on the pathbreaking work of Aurelian Craiutu,[44] after a general introduction to this specific virtue, we briefly refer to the Aristotelian idea of balance, which is followed first by its connection with civility and later, with the conservative sceptical concept of trimming in politics, a concept that can be traced back to the debate on the politically disastrous effects of religious passions during and after the seventeenth-century British Civil War.

In a number of works,[45] Craiutu, a political philosopher of Romanian background with a wide Western horizon, developed the idea that 'political moderation constitutes a coherent, complex, and diverse tradition of thought'.[46] He recovered the conceptual history of the term and the specific discourses (mainly within French politics) which made significant use of it, and pointed out the contemporary relevance of the concept. Craiutu, rather a classical liberal, admitted that 'moderation may sometimes imply a conservative stance'.[47] He claimed – just as we did in connection with prudence – that there is 'no "ideology" (or party) of moderation in the proper sense of the word',[48] and argued that 'moderation cannot be studied in the abstract, but only as instantiated in specific historical and political contexts and discourses'.[49] From the half dozen authors he discusses in his book, two are specifically relevant for our present concerns: Raymond Aron and Michael Oakeshott. A third author, Tocqueville, is relevant to both of us, but for different reasons he will not be dealt with either by Craiutu or by the present project. We will concentrate here on what Craiutu labels 'the ethos of moderation'.[50]

The starting point is a quote from Simone Weil: 'Modern life is given over to immoderation. Immoderation invades everything: actions and thought, public and private ... There is no balance anywhere.'[51] This is a valid criticism on different fields of modern life, but perhaps more pertinently on the field of politics in the twentieth century, where indeed extremist totalitarian regimes took the lead even in Europe, traditionally regarded as the most politically cultured, and therefore politically the most moderate continent. Moderation, as Craiutu understands it, is 'a legitimate reaction to the violent age of extremes in which we have lived'.[52] It is therefore not a soft and simply defensive way of thinking, but 'a fighting and bold creed',[53] even if it is not an ideology in the proper sense of the word. Unlike ideologies, 'it implies a good dose of courage, non-conformism, flexibility, and discernment'.[54]

This is a view of politics that starts out not from *a priori* principles, but from the historically conditioned reality of the community in question. We have seen, too, in Chapter 2 on early modern prudence that moderation was closely connected in the seventeenth century to the debate on political theology.[55] Basically, all the main points of reference in the prudential tradition, including authors such as Aristotle, Montesquieu, Burke and Tocqueville, kept emphasizing the significance of moderating inclinations, and the worth of bargaining and compromising in political life. No doubt, the non-utopian, practical nature of the virtue of moderation explains why new supporters of moderation, including Peter Berkowitz and Paul Carrese, 'made a strong case for linking conservatism and political moderation viewed as a constitutional imperative'.[56] This is a point where the present author distinguishes his own position from that of Craiutu. Craiutu does not commit himself to a conservative stance, but keeps a widely defined classical liberal position, his reference being a pluralist society, while the present author deals with the virtue of moderation in the context of a conservative understanding of political prudence, where moderation is closely linked to the aforementioned constraints on the individual actor in the realm of politics by the human condition, and to his or her necessary reliance on the traditional wisdom of his or her community. In other words, here a combination of prudence and moderation is investigated within the context of communities with a specific historical identity.

If we try to collect the key terms of a theory of moderation within either a liberal or a conservative framework, we soon arrive at an ethics of responsibility, which encourages sobriety in political aspirations. As opposed to Nietzsche, who looked at moderation as 'proper only to a conformist herd',[57] supporters of moderation agree with Montaigne, who showed that it is easier to find your way 'along the Margins' than to 'take the wide and unhedged Middle Way'.[58] It requires 'vision, audacity, and firmness as well as a certain degree of nonconformity' to abstain from exaggerated reactions.[59] To be sure, in certain moments, even a general attitude of moderation admits a certain degree of immoderation. Interestingly enough, it is in this context of moderation, non-conformity and courage that the seventeenth-century ex-Jesuit writer Baltasar Gracián is also referred to by Craiutu, arguing in favour of boldness, moderation and prudence: 'A grain of boldness is everything. This is an important piece of prudence.'[60]

Aristotelian balance

Montaigne's Middle Way, of course, refers to Aristotle. After all, prudence is the Latin equivalent of Aristotelian *phronesis*. However, in connection with moderation, the key terms we associate with Aristotle is 'balance' and the 'golden mean'. Aristotle famously pointed out that virtue is nothing less than 'to feel such things when we should, though, about the things we should in relation to the people we should, for the sake of what we should, and as we should'.[61] It is in this description of virtue that he calls a virtuous feeling or action one that finds the mean. The relevance of the mean derives from the fact that it lies midway between the two opposite poles of mistaken excesses: 'In everything continuous and divisible, then, it is possible to take more, less, and equal, and these either in relation to the thing itself or in relation to us – where equal is some sort of mean between excess and deficiency.'[62] Mathematically, it seems to be easy to find 'since it exceeds and is exceeded by an equal amount', but in moral questions the mean is often to be taken 'in relation to us', and in politics, presumably, it must be taken in relation to the good of the whole community. It is, therefore, not something that can be given in absolute terms, but something that is relative to the circumstances – which does not turn it into something subjective. On the contrary, the Aristotelian description of virtue as balance suggests that one should find the right moral feeling or political action in reference to things external, but related to oneself or to the community of which one is part.

The same theme returns in the twentieth-century British conservative thinker's ruminations. Michael Oakeshott, whom we have already discussed in connection with his notion of practical knowledge, regarded himself an admirer of 'the relative importance, in the given circumstances, of the numerous, competing normative and prudential considerations which compose our tradition'. As he saw it, what you had to find in politics was the balance between these competing considerations: 'What is sought is a decision which promises the most acceptable balance in the circumstances between competing goods.'[63] The important point for Oakeshott in this respect was a refusal to submit to a teleological account of political action. Famously, he found it impossible to provide a roadmap in politics with a final aim to arrive at. His favourite metaphor for the challenge of the political was that of a ship on the open sea, without a final destination ahead, simply concentrating on keeping afloat, avoiding the risks of sinking or wrecking or crashing over: 'In political activity, men sail a boundless and bottomless sea; there is neither harbour for shelter nor floor for anchorage, neither starting-place nor appointed destination. The enterprise is to keep afloat on an even keel.'[64] His criticism of rationalism, one of his major ventures in political philosophy, was a sceptical position about overambitious projects in politics, so characteristic of modern politics. The modern rationalist politician reminds Oakeshott of the character of the engineer. 'He believes that the unhindered human "reason" ... is an infallible guide in political activity.'[65] Therefore, the social engineer discounts bargaining, devaluates compromises and prefers destruction and creation ex nihilo to acceptance and reform. Oakeshott presents Voltaire as the paradigmatic case of a rationalist in politics, who thought that 'the only way to have good laws is to burn all existing laws and start afresh'.[66] Conversely, the real politician, as Oakeshott describes him or her, starts from what is given historically, takes into consideration the tradition of the given political association and aims his or her efforts at balancing between the different passions and interests of the stakeholders. The trope of the ship is fitting in this respect: ideologically driven or rationally built interests and unreflected passions can provoke strong political upheavals in the state, which compare to strong and crashing winds on the open sea, when the captain and crew need to maintain full control of the ship to avoid it keeling over. In this respect, balancing is a reactive kind of activity, and minimalist in its aspirations as it only wants to keep the ship of the state in balance, on the surface of the sea.

Civility

Civility, the term often associated with moderation and balance, plays a major role in Oakeshott's discussions of traditions and traditional political knowledge. After all, British politics was for a long time determined by an aristocratic elite, distinguishing itself from the rest of society by its standards of politeness and civility. However, after the European shift to the left in 1945, the fall of the empire led to a downgrading of the notion, and Oakeshott's reference to it is a criticism of mainstream European liberalism, which eradicated notions of civility as politically incorrect. Oakeshott refers to the adjective civil partly in a historical context in connection with Hobbes's notion of civil association, where civil is opposed to natural, and where it refers to 'the voluntary actions of man in commonwealths'.[67] But based on that historical reconstruction of the term, Oakeshott works out his own normative account of civility, in the form of the distinction between civil and enterprise associations. While the latter means a coming together to solve well-defined practical and utilitarian aims, the former refers to an association that is designed to allow members their own private life aims within a well-defined and honoured framework of rules and institutions. In other words, civility means mutual respect between individual *cives* as well as between citizens and (representatives of) the state. Civility 'is a vernacular language of civil understanding and intercourse; that is some historic version of what I have called the language of civility ... the instrument of that conversation in which agents recognize and disclose themselves as *cives* and in which *cives* understand and continuously explore their relation with one another'.[68]

After Oakeshott's rather idiosyncratic, historico-philosophical account of civility, let us observe a more sociologically oriented notion of civility, worked out by Edward Shils in his classic essays collected in *The Virtue of Civility*. Starting out from sociological axioms, Shils, too, tried to explain the concept of civility in accordance with the ancient Roman, Ciceronian, republican use of it. He stressed that civility implies the existence in a society of 'a norm which gives precedence to the interest of the collectivity over the individual or parochial interest'.[69] This norm helps to create a smoothly operating society. As Shils put it: 'Civility is a belief which affirms the possibility of the common good: it is a belief in the community of contending parties within a morally valid unity of society'.[70] This norm will have a direct effect on the way of thinking and also on the choices of individual members of the community – when conditioned, it works as a virtue. 'Civility is a virtue expressed in action on behalf of the whole society. ... Civility is an attitude in individuals which recommends that consensus about the maintenance of the order of society should exist alongside the conflicts of interests and ideals.'[71] Shils also connects the term with a moderating effect on the conditions of the legitimate use of power, where it is arranged in a balanced manner, involving both the government and the general populace: 'It attempts to keep a balance among the parties to the conflicts by an example and insistence on self-restraint.'[72] In addition to legitimacy, Shils also connects civility with authority: 'Civility is on the side of authority and on the side of those over whom authority would rule.'[73] In Shils's account, civility stands for an attitude aimed at others, one that presents it as the virtue by which society can be kept governable and together.

Trimming and the art of compromise

In addition to balance and civility, a third term 'trimming' helps to make sense of the virtue of moderation. The term 'trimming' became important in the seventeenth century following the extreme conflicts of the British Civil War.[74] In his presentation of the art of trimming, Craiutu lists the variety of meanings associated with the verb to trim: 'To prepare, to put something in proper order ... to clip ..., to cut something down to the required size, to balance a ship by shifting its cargo or an aircraft by adjusting stabilizers, to modify according to expediency, to adjust one's opinions, actions, expenditures ..., to adapt ... to ever changing conditions and situations.'[75] Craiutu then presents the main political protagonist associated with the birth of the term, George Savile, Marquis of Halifax (1633–95), and his original definition of the word trimmer: 'If Men are together in a boat, and one part of the company would weigh it down on one side, another would make it lean as much to the contrary.'[76] But, Craiutu seems to imply that the actual political activity of the marquis was even more important than his succinct definition of the key term, for it embodied the idea behind the concept in a practical and easily discernible fashion. Craiutu characterizes this activity in the following way: Halifax 'remained politically uncommitted and refrained from joining any political association, party, or group'.[77] He confirms that this political attitude, defined by 'flexible tactics, forward-looking attitude, and conservative interests' is to be distinguished from opportunism, or from the changeability of the weathercock. In the case of trimming, the political effect of cautious moves was described as 'an art of balancing different ideas, groups, and interests', and those who repeatedly used them as 'moderates concerned with the preservation of political equilibrium'.[78]

As the direct opposite of political partisanship, trimmers were not idealists, but practical politicians fighting on realistic ground for compromise, if not for consensus. They could be easily attacked as timid, vacillating or neutral – as was the case with the hesitant behaviour of Prince Hamlet in Shakespeare's play. It is impossible to imagine that a whole political system be grounded simply on the ideal of the art of trimming. Yet, it is easy to understand that it can be a very positive influence, especially so in times of sharp political conflict. It should also be welcomed in every political society as an alternative to the disastrous activism of the radical.

If we look for further exemplification of the art of trimming, no doubt, Montaigne can be easily referred to as a trimmer. Craiutu makes use of Montaigne's sceptical non-partisanship in an argument for a non-Burkean that is a non-partisan version of conservatism: 'Burke, Oakeshott admitted, displayed political moderation but lacked speculative moderation, a virtue that Oakeshott valued highly in Montaigne and Hume.'[79] In addition to Halifax, Hume and Montaigne, Craiutu refers to Henry Adams and de Tocqueville as further representatives of the art of trimming. In connection with de Tocqueville, in his autobiographical writing, Adams mentioned the timidity and hesitancy of trimming, yet regarded it as 'high wisdom in philosophy'.[80] A further author who apparently exercised the virtue of trimming was Raymond Aron, who again referred back to de Tocqueville's example. Aron, the hero of Craiutu in twentieth-century France, whose judgement was generally much more reliable than that of 'Sartre, Merleau-Ponty, Althusser, or Foucault',[81] and only comparable to that of de Tocqueville, called attention to the relevance of *mores* in political life, and found that a lively political culture might be more relevant than the most perfect institutional arrangement. He diagnosed a 'moral crisis' at the heart of the liberal democratic regimes of his age, and for that very reason advocated 'a reconsideration of our civic duties'.[82]

Having looked at Aron's example, we can sum up the main thesis of the whole chapter. Presenting the resources of the individual political actor, it was argued that an understanding of political action and thought is hardly possible without a close look at the intellectual and practical support of thought and action by virtue, or practical intelligence, a habituated form of excellence. Virtue helps the development of an attitude or inclination to take care of the community of the agent, made possible by character formation. We also argued that in order to let virtue have its positive effects, besides prudence there is a need for a further virtue, that of moderation, an ability to downscale one's passionate drives, as was explained by Plato in the chariot allegory of Phaedrus. Yet, the main reference point here again was Aristotle and Cicero, while the key analytical points were that to remain moderate it was necessary to keep a balance, to rely on the ability of civility and to practice the delicate art of trimming.

Let us take one last step and see what happens when all these resources are not enough to arrive at a reliable judgement and proper action. If the individual agent's resources are not enough, one needs to turn back to communal political resources.

8

The prudent community's resources: Tradition and political culture

So far, we have seen that although politics is primarily dependent on an individual's activity, there are serious constraints on the individual's mental, spiritual and practical make-up. To counterbalance these drawbacks, it is crucial whether the agent is in possession of political virtue, based on experience and practical intelligence. We have also seen that political virtue depends on the character of the agent. It needs a character to domesticate passionate political impulses, to achieve the virtues of moderation, civility and the art of trimming. Yet, all these elements of an individual's toolkit are not enough to establish and preserve a stable regime. To achieve this, it is necessary to mobilize the community's common set of political experiences: the habits, customs, traditions and manners of the political community of which the agent is part. In this chapter, we look at the connection between individual practical wisdom and the communal reservoir of politics in conservative thought.

Institutional order: The rule of law

When reconstructing the origin of the struggle for liberty so characteristic of European political regimes since the start of the process of modern democratization, historians of political thought such as Montesquieu and Alexis de Tocqueville and historically minded political philosophers such as Friedrich Hayek recognized the distinction between political virtues and institutional order. By the eighteenth century, it was already obvious that a well-ordered political society required an institutional framework that provided for the smooth operation of the government's bureaucratic apparatus, offering 'justice as fairness' (Rawls) even if political virtues would be otherwise missing. This claim can be seen as the result of an early modern development, of a separation between two characteristically different political discourses, or frames of mind, one of which can be labelled civic republicanism, while the other one as a juristic approach to government. Reconstructing this conceptual polarity, historians of political thought usually start with the Italian Renaissance humanist authors, most of whom were engaged in what is called a civic republican language, emphasizing civic duties and moral virtues as prerequisites of the free workings of a political society. Conversely, some historians such as Pocock and historians of the early modern natural law discourse claim that some humanists, mainly those also educated in the law, civil and divine, better trusted a juristic account of governmental order. The first was an Aristotelian–Ciceronian 'humanist vocabulary of *vita activa* and *vivere civile*', which 'entails the affirmation that *homo* is naturally a citizen and most fully himself when living in a *vivere civile*.'[1] In this paradigm, called 'civic humanism' or 'classical republicanism', the existence or the lack of individual virtue made the difference. Also in this paradigm, participation in the affairs of the *res publica* was the prerequisite for freedom. In the other conceptual framework, law was regarded as the final instance, either already in existence for times immemorial or pronounced by the voluntary will of the legislator. Law did not require the active and direct support of the citizen for it to become valid – in this sense, it simply prescribed the norms of behaviour and the procedural rules within the political community and remained neutral as far as political values were concerned. Envisaging law as negative and individualistic, this concept of a stable juristic background to political life can also be labelled 'apolitical': the rights and duties of the individual and his or her groups were clearly defined as well as defended by legal provisions, and no political action was needed to verify or even to apply it. Pocock's examples within the British context were Harrington, representing the positive, participatory concept of liberty, and Hobbes, presented as the defender of 'the vocabulary of the law'.[2] While the civic republican discourse had virtue at its centre, right was the keyword for the juristic account. Pocock also referred to the political philosopher Hannah Arendt, a chief representative of republican political theory in the twentieth century, when he described the opposite of the legalistic approach: 'Jurisprudence can be said to be predominantly social, concerned with the administration of things and with human relations ..., as opposed to a civic vocabulary of the purely political.'[3] He criticized historians of political thought such as Richard Tuck, who focus on the central concept of rights in their historical reconstruction of the early modern period. He attacked what he called 'the liberal synthesis', which was too focused on the birth of the bourgeois – in the sense of the property owner and the entrepreneur – and disregarded the historical role of the citizen – in the sense of the active participant in the *res publica*, the common things. Pocock also kept emphasizing that though the two paradigms existed side by side, they did not easily negotiate with each other. But his real interest was in the eighteenth century, a period that was not examined by Skinner, whom he took as one of the key figures behind the (re)construction of the early modern republican discourse. Pocock's main heroes, like the Scottish historians and moralists, had to reflect on the context of the birth of commercial society, when active involvement in politics was not yet available to the majority of people, but which offered an unprecedented growth in the degree of freedom enjoyed in the private sphere of the individual. Yet, his story was not the outdated one of A. O. Hirschman or C. B. MacPherson.[4]

Pocock's story of the birth of a legal order as the structure of government is crucial for the history of political thought. He connects his story of natural jurisprudence with the notion of manners or *mores*. First, he seems to identify manners with virtue redefined. But later, he claims that it is 'a term in which the ethical *mores* and the juristic *consuetudines* were combined, with the former predominating'. As the author of commercial society saw it, 'it was pre-eminently the function of commerce to refine the passions and polish the manners'. It is this form of looking at the function of commerce in society that is of interest to Pocock: he presents his case for what he calls 'commercial humanism', apparently as an alternative to civic humanism.[5] His point is this: natural law theorists have a compelling story of limiting the arbitrary use of power by the ruler or his government against citizens. Yet, Pocock thinks that the achievements of a growing global commerce were not simply the construction of a legal order that guarantees the security of property ownership, as well as of contract and profit. He finds it even more important politically, that the legal order behind commercial society led to a political culture which is even more relevant, as it conditions the political agents internally, instead of simply threatening them externally. Internal conditioning, of course, was not independent of external recognition, of social rank, and in this sense political culture is a social achievement, and not an individual one, even if it might be an unintended consequence of preceding events or states of affairs, rather than the result of some sort of a social contract (and even less one drawn behind the veil of ignorance).

The founding father of this paradigm, in which a legalistic frame of mind is transformed into an internalized polite culture of procedural justice was, Pocock claims, Burke. He quotes Burke: 'Manners are of more importance than laws ... they aid morals, they supply them, or they totally destroy them.'[6] Yet, for Burke, unlike for his Scottish contemporaries, Smith and Hume, manners must also 'precede commerce', and as he saw it 'modern European society needed and must not sever its roots in a chivalric and ecclesiastical past'.[7] Here, Pocock's argument returns to his earlier volume on *Burke and the Ancient Constitution* when he declared: 'If "manners" were *moeurs*, refined and enriched by the progress of society, they were also *consuetudines*, disciplined and reinforced by the memory of society; and presumption, prescription and prejudice were signs and means of society's determination to keep its memory alive.'[8]

In what follows, we follow Burke's logic and first concentrate on the classical liberal idea of the rule of law. Next, we point out the criticisms against that view, which led to the introduction of further safeguards into a political theory of conservatism to defend the institutional framework together with the whole regime: namely, customs and traditions. This is followed by a short analysis of the rather vague, but the more pertinent problem of political culture and the education to obtain it. Together, these concepts, in this order, show how individual virtue, the right character and an inclination to moderation might be helped by social means to guarantee that a society might operate smoothly in the long run.

First, let us examine the classical liberal idea of the rule of law, a key concept of 'commercial humanism', and the first level of communal resources to balance the individual's constraints, in order to help the ordinary individual political agent act prudently.

When in full swing, the rule of law is meant to provide the institutional framework for political activity within a political community. This institutional framework will ensure that even if human beings cannot become the virtue-driven characters we should be, and still remain to some extent driven by personal self-interests, our decisions and actions should be in harmony with the interest of the whole community. As Jeremy Waldron defines it, 'The Rule of Law comprises a number of principles of a formal and procedural character, addressing the way in which a community is governed.' Among the formal principles he mentions are 'the generality, clarity, publicity, stability, and prospectivity of the norms that govern a society', while the procedural ones 'concern the processes by which these norms are administered, and the institutions – like courts and an independent judiciary that their administration requires'.[9] He also adds that some theorists would include in the list of what makes the concept of the rule of law complete, certain 'substantive ideals', such as a 'presumption of liberty and respect for private property'.[10] We are not in a position to decide on the internal debate of the theorists of the rule of law whether this substantive dimension is indeed a part of it. Yet, the fact seems to be untouched by the debate that the formal-procedural principles of the rule of law are designed exactly to help agency-constrained politics, including the government to operate in a smooth fashion and for the benefit of the public, even if moral virtuosity is not given for human beings. Waldron, too, concentrates on the rule of law to counterbalance the potential moral corruption of practitioners of politics: 'The most important demand of the Rule of Law is that people in positions of authority should exercise their power within a constraining framework of well-established public norms rather than in an arbitrary, ad hoc, or purely discretionary manner on the basis of their own preferences or ideology.'[11] Instead of discretionary rule, publicly announced norms should be followed by those who govern, in order to minimize the risks caused by the agency-constraint of infringing the liberty of citizens. If law rules, instead of men, as Aristotle puts it,[12] the chances of misusing power can be lowered, and means are made available to counteract misused power. But the rule of law is not only about limiting the power of the rulers. The rule of law also obliges ordinary citizens. As Waldron puts it: 'It requires also that citizens should respect and comply with legal norms, even when they disagree with them.'[13] This side of the principle reveals that the idea of the rule of law is not simply about the smooth operation of the organs of the state, but also demands certain things from the ordinary citizens of the political community. In this sense, it is not simply Berlin's negative freedom. The introduction of the principle of the rule of law does not make the norms of civic engagement unnecessary, it simply provides further safeguards in case human virtues are missing.

As for the relationship between a virtue-based concept of politics and a rule of law-based concept of politics, a conservative political philosophy of prudence does not regard them as contradictory. In fact, as the first great practically informed theorist of the state, Aristotle was aware of the mutual dependence of these two attitudes. What is more, he, in fact, succeeded in reconciling these two perceptions. When he was asked whether the laws or virtuous men should be in power, he answered: 'The laws, when correctly established, should be in authority, and … the ruler, whether one or many, should have authority over only those matters on which the laws cannot pronounce with precision, because it is not easy to make universal declarations about everything.'[14] So for Aristotle, too, laws take priority, and practical wisdom is needed only within the confines of the restrictions of laws, or if the laws do not regulate the given field of activity.

The question, however, of the basis of the laws remains open. Natural jurisprudence has an answer to it, but it does not necessarily work in a secular context. But if unfounded, how can we know that our laws have been correctly established? And who is to judge their correctness? And what procedures and standards should be used when making those judgements? These are very hard questions and I guess there is no standardized answer to them. Let us rely on Friedrich Hayek's own explanation of the practical mechanism of the rule of law.

To understand Hayek's starting point, we have to refer to his early masterpiece, *The Road to Serfdom* (1944), which warned democratic states of the dangers of direct political control over civil society in wartime conditions. This direct control leads to serfdom, he claimed, while clearly formulated rules will allow people as much liberty in their own sphere as possible in the given social milieu. Individual citizens would be defended by these rules from the intrusions of both the state and their compatriots – the rule of law in this sense opens up a sphere of non-interference and independence for individuals.

The distinguishing mark of Hayek's theoretical concept of the rule of law is that he thinks about legal rationality in the same way as he thinks about economic rationality. In both cases, the individual's knowledge is necessarily limited, due to the previously discussed knowledge-constraints. In both legal and economic rationality, it is better therefore to rely on the help of the invisible hand, which is supposed to create what Hayek calls a spontaneous order without people's conscious involvement. In economic matters, the invisible hand is an abbreviation for the sum of market operations that provides the actual price of commodities.[15] In the legal realm, the decision-based nature of British common law can be looked at as being under the spell of an invisible hand: case-based decisions provide legal principles for later decisions, and the transparency of the law excludes the arbitrary power of the legislator, who cannot be supposed to have a non-political, neutral stance when drawing new legislation. Precedents in the common law system are the result of a trial-and-error method. The judge compares the interpretation of the law in the earlier case, considers the legal argument, which supports the judgement, which needs to mirror the internal logic of the law, as it is extracted from the judgements of the facts of the particular case.

Hayek seems to have been influenced in this respect by his analysis of David Hume's historical account of the birth of justice.[16] Hume had already touched upon the problem of the birth of justice in human societies in his *Treatise*, where he argued that humanity found principles of justice through a trial-and-error procedure, instead of establishing it voluntarily, as the social contract tradition supposes. In his later essays, he returned both to the random birth of institutions of the rule of law, and to the fact that no wise and omnipotent legislator is required to have good laws and preserve freedom: 'The government, which, in common appellation, receives the appellation of free, is that which admits of a partition of power among several members ... but who ... must act by general and equal laws, that are previously known to all the members and to all their subjects.'[17] This knowledge is a practical (or even tacit) knowledge in Hume's case as well. He refers to common law as his basic example, where 'frequent trials and diligent observation can alone direct' improvement.[18] In this respect, Hume prefers republics to monarchies, as they provide more opportunity to have trials, and although Britain was a republic for only a very limited period, he still finds in its political and legal framework strong republican elements. These republican elements are going to be crucial for the conservative political philosophy of prudential urban republicanism this book purports.

Another important note is that Hayek's reference to the invisible hand at work in a well-developed, precedent-based judicial system, and Hume's references to the trial-and-error nature of the development of the concept of justice, both point to the insight that the rule of law understood as a rational construction would not really work on its own. The legislative act in itself cannot solve the problems covered by the three constraints (knowledge, temporal and agency-constraints). It simply provides a legal-institutional framework, which excludes certain possibilities, but which allows freedom for individual decisions to be made and for actions to be performed. In what follows, we see how public control can permeate the sphere of individual freedom in a less obvious way, and how public norms can control individual agents' judgement and performance without written collections of (basic) norms and legislative constructions. Here, we build on the wider meaning of the Greek concept of *nomos* and the common law notion of the law.

Customs and traditions

Nomos in ancient Greece was a concept with a wide range of meanings. Aristotle made many references to human rationality (*logos*), and therefore often associated *nomos* with *nous* and *logos*, as in the following quote: 'The law, however, does have the power to compel, being reason that derives from a sort of practical wisdom and understanding.'[19] But law is traced back here to practical reason, more exactly, to *phronesis*, the Greek equivalent of prudence, and through that an appetitive and purposive element is also introduced into its meaning, bringing it down to earth and nearer to the actual reality of the fragile human social world: 'For Aristotle moral action was reason penetrated by desire, and law was the handmaid of morality; it existed to habituate men to virtue. Law must therefore share the appetitive and purposive element which is found in virtue itself.'[20] The crucial point of the foregoing succinct narrative is that law and virtue are no longer separated as they were in the early modern context, but rather depend on each other.

Aristotle, however, does not always identify *nomos* with *logos*, but uses the term in a somewhat different, wider sense, including among its elements both customary law and convention. Murphy claimed that 'whenever Aristotle adopts the Sophistic contrast of nature and convention (*nomos*), he uses *nomos* broadly to include customs and laws'.[21] The important point for us here is to see that *nomos* covers social norms that are not born by human deliberation but are the results of unreflected practices.

However, Murphy also stresses the Janus face of the Greek notion of custom. He starts out from Hayek's criticism of the distinction between nature and convention, in the context of his explication of the concept of spontaneous order, a criticism based on views elaborated in the Scottish Enlightenment by authors such as Adam Ferguson. Unlike Hayek, however, Murphy distinguishes the two faces of custom, one closer to habits, the other reminiscent of stipulations. As he puts it, custom has the potential to turn something artificial into something natural by habituating us in(to) it. Natural languages are examples of this development. This is made possible by 'the close psychological relation of habit formation and social convention. If our habits were not shaped by social convention and if our social conventions were not generally habituated, there would be a deep chasm between our natural propensities and our social conventions.'[22]

Illustrating the dual sense of the concept of *nomos* as well as of the concept of custom, Murphy shows us that ancient Greek politics, as worked out by Aristotle, meant by the rule of law not simply a constitutional order designed by a legislator or lawgiver to suit particular political purposes, but rather a system of unreflected habits, *mores* and explicit rules, which together channel the behaviour of individual citizens as well as the deliberations of a specific body. Yet, by widening the concept of the law, the connection between legal regulations and other, habituated forms of exercising social control over individual activity is made visible, in other words connections between community demands and individual aspirations, between common laws and individual virtues or the lack of them. This way, we are reaching the insight that the three constraints on the individual agent and the sources of the constraint over his or her political virtue are to be handled by the whole culture of a political community, instead of simply providing a well-ordered institutional setting.

Thus, more needs to be said about political culture itself. However, before that, there is a further task: we have to analyse customs integrated into a compact whole, which is commonly designated as tradition.[23] The survival and persistence of customary law, for example in the UK, even after the introduction of the enlightened practice of creating statute books and constitutional blueprints, was based on the assumption that law is a form of customary wisdom. In European politics, in general, however, the struggle for liberty pushed aside traditional knowledge in favour of understanding law in light of the epistemological revolution of Descartes and Kant. The intellectual hubris of science-based progressivism in the nineteenth and early twentieth centuries made the case even more radicalized. But after the deluge of totalitarian regimes, based on the modernist-technocratic creation of law ex nihilo in the name of liberty and egality, or of scientifically supported claims of racial and civilizational superiority, a return to tradition might have very good reasons. The list of important postwar thinkers of a re-examination of social and political traditions included such diverse authors as T. S. Eliot, Edward Shils, Hans-Georg Gadamer and Alasdair MacIntyre.

The political relevance of the renewed interest in tradition is due to the fact that liberal individualism has no theoretical answer to the problem of how to make sure that liberal values survive and live on. If the values that individuals cherish are up to individual choice, how can the political community ascertain that the sins of the past will not be repeated?

Tradition is relevant for a political community because it can code the experiences of earlier generations, together with the conclusions the forefathers drew from their experiences in a way that can be transferred to later generations and decoded by them. *Traditio* was originally a Roman law concept, meaning the transfer of certain property from the owner to the transferee. The root of the term was *tradere*, meaning to teach, and Iustinian used the term as a synonym for *docere*, in the context of teaching the law. Which means that from its very origins there is a sense of the term when it refers to the transfer of some intellectual or spiritual possession from one generation to the next. It is this meaning that is widened in the Christian theological meaning of the category, where the Sacred Tradition means the actual teachings of Christ, as given over from generation to generation, in a living tradition.[24] A somewhat similar understanding of the term is present in Judaism, where the meaning of the foundational text, the demands of the law and oral teachings are also passed on in the form of a religious tradition (*halakha*). Secular, and more politically loaded contexts of the word include an understanding of the ancient constitution as something that comes from the immemorial past, an ideological construct of the common law jurists, among them Edward Coke, in their struggle against the arbitrary rule of the king in the seventeenth century. All of these ancient Roman, Christian, Hebrew and British religious and legal uses of the term suggest that tradition is still a useful concept to understand the continuity of certain forms of communal (common) knowledge within societies, which have oral, visual and written ways of self-expression. For the present purposes, tradition is a way of accumulating certain experiences, recognitions and habituated norms, in the form of written or spoken texts, patterns of thinking and perhaps even more importantly, by posture, gesture, picture and general behaviour, ways of reflecting on communal and individual identity and drawing visions of the external world.

When we understand the rule of law as providing an institutional framework within which individual political agents can interact, we can draw certain conclusions. One conclusion is that when law is habituated, its close relationship with virtue becomes obvious. A second conclusion is that to have a real effect upon the next generation, it is not enough to transfer an institutional framework, but the political community needs to '*tradere*' in encoded, written and unwritten forms, in behavioural, thought and pictorial patterns, and finally, as manifested in the example of the ways of individual and communal life of the present generation, the experiences it gathers and the reflected and unreflected conclusions of those experiences. The teaching programme of humanist civic republicans was aware of these communal tasks, learning them from classic texts such as Cicero's writings. During the early modern and modern period, education was still seen as character-forming for young men (and a little later for young women) for the benefit of all. After the victory of an individualist ethos in the nineteenth and twentieth centuries, in parallel with the rise of late capitalism, Western constitutional democracies forgot about the common good as one of their core values. This oblivion seems to be a crucial problem in the present day, as made explicit in the Böckenförde Dilemma, which states that

> the liberal (*freiheitlich*), secularized state lives by prerequisites which it cannot guarantee itself. This is the great adventure it has undertaken for freedom's sake. As a liberal state it can only endure if the freedom it bestows on its citizens takes some regulation from the interior, both from a moral substance of the individuals and a certain homogeneity of society at large. On the other hand, it cannot by itself procure these interior forces of regulation, that is not with its own means such as legal compulsion and authoritative decree.[25]

When asked to make the claim more explicit, Böckenförde, an earlier constitutional court judge of the German Federal Republic, clarified it the following way:

> To conceive of such a state the liberal order needs a unifying ethos, a 'sense of community' among those who live in this state. The question then becomes: what is creating this ethos, which can neither be enforced by the state nor compelled by a sovereign? One can say: first the common culture. But what are the elements and factors of that culture? Then indeed we are dealing with its sources such as Christianity, Enlightenment and humanism. But not automatically any religion.[26]

Here, it is not possible to analyse in detail the references of this quote, which would require Europe-wide political debates in the present European-wide crisis.[27] But it is important to recognize that the liberal order of the rule of law is not standing on its own, but presupposes this sense of community, an ethos, which depends on the 'common culture', itself rooted in religion and the secular *Weltanschauungen* of the given political community. In what follows, therefore, we have to deal with the notion of political culture, and education as a way of cultivating it in an intergenerational manner. For a political regime where prudence and moderation can thrive requires not only a constitutional regime based on the rule of law, not even just common customs and traditions, but also a common political culture and a common will and a traditional programme of educating youngsters that takes care of transferring not only culture as the movable and immovable property produced by the forefathers but also its universe of knowledge and the strong emotional attachment to this very universe. All these requirements seem necessary to compensate for the heavy constraints upon political activity caused by an egocentric human nature, and to safeguard the individual resources of virtue, character and moderation. Only through an appreciation of political culture and education can we arrive at the proper action, the main aim of any practice-oriented political philosophy. The regime where political culture and education are appreciated for these very reasons is nothing less than what I call a conservative republic.

Political culture and education

As we have seen, Hayek had already picked out culture as key to understanding the political machinery in a political community. His concept of spontaneous order was defined as a go-between connecting natural phenomena and artefacts, that is products of human design. He argued that much of what we experience in human interactions, including language, the market and the law, were born in a process that was neither natural nor artificial, but somehow both. As he put it: 'Yet much of what we call culture is just as much a spontaneously grown order (e.g. custom), which arose neither altogether independently of human action (nature) nor by design (stipulation), but by a process that stands between these two possibilities, which were long considered as exclusive alternatives.'[28] In other words, culture is an unintended by-product of human actions and interactions and as such, it limits and orientates later actions and interactions. If political actions and reactions happen on a regular basis in a given community, they will have longer-term direct effects, in accordance with the aims of the actors, or against their intentions, but there will also be certain side effects, not aimed at, neither intended, nevertheless very much influencing later interactions themselves. The experience of earlier actions and interactions and the memory of their consequences and side effects create a capital of reflected and unreflected knowledge in the political community, which will determine the limits of what is imaginable in the political arena. Later actors entering politics will find a cultivated political field, with its specific requirements, explicit and implicit standards, the successful examples defining what is acceptable and the narratives of how to lose and what counts as loss, and this will have a significant, although not fully deterministic impact on their attitudes, beliefs, values and aims. Political culture in this sense defines the political imaginary of a given community, creating a bubble that confines the way people think and act politically. In this sense, political culture is both an obstacle for the individual political agent and a source of power, which borrows for the political agent the resources of communal identity.

If we want to see the origins of a reflection on the cultural dimension of politics – that is on the side effects of political actions and their reactions – again it was Aristotle, who in his talks about the way of life in the Greek *polis*, embedded his analysis of politics into a general description of community life in a city. Take the relationship between his normative books (most famously the *Nicomachean Ethics* and the *Politics*) and their relationship to his books on communal culture, including his *Poetics* and *Rhetoric*. The single example of how he recapitulates the cultic events of Athenian theatrical festivals shows us that he was aware of the feedback mechanisms of reflections on politics in dramatic dialogues, and their political relevance. Also, his concept of *eudaimonia* as the final aim of a flourishing human life, consisting of a virtuous character and friendship, his vacillation between the active and the contemplative life shows that he viewed politics as an integral part of a whole human life, individual and communal. The teleological description of human life that Aristotle provides is based on the assumption that the fullness of a human life means the achievements of the potentials inherently given at the time of the individual's birth. In the long deliberation about participation versus contemplation in the *Politics*, Aristotle is arguably 'cagey, dialectically balancing the claims of the political life against the philosophical, but not giving decisive precedence to either'.[29] So, it seems that he thinks that both of these alternatives might offer the individual ways to achieve a life completed by a perfect friendship based on character, benefiting the other for the sake of the other. In the human interpersonal relationship called friendship, the individual can reach out and get in contact with the other one, and through that (in Aristotle's case, most of the time) he or she is able to feel sympathy with his or her closer and wider community, present and past. This concept of cultivating one's character through socializing, and in this way producing products of culture is also present in Cicero's own views of a perfect human life. In fact, we owe Cicero our concept of culture, which comes from the Latin expression for cultivating the soil. In Hannah Arendt's summary, Cicero's achievement was

> Culture, word and concept, is Roman in origin. The word 'culture' derives from colere – to cultivate, to dwell, to take care, to tend and preserve – and it relates primarily to the intercourse of man with nature. ... It seems it was Cicero who first used the word for matters of spirit and mind. He speaks of excolere animum, of cultivating the mind, and of cultura animi in the same sense in which we speak even today of a cultured mind.[30]

Among twentieth-century thinkers, one can refer to Alasdair MacIntyre and Martha Nussbaum as examples of thinkers who kept emphasizing the relevance of the cultural dimension in ancient political thought. MacIntyre, for example, in one of his polemical essays on how to interpret Aristotelian political theory, sheds light on the connections between Aristotle's theory and the social and political practice of contemporary Athens. As he saw it, an Aristotelian community was 'informed by shared deliberation', and therefore it had to have a practice 'in which there is sufficient agreement about goods and about their rank ordering to provide shared standards for rational deliberation on both moral and political questions'.[31] In short form, what is required by Aristotle's account is 'a type of community that exhibits a common mind in its practice arising from its shared goals'.[32] MacIntyre is aware that this is a rather strong demand, one that our own political communities (meaning the modern European-type nation states and their large-scale market economies) cannot perform. MacIntyre is aware of this state of affairs, and in his own philosophical programme he focuses on smaller communities, where he thinks we can still today find remnants of this density of shared standards, including 'households, fishing crews, farming cooperatives, schools, clinics, neighbourhoods, small towns'.[33] Yet, even here, there is a third requirement: shared standards of rational justification are also required, ones 'that are independent of the de facto interests and preferences of their members'.[34] What is more, these standards should clearly 'define the community's common good', and members will have to be loyal to that common good. This third requirement shows that the supposition is that a community's common culture is no less than a harmonization of views about the ranking of goods, of deliberative standards as well as of the standards of rational justification. In other words, MacIntyre's account of the social and political practice of a well-founded political community supposes a remarkable attachment between members and the community, and an identification with the common good of the community, even if it is in conflict with the individual's own self-interest – a strong requirement closer perhaps to the German concept of *Gemeinschaft* than to *Gesellschaft*.[35]

Martha C. Nussbaum is another late twentieth-century author dealing with ancient Greek political thought and its connections to the general culture of the *polis* of the age. In her influential work, *The Fragility of Goodness: Luck and Ethics in Greek Tragedy and Philosophy* (1986), she compared the philosophical and dramatic works of ancient Greece in search of answers for her ethical questions. She seems to have been influenced by the provocative criticism of modern philosophical Kantianism and utilitarianism, while she highly appreciated ancient Greek philosophy and literature, also influenced by Bernard Williams, Nussbaum not only showed that literature sometimes opens a better window on Greek thought than philosophy but she also pointed out that the Greeks were right in their claims that no matter how morally good a person is, or wants to be, his or her moral standing is extremely fragile due to external circumstances that he or she cannot influence directly. This lesson closely parallels some of the findings of Williams in his famous *Ethics and the Limits of Philosophy* (1985). Yet, Nussbaum's achievement is her pronounced claim that ancient tragedy as an artistic form was more suitable to express this lesson than formal philosophy. Nussbaum's expertise in the principles of the ancient Greek theatrical tradition led her to utilize for political thought the historical fact that 'Greek tragedy was necessarily "political": its subject matter was the well-being of the polis, and its performance was part of what turned a collection of men into a polis'.[36] Nussbaum was also more straightforward than Williams in showing that the ancient Greeks' way of life and ideas were closely connected to each other, a point that brings her view close to Pierre Hadot's argument that in ancient Greece practising philosophy meant the choice of a particular way of life.[37] Her conclusions of fragility and vulnerability return once again in a different context in MacIntyre's *Dependent Rational Animals* (1999). In this book, MacIntyre is starting to leave his Aristotelian phase, and gets closer to a Thomistic Christian virtue ethical position, claiming that 'vulnerability and disability ... pervade human life'[38] and that therefore we are destined to depend on others. This move by MacIntyre shows us that there is a continuity in the virtue ethical tradition, connecting the ancient Greco–Roman to the medieval Christian phase of it.

Neither Williams nor Nussbaum nor MacIntyre disclaimed rationality as the distinguishing mark of human nature. Yet, their reconstructions of Greek thought revealed the inherent risks of individual human life – in both a moral and a political sense, even if planned and executed in a fully rational manner. The conclusion they drew, however, from this description was rather different. MacIntyre already established in his *After Virtue* (1981) that indeed the Greeks had a certain way of *polis* life, which connected individuals to each other and the community with strong ties. In the Greek *polis*, the individual had to cooperate with the other citizens on a regular basis. The members of the *polis* had a shared identity in which the communal belonging was just as important as one's own personal experiential horizon. MacIntyre's interpretation of Aristotle, however, labelled as the social Aristotle, seemed to be too idealistic for Nussbaum. She criticized MacIntyre for distorting historical reality when he presented an ancient Athens where individual life was supposed to have been lived in harmony with other persons' lives and with that of the community. Nussbaum's supposedly more realistic, non-harmonic view of *polis* life was meant to undermine MacIntyre's romantic views on community in ancient Greece. We are not entitled to decide that debate. However, for our present purposes, it is enough to say that MacIntyre's and Nussbaum's differing approaches to Greek culture reflect a twentieth-century conflict between a liberal view of the individual's autonomy and that of its critics, usually labelled as communitarians, who wanted to show that even in a liberal regime individuals need to have interpersonal and even communal dependencies.[39] For us, what is relevant from this debate is that the political virtues of the individuals are not enough to make the political community flourish, and that political culture is a non-negligible resource for the individual or communal agent's deliberations, and his or her execution of political actions. Böckenförde's paradox showed that a community's culture determines certain dimensions of the human identity, and therefore political culture and education are a necessary condition for the right operation of a political community's common political prudence. From the Aristotelian ideal that a *polis*-like community needs a shared horizon of values and shared final aims, it is only one step towards the interpretation of Aristotle that both MacIntyre and Williams and Nussbaum suggest. This interpretation presents the individual as fatefully fragile, and therefore obviously dependent on the shared culture available in the community.

Let us take another example. In their path-breaking analysis of the historical regions of medieval and early modern Europe, entitled *The Three Historical Regions of Europe: An Outline*,[40] Jenő Szűcs and his co-author presented the three parts of Europe – Western, Eastern and Central – as having three different historical traditions, resulting in three different approaches to politics, three different institutional settings as well as three forms of political life, in short: three different political cultures. Although by now this classification – in spite of the faults of some of its details – is generally accepted, the question is not whether its historical geography is correct or not. For example, whether Central Europe's borders are where Szűcs and his co-author supposed them to be. The issue relevant for us here is that if the theory of historical regionalism is right, and if it is correct that it led to alternative political cultures in the different regions, which has a decisive impact on present-day political realities, this is a further argument that the tradition-based political culture of a political community can indirectly limit the available possibilities of political actors even today. Considering the main issues why the V4 countries decided to form a political group, we cannot avoid the supposition that the group's formation expresses a political reality: a divide between the Western and the Eastern part of the continent, as far as their inhabitants' experiential horizons are concerned. This dissimilarity is mirrored in the political attitudes of the relevant communities, which may lead to different available answers to the challenges of the day.[41] Apparently, the political aim to unite the continent after the fall of the Iron Curtain was based on the hypothesis that inhabitants of Eastern European countries would happily follow the guidelines of their senior Western partners. Most of these countries did not have a substitute-elite, which could have taken over the role from the elite of the communist period. And certainly, both the general public and the local elites of these Eastern European countries were habituated in the manners of the totalitarian regimes of their countries, under the oppression of communist Russia or Nazi Germany. Although institutional structures could easily be rearranged in 1990, after the fall of the Iron Curtain, the mentality, the imaginary and the behavioural patterns of the populace and of the elite were not so easy to change, if anyone would have been aware of its significance.

It is unquestionable that the past of the Central European region has had an effect on its nations' attitudes towards the West and towards each other. In fact, already in the medieval period there were strong similarities connecting the countries of the region, and cutting them away from the more centrally positioned parts of the continent: 'Despite differences, enough significant similarities existed in political, socio-economic and cultural terms to warrant examining the early history of this region together, in a comparative perspective.'[42] As we see from this quote, historians, too, look for regional answers to the political and socioeconomic situation, including cultural patterns of the past. The argument from architectural history is well known: if you travel in the region, you will see in architectural terms how far the Central European cultural region stretches. Certainly, present-day political borders do not follow the cultural geographic patterns in a straightforward way, but one can argue that from a bird's eye view the patterns of political and cultural attitudes indeed largely coincide.

If this thesis holds, it can help to convince us that there are indeed soft, but hardly avoidable cultural determinants of political behaviour. To understand a political agent, you need a thick description of his or her political inclinations and habits, to use a term first introduced by Gilbert Ryle and later elaborated by cultural anthropologist Clifford Geertz. For it is, most probably, not simply his or her personal reservoir that is mobilized by the agent when he or she deliberates, makes decision and acts, but his or her political behaviour that is embedded in the political culture into which he or she was born or habituated.

This is not an argument for any sort of social determinism. We should not think that an agent's behaviour can be fully dictated by his or her cultural environment. Not at all: it is only a note that the methodological individualism of much liberal theories of political (as well as economic or social) behaviour is not realistic, and that we can give a more convincing picture of it if we take into account the cultural framework in which the agent is embedded. The political impulses of an Athenian and a Spartan would be different, even if their rational political calculations coincided, and even if they aimed to do similar things. When he made his famous comparative analysis of forms of constitutions, Aristotle was not simply interested in the institutional question 'Who should rule?' He, too, tried to understand the inner logic of the political community in question, which could only be done if he looked at the whole cultural identity of the given *polis*. A *polis* operates in a particular manner to achieve flourishing or happiness, which is not simply a political target, but one on which one's life narrative might depend. The constitution, too, he thought, needs to be explained as embedded into a much wider realm than the framework of the actual institutional arrangements themselves: 'It is by seeking happiness in different ways and by different means that individual groups of people create different ways of life and different constitutions.'[43]

As with Aristotle's rational nature, one's political virtues are also embedded in a cultural context, in which they make sense. It is therefore logical that in Aristotle's theory, education is crucial for a flourishing *polis*, and that the form of education in a particular *polis* should suit the constitution and the ways of life characteristic of the given political community. Education opens up the intellectual capacities of citizens, enabling them to make use of their own personal resources. Education also habituates citizens in the practices of the community in accordance with the political and cultural norms of the *polis*, thereby making available the communal resources: 'Aristotle argues that virtues and the education that inculcates them must suit the constitution.'[44]

The connection between education and the constitution and culture of a community is complex and multidirectional: the education needs to suit the constitutional culture while the constitutional culture can be reinvigorated by education. In an earlier paper, the present author argued that, according to Aristotle, imitation is crucial in the learning process of the individual: the disciple or the son follows the example of (i.e. imitates) his master or father.[45] For Aristotle, philosophy, history, drama and myth all provide examples of human character, behaviour, good and bad choices, and the consequences of them. The humanities are crucial within the educational process, because the narratives they make available help to form the disciple's character, to inculcate his virtues and to illustrate how to behave virtuously in hard cases. Through either lively narratives or real-life experiences, the disciple learns to consider the antecedents and consequences of a decision in a given situation, and learns how to enlarge his own perspective to include further temporal and communal dimensions.

Political culture, therefore, is not something that can be easily taught and learnt, it is the opposite of liberal *tabula rasa*. Past generations' experiences are encoded in the culture inherited by the present one, and this way the quintessential conclusions of long histories of the community can be preserved. Political culture, however, itself needs cultivation – think once again about the concept of culture in Cicero's work. And think about the problem raised by the fact that political culture needs to be picked up by members of new generations of the community. Without a consistent programme of education, past experience, valuable customs and identity-forming cultural remnants will be lost to the next generation and onwards. Therefore, a prudent community will always take care of how to transfer its political-cultural heritage to the next generation. In other words, prudence at the community level requires an awareness of, and even an answer to the Böckenförde Dilemma. Educating youngsters in the political culture of a community is a crucial condition of a conservative political philosophy of prudence.

How to find the proper action in politics

Prudence, or this-worldly wisdom, reminds humans that perfection is not available in this world. A conservative political philosophy of prudence needs to give up perfectionism, starting out from the presupposition of Anthony Quinton, as the title of his famous book, *The Politics of Imperfection* (1978), a short historic overview of mainly British conservatism, suggests.[1] In this book, originally given as a series lectures at the University of Kent at Canterbury, Quinton provides a narrative of the history of English (rather than British) conservatism, religious and secular. As the title suggests, Quinton finds a denial of perfectionism at the core of the conservative message. The political philosophy of prudence agrees with Baron Quinton that perfection is unavailable in real politics. Quinton wants to help his readers better understand what is at stake in conservatism. This is how he explains the fundamental principles of it: conservatives, he claims, 'express a conviction of the radical intellectual imperfection of the human individual, as contrasted with the historically accumulated political wisdom of the community as embodied in its customs and institutions'.[2] This formulation is relevant to our discussion for more than one reason. First of all, because it contrasts the imperfect intellectual capacity of the human individual with communal wisdom, and secondly, and no less importantly, because it stresses that the content of communal wisdom is something that cannot be conceptualized but which can only be grasped through its embodiments, through customs and institutions. In the mirror of this comparison, the imperfection of the knowledge of the individual leads to the denial that political ideas could be meaningful when expressed in *a priori*, abstract formulas. The imperfection of individuals explained in the book also leads the readers to a reflection on communal wisdom as practical wisdom, in the sense that it is the result of a long trial-and-error method, and its first premise is Socratic self-criticism. It claims to be, by definition, imperfect, and therefore does not allow the sort of universal abstraction so characteristic of the philosophers' intellectual pride. This is why traditionally conservative politics is not enthusiastic about theory in the proper sense of the term.

Intellectual imperfection, however, is not the only form of imperfection in Quinton's account. It is accompanied by what he calls moral imperfection. This latter, he argues, plays a far less significant role in conservative thought than intellectual imperfection, nevertheless it has its own relevance. These two imperfections are conclusions of the imperfection of human nature as such. In the case of intellectual imperfection, politics needs to avoid relying on grandiose and abstract designs, created ex nihilo by individual thinkers, who are themselves isolated from the daily realities of political life. In the case of moral imperfection, each and every individual, including the prince, is open to making wrong decisions as a result of their reliance on their unchecked inclinations. Morally fallible humans are in need of the control mechanisms provided by customary law, law in general and institutions. Subjective and personal impulses can be controlled by objective and impersonal barriers. As a result of Hobbes's pathbreaking *Leviathan*, government is usually taken as the remedy for individual and collective sinfulness. Conservatism specifically regards government as the antidote to the intellectual incapacity of humans, but it is also cautious with humans taking part individually or together in government. As opposed to Hobbes, who is arguing in favour of a strong government to check powerful individuals and influential groups in civil society, conservatives claim that the intellectual and moral corruptibility of individuals calls for control mechanisms, even if the individuals are themselves parts of governments. They rather trust the authority and wisdom of the community, as expressed in long-standing institutions and unwritten customs, which have a coercive power even over legally entitled political actors.

Finally, intellectual imperfection also returns in the description of the third principle that Baron Quinton attributes to conservatism, namely of political scepticism. It is defined as 'a direct and obvious application of the thesis of man's intellectual imperfection to the domain of the political'.[3]

This scepticism about the potential of individual human intelligence in the realm of the political is crucial for the conservative political philosophy of prudence. Conservatism is a political attitude that tries to redress the problem pointed at by the sceptical: its standard of propriety is partly served by the traditional wisdom of the well-performing human community. This is the reason behind Quinton's returning references to the communal aspects of conservative politics. It is not collectivism – it is simply a recognition of the relevance of communal life in human society. Besides political scepticism, therefore, Quinton picks out traditionalism and organicism as the characteristic principles of conservatism. As he sees it, 'a historically evolved social order incorporates the accumulated practical wisdom of the community, it is a collective product, the outcome of innumerable adjustments and modifications made by politically experienced individuals in circumstances'.[4] This ad hoc, pragmatically born traditionalism is connected to organicism, 'which takes a society to be a unitary, natural growth, an organized, living whole, not a mechanical aggregate'.[5] Together, these three principles (traditionalism, organicism, political scepticism) serve in Quinton's framework as pillars describing politics understood practically and realistically, as the realm of the possible. Political scepticism suggests that embodied forms of social experience (customs, laws and institutions) have a much better chance of serving as external controls to individual political decision-making than abstract individual rationality or moral virtues. This scepticism about individual political decisions and actions directly leads, therefore, to traditionalism, honouring existing manners and customs, and proposes to avoid radical changes in the texture of society or in the web of political institutions. This sketchy recollection of Quinton's analysis of the three pillars of conservatism helps to point out the parallels between our understanding of prudence as the practical virtue in politics and conservative political attitudes.

If we accept, therefore, the narrative of Quinton about human imperfection as an unsurmountable barrier before political rationalism, we will exclude the search for perfection from our perspective, too. Instead of encouraging the agent to find the perfect solution to his or her political dilemma, the aim of the conservative political philosophy of prudence is much more moderate: it proposes to talk about a proper act and a proper way to speak in politics as its agenda, in a tradition-based context.

Political prudence and the proper way to speak and to act

To talk about the way to find the proper act and the proper words in politics, however, is not a new enterprise. In what follows, Cicero's understanding of the term *decorum* in his description of the ideal orator will once again be recalled.[6] To make that possible, however, two points will be needed from our earlier historical recapitulations of Ciceronian thought.

The first is the connection of action and speech in politics. Cicero was both a practising statesman and a rhetorician and thinker, who was well aware that in politics no one can survive without an ability to properly express himself or herself in speech, and to act as prompted by his or her political circumstances. And the two things were intermingled: speaking properly was a politically valuable act, and performing a certain act was itself a form of self-expression, an utterance.

Secondly, it was Cicero who, in his considerations of rhetorical excellence, connected questions of content with stylistic issues. In other words, he connected politics and morality with aesthetic appreciation. When you judge, he argued, how a statesman acts and speaks, you evaluate his speech and action both rationally and – so to say – sensually, judging how far it fits your expectations of the proper way to act and speak. Decorum, the key term of Cicero's understanding of what appropriateness means in speech and act, is a term that includes both a moral–political and an aesthetic dimension.

Let us see how Cicero defines appropriateness in speech and action: 'In an oration, as in life, nothing is harder than to determine what is appropriate. The Greeks call it *prepon*; let us call it *decorum* or "propriety".'[7] Propriety or appropriateness is a relative term: what is appropriate matches something else, which is either internal or external to the agent. For example, something can be fitting as far as the occasion or the person is concerned: '"Propriety" is what is fitting and agreeable to an occasion or person.'[8] This ability to relate one's position and motivational basis to the circumstances is needed when preparing for action. Also, to know the audience one is addressing in one's speech is crucial to find the proper action/words. As it turns out, in Cicero's narrative it is prudence that will help the individual to position himself or herself and to find the right words and actions. But in Cicero's scheme it is not only the active partner who needs the support of prudence: the same is true about the audience of the agent. The audience will also use prudence to judge him or her: 'The eloquence of orators has always been controlled by the good sense (*prudentia*) of the audience.'[9] Cicero's important point here is that prudence can relate to the judgement of speech, not only the judgement of action. This judgement can also be made by the agent or about the agent. The agent and the rhetor are not that different from the audience – or to put it differently, everyone needs to be able to judge speech and action, 'for to discover and decide what to say … is a matter of ordinary intelligence (*prudentiae*) rather than of eloquence'.[10]

In his paper on Cicero's *decorum*, Kapust differentiates between two ways of using prudence in Cicero's writings, one relating to political wisdom (*civilis prudentiae*) and the other referring to the term in rhetorical theory. But as long as the term is the same, the contexts of these alternatives will be connected with each other. What is more, rhetoric was not for its own sake in republican Rome: words and deeds related to each other, as well. Therefore, the present account of prudence does not share Kapust's view that Cicero made a systematic distinction between his different uses of prudence, rather it suggests that the same ability called prudence helped to judge speech and action, actively (as agent) and passively (as audience or receiver of action). It is also relevant that in Cicero's view judging the practical case did not require expert knowledge. On the contrary: 'Considering the great difference between the expert (*doctum*) and the unschooled (*rudem*) in terms of performance, it is remarkable how little they differ when it comes to making a judgement (*in iudicando*).'[11] This is important as it shows that indeed prudential judgement has a natural basis in human beings, usually identified as common sense. Cicero's account of prudence prepares the ground to broaden the discussion from the virtue of the political elite, and to relate it to the citizens of a conservative republic. As the source of prudential judgement, common sense makes it possible for the audience to judge the content of the message as well as the style of the speaker, and to consider the consequences of both on the common good together with the effects of the action itself.

In other words, Cicero wants to leave behind the purely formal, stylistic understanding of the success of the orator, and particularly in his *On Duties* made an effort to give *decorum* an 'ethical content'.[12] Here, *decorum* takes the role of temperance or moderation, as one among the cardinal virtues. It is *decorum* that helps to define order and find 'limit to words and deeds'.[13]

The expression used for *decorum* in English is 'seemliness'. For Cicero, seemliness entails 'a sense of shame (*verecundia*) and what one might call the ordered beauty of a life, restraint and modesty, a calming of agitations of the spirit, and due measure in all things'.[14] Cicero's virtuous person, the one who behaves with *decorum*, is in search of this measure in all things; he never gets tired of judging appropriateness, and relating things and persons to each other. Actions and words that survive this test of the judging person are called proper acts and words. But *decorum* is not self-centred, even if it judges the actor's and the speaker's propriety: virtue relates the agent to the other, in the sense of mutuality and a shared experience: *verecundia* in this sense is 'the essence of the emotion as a force of social cohesion'.[15] This social dimension as the basis for the demand for *decorum* is crucial for the present venture: it is clear that within the Ciceronian universe individual virtues are interpreted within a social-communal framework. The proper act is not only proper in relation to the agent and his or her political circumstances but also proper in relation to the social whole with which the agent is identified.

Next, we have to tackle one further challenge: if prudence is indeed so crucial in politics, how does Ciceronian prudence as the virtue leading to the socially good and proper act and words relate to the prudence of the political realist, such as Machiavelli, for whom it is nothing more than cunning and finding the right means to achieve politically (in other words non-morally) defined aim.

Political prudence and political realism

The challenging claim of political realism, recently becoming quite popular in political theory, is the following: no abstract standards could help us identify the proper act and words in politics context-independently.[16] For Machiavelli, prudence turns out to be nothing more than the art or technique of winning over an audience, determining who was right in a certain situation, or simply having the final say and/or move in a debate or acting as one wants to in a 'hard case' political situation. Obviously, this means relinquishing a normative theory of politics.

To remain normatively defendable, the political philosophy of prudence needs to answer the challenge of theorists well versed in the practice of power politics such as Machiavelli or contemporary philosophical realists such as Bernard Williams or Raymond Geuss. A way to do this could be to analyse these theorists within their own political contexts. One could show that Machiavelli's *The Prince* (the usual reference work for realists, as opposed to republicans who usually refer to his *Discourses*) is in fact an answer to the loss of vigour of the Florentine republican regime, of which he was an office holder, and the abrupt rise of the princely rule of the Medicis at the beginning of the cinquecento. Alternatively, one could point out that Williams and Geuss had very strong contextual reasons to argue against the depoliticization and loss of vigour of late twentieth-century Western liberal politics. They wrote in the very moment when this liberal democracy started to weaken. But neither of those answers would directly provide theoretically satisfactory answers to the problems we face. To achieve that, we need to see in what sense Machiavelli's argument in *The Prince* differs from the classic theory of republicanism, as proposed by Cicero, and in particular what does it mean that the Ciceronian view of the ideal statesman is normative, while Machiavelli's own one is simply descriptive. In what follows, I argue that it is not by chance that Cicero's republican views had a religious dimension. Also, I would like to argue that Roman political virtues, among which prudence had priority, were continuous in the Roman context with law understood as public wisdom, connecting Latin *mores* to Greek *nomos* and Roman law *ius*. Comparing the Renaissance author to his Roman republican predecessor, it will be argued that the lack of public dimensions in his considerations of politics results in Machiavelli's own concept of prudence being theoretically shallow because of being cut away from the larger and socially embedded framework characteristic of Cicero's and the Roman republicans' understanding of prudence. I argue that, in fact, Machiavelli's acclaimed realism is not more, but less political, if we define the term 'politics' as a thick concept, meaning the close connection between the individual and his or her community which is, I argue, the Aristotelian-Ciceronian heritage in political thought.

One can certainly argue that Cicero as an eminent rhetor used references to eternal, moral and cultural values in a rather pragmatic way, relying on them only as part of his rhetorical tactics. The present interpretation depends on the claim that this ideology of a normative basis of politics was more important for Cicero than that, in other words, that he used this discourse for substantive reasons. The demands of eternal, moral and cultural values that he associated with politics were integral parts of how he looked at himself, philosophy and politics being continuous in his mind.[17] One can argue that Cicero's political vocabulary with its returning references to values beyond politics is only wishful thinking in a political context, and the normative use of prudence disregards the demands of the moment, so characteristic of actual political deliberations and actions. Machiavelli, according to this criticism of Ciceronian normativity, was the first to dare to talk about the realities of political conflicts. The answer to this criticism is that in Machiavelli's account of the realist prince, the statesman is cut away from his community. This is absolutely impossible within the Roman political context – except for Nero-like tyrants, who, however, violated the basic republican principles of the Roman heritage.

To show what a thicker concept of political normativity might mean, let us take a look at the classic work on the religious dimension of city life in ancient cities by Numa Denis Fustel De Coulanges, which called attention to the metaphysical sphere of the ancient understanding of politics.[18] Fustel's aim was to show that city life in ancient Greece and Rome was dominated by religious ideas.[19] His thesis was strong in an age when the French state's neutrality in religious affairs became dominant. He succeeded in showing that the concept of the city itself belonged to the religious imaginary in the age of Pericles or Cicero. Not only did the Gods have a major role in the establishment of the city, but the daily communal life of its inhabitants was also marked by a strong theological dimension: the family, marriage, domestic activity, the law, urban rituals, war and peace, city government – all were in fact phrased in religious terminology. Remember Antigone's relationship to the dead in the tragic conflict of Sophocles's *Antigone*. She thought that she had an obligation to bury the dead (even more, the dead who were her relatives), although they had attacked the city, and therefore had to be taken as enemies. Sophocles's play reveals the political relevance of the issues concerning the dead already in the context of the Greek *polis*.

Fustel De Coulanges's work is important for us to highlight the fact that life in the ancient city state was yet a part of the religious universe, where human understanding was based on religious dogmas and mythical narratives. By the time of the Roman republican regime of Cicero (first century BC), it was a more sophisticated system than the paradigmatic type of ancient city immortalized by Fustel. It is noteworthy, therefore, that Cicero played such a major role in Fustel's historically informed narrative.

When Machiavelli wipes out the religious dimension from his picture of the Italian city states, it is indeed a radical move, which is diametrically opposed to Cicero's more tradition-bound way of thinking,[20] and necessarily leads to a distortion of the understanding of politics of the city states. Machiavelli seems to have been quite antipathetic towards religion. Within religion, he was even more antagonistic with its Christian form than with the ancient pagan version, which he found better suited to urban politics than Christianity. But he did not present a religious imaginary in the background of his analysis of the prince or of the republic. This decline of the religious universe from behind the remaining vocabulary of politics is crucial when we try to understand the novelty of Machiavelli's way of approaching politics.[21]

> The contemporary of Cicero speaks a language whose roots are very ancient; this language, in expressing the thoughts of ancient ages, has been modelled upon them, and it has kept the impression, and transmits it from century to century. The primary sense of a root will sometimes reveal an ancient opinion or an ancient usage; ideas have been transformed, and the recollections of them have vanished; but the words have remained, immutable witnesses of beliefs that have disappeared.[22]

Cicero, the ideal rhetor, keeps referring to 'ancient opinion or an ancient usage', to what is labelled *mos maiorum* in the contemporary discourse. The conservative interpretation of Cicero tends to take him seriously on this point. 'Throughout his works Cicero says much about what it means to be Roman citizen: it is determined by "ethical continuity" (*mos maiorum*), which includes culture, descent and political identification with the *res publica*.'[23] In other words, as he sees it, human identity is to a large extent determined by culture, in its most general sense, in the sense of *mores* (the equivalent for Cicero of Greek *ethos* but also including elements of *nomos*). As Cicero sees it, human beings are helped by a common sense (*sensus communis*), shared not only by all rationally endowed human beings but also by long-established routines, by the experiences of earlier generations, in other words by the customs of the community. In his survey of Roman political thought, Atkins sums it up: besides nature 'Rome's customs and constitution provide another means of shaping opinion and guiding appropriate judgments'.[24] To which he adds the following enumeration from *De oratore* of what he calls 'republican institutions': 'The *forum*, *contio*, law courts, and senate (I.35, 44), the Twelve Tables and other public law (1.194) establishing Roman political culture (I.193-6), and the "spirit, customs, and way of life" (*mens, mos, disciplina*) of the fatherland that Romans love (I.196).'[25] He also adds that both sources of judgement, that is nature or character (*natura*) and customs or character (*mores*), are words that Cicero used for the Greek term for character (*êthos*).[26]

But what if all these references to the forefathers is done in a simply technical fashion, if this reliance on the practical wisdom of the glorious Roman past is nothing more than a way to attract attention and search for the support of one's audience? Cicero seems to be a firm and honest, though sometimes more cautious and sometimes more ideology-driven supporter of the glorification of the Roman tradition: his political *persona* is based on his trust in the ways of the forefathers. Obviously, this discourse referring to ancient wisdom was not his own invention, it could be traced back to the gradual historical birth of Roman law from 'statements of customary and religious norms, concerning marriage, family relations, funeral rites, and so forth'.[27] But in Cicero's own rhetorical universe, ad hoc references came to be arranged into a well-defined framework of concepts and phrases idealizing the *patria*'s past, with its wisdom, and Roman experience as exceptional in the political history of humanity. Western thought did little more than take over from Cicero this confidence in common sense and in communal *mores*, until Machiavelli separated the public and the private realms.

The present chapter wants to argue that, in fact, Machiavelli's brave move to separate the interest of the ruler and his community, of politics and morality was disastrous to what counted as politics, and also to morals. Machiavelli's description might give a more realistic account of the inclinations of ordinary, guilty human beings than Cicero's own summary of Roman republican statesmanship. But excluding the normative dimension from the theoretical considerations of politics by Machiavelli meant not only an allowance but also an encouragement for the political agents to do whatever they felt was necessary not for the community, but for preserving their own personal power over the community. In this sense, *The Prince* is not only the direct denial of the basic principles of Ciceronian ideas of the relationship of individual political agents and community, still present in the *Discourses*, but it also had a disastrous influence in the time of the rising royal absolutisms in Europe. Conversely, one should also admit that Cicero's own description of the relationship was neither unproblematic nor always followed by Cicero himself – which was not favourable for the legitimacy of that discourse, either.

The point of the foregoing argument is this: a major break has occurred between the Ciceronian paradigm still alive in medieval and early Renaissance Europe (as reconstructed in the *Discourses*) and Machiavelli's own innovation in *The Prince*. To make sense of this break, one should refer to Viroli's distinction between the Machiavellian discourse as 'the art of the state' (*arte della stato*) and what Viroli calls the 'art of the city' (also referred to as that of the '*civitas*' or the '*vivere politico*').[28] As Viroli interprets him, Machiavelli's art of the state is 'not the equivalent of the *civitas* or the *vivere politico*'.[29] The difference between these paradigms is in the aim of their use of political prudence.

In the classical sense, individual prudence led to the flourishing of the political community, by serving the common good. In Machiavelli's *Prince* it already means 'the talent for preserving, and if possible, improving one's status'.[30] While individual agency is also important in the classical tradition, the '*politikos*', the '*civilis vir*'[31] cannot concentrate on his own well-being, as he is required to fulfil the requirements of all four cardinal virtues, in other words he 'must be temperate, constant, prudent and just'.[32] The statesman has to keep a balance between these values, and has to find harmony between individual and communal interest. Machiavelli gives up this effort for a balanced, harmonious and moderate view of the relationship of the personal and the communal. This was the source of the scandal around him, and the cause of what is labelled as the Machiavelli problem, that is the diametrically opposite message of *The Prince* and *The Discourses*. Cicero thought that the conflicting and partial interests of different groups in the city could and should be moderated and pacified, or at least balanced, finding its proper place (*loco suo collocare*). Machiavelli does not deny this demand explicitly, on the contrary, he reaffirms the demand for the good man in politics, too. Yet, he makes it clear, as Viroli sums it up, that 'a man who wants to be good under all circumstances' can cause serious problems not only for himself but also for his own political community, as he 'will certainly come to ruin among the many who are not good'.[33] To learn how and when not to be a good man is part of the art of the state, which is needed in republics as well in times of urgency, and not only for new empires but also for the conservative task of restoring political life in a corrupted city. Viroli might be right, that Machiavelli was in fact in favour of the republican model of the good political man, yet he opened a new discourse of monarchy, the state of urgency, the art of the state, which, as Viroli claims, replaced the art of the city. He was contemporary with the birth of the territorial state and its competition for dominance in Europe. If we do not accept Machiavelli's proposal that the politics of the nation states is an art of the state, what we need to show is that it is possible to learn how to control and moderate this push to step over boundaries. We have to show that it is enough to commit moral sins only when it is proper to do so, as is explained in the 'problem of dirty hands'. In this way, the norm to do what is right can be kept on a meta-level. It is right to do what is required by the moment (even if it is morally sinful), when the choice is between bad and worse, a political situation described by Sartre, Walzer and Bernard Williams as that of the dirty hands.

Surely, the ideal vision of Aristotle and Cicero, concerning a city of concord and balance, of *decorum* and propriety, is not always realizable, but the description of political realists of a world of ineliminable conflicts at the centre of politics is perhaps the other extreme. The question is whether or not the discourse initiated by Machiavelli is still viable. The question is if one can draw radical conclusions of amorality from the insight that there are moments when politics requires discarding the unity of the virtues in order to keep one's potential to act. Surely, there are moments when it would be unwise to remain good, either for yourself, or for your community. Yet, the argument is that Machiavelli lost sight of the normal operation of politics as understood in the discourse of the art of the city. While Viroli might be right that in international conflicts, or even on the national level, the art of the state cannot be disregarded, one should remember that the art of the city is still available for lower-level units of politics, in peacetime. The political philosophy of prudence is built on the historical evidence that lower-level units of political community, such as city magistracies in the Western political world, could very well function under very different external circumstances, irrespective of the political regimes they had to suffer. Even under oppressive state-level regimes, they could still keep their standards of political balance alive for relatively long periods of time, and despite historical challenges attacking them from time to time. The claim of the conservative political philosophy of prudence is that these lower-level communities can organize their own common affairs according to the standards of what Viroli calls (borrowing from Machiavelli) the art of the city, and what is going to be labelled here as the standard of conservative republicanism, even if their national or state-level leaders might have learnt a lot from Machiavelli's art of the state. To act properly is to find the proper place for both kinds of arts. The way to combine these arts, the art of the city and the art of the state, adequately for the benefit of both the individual agent and his or her community, requires the Aristotelian approach introduced in this book. It is still possible to achieve such a delicate balancing between individual and communal interest, and when and where this is done successfully, defending the rights and fulfilling the duties of the local community within the state, it is called conservative republicanism.

Prudence and conservatism: The example of early modern Dutch urban republicanism

In what follows, finally, an early modern example will be reconstructed, where the shift from politics to the art of the state (in other words reason of state) was not so direct, and instead the art of the city (republican participation) and the art of the state could survive side by side: the example of early modern Netherlands.

As a first step, let us see how a combination of conservatism and republicanism can be conceived, and how it is to be distinguished from the modern notion of the republic where the art of the state is in full swing. In Continental Europe, republicanism usually means the French model: it is a progressivist liberational ideology against the oppressive power of the state, or the French emperor, who obtained almost absolute power over his subjects. The art of the state in that context meant the art of building an empire, and Richelieu was the major influence behind it. The progressive republican movement led to a wave of revolutions against that autocratic state from the time of the great French revolution to its nineteenth- and twentieth-century mimicries. In a certain sense, the French revolution represented a return to politics (in the sense of the art of the city), but this time the political community meant the French nation. In this sense, continental republicanism was first an art of the nation, and then its ideology became step by step an international art of uniting the citizens' power against an oppressive state and its bureaucratic power. It was with the help of that international republican ideology that Napoleon first tried to unite Europe under his own yoke. He combined the art of the state with the art of the nation and the French version of progressivist republicanism – a rather strange mixture.

The French narrative of the republic was an ideological construct – a vision of liberty, equality and fraternity. Although the American republic was not as subversive, it, too, was to a large extent an ex nihilo political creation, which turned the republic into an experimental project. It was based on the British tradition of Protestant republicanism, as exemplified by Algernon Sidney or Harrington. In the eighteenth century, the Commonwealth men still had their radical views, and a nationwide ideology played a major role in the outbreak of the American Revolution.[34] As Tocqueville explained, nineteenth-century American democracy (the concept taking over the main role of a modernist ideology from republicanism) took the lead, and paved the way for the federal project.

Yet, there is an alternative concept of modern republicanism – when it is associated with the ideology of a city or (local) commune. This concept is neither progressivist nor revolutionary – rather, its function is to secure cohesion, save continuity and help preserve the status quo within the particular face-to-face community.

The claim of a conservative political philosophy of prudence is connected to this second understanding of republicanism. The conservative republican paradigm is an urban phenomenon, European, but non-French, modern, but mostly, early modern. References in the discourse of the conservative republican paradigm included ancient Athens in the age of Pericles and republican Rome in the time of Cato and Cicero, but its real forerunners were the medieval free cities or the Renaissance Italian city states or *comunes*.

In the early modern period, the main reference points of the discourse of European urban republicanism were the early modern Dutch Republic and Venice. In both of these cities, citizens of the political community had to and did play a major role in operating the political institutions of the community. In the ancient Roman sense, they could easily be called republics, where citizen participation in the affairs of the political community was highly expected.[35] But the active patrician or middle-class elites of these republics did not have a progressive and subversive ideology (except for some periods of the history of the Florentine republic, when it had such a subversive ideology as well, causing internal struggles and finally the loss of liberty). These citizens and their bodies had not envisaged themselves as the opponents of the holders of state power, even if liberty was a key concept in their ideology. On the contrary, they and their communities, the cities and the commercial companies were loyal supporters of the monarch, the pillars of the state's sovereignty. Let us take a brief look at how the Dutch Republic was characterized by its observers, and how their citizens understood their political role and in what sense they relied on the virtue of prudence.

The first question about a republic was whether it should be belligerent, as ancient Rome, or rather neutral and possibly peaceful, as Athens was, and as a premodern commercial centre should be. The answer was, claims Franco Venturi, a definitive yes to peacefulness: 'The old republics could survive only if they withdrew from the conflicts of the great powers ... Both Holland and Genoa ended by admitting that Venice was right.'[36] As the historian of the Dutch Republic, E. H. Kossmann understands it, 'Venturi's republican tradition is the tradition of the peaceful commercial commonwealth, politically conservative, inclined to insist on the rights rather than the duties of its citizens whereas Pocock offers us in great and impressive detail a tradition of anti-commercial republicanism, agrarian, combative.'[37] Kossmann is right: a detailed account of the Dutch experience is painfully missing from Pocock's reconstruction of the Atlantic republican tradition. But Kossmann's strong point is his own characterization of the Dutch experience:

> The Dutch thought in terms of the city state. The city state, or a league of city states, represented for them normality and tradition. ... The more or less democratic republic which they envisaged as the best form of government in this sad and imperfect world was a city, large certainly, with tens of thousands of inhabitants, open to foreigners and drawing its prosperity from trade and industry.[38]

The connection between trading interest and republicanism was already established by Sir William Temple in his 1673 work on Dutch trade.[39] In this work, the former British ambassador claimed that most of the trading communities of Europe had been republics, including Athens, Venice and Holland.[40] Yet, the most important factor for a trading community was, he added – only a few years after the Cromwellian experiment – to avoid 'Arbitrary and Tyrannical Power'.[41] In other words, trade required 'security and order', 'the legal registration of property': all these factors contributed to a regime of order and peacefulness, together with a potential to (economical) grow and the spontaneous development of certain manners of social behaviour (culture). In his analysis of Temple's work, István Hont cites the terms used by Temple to describe these non-legislated *moeurs*: '*General habits, dispositions, affections, customs, veins, use, opinions, education, and humours* of people'.[42] In our present context, all these terms are crucial, as they point to what is nowadays called political culture: the way politics is practised unconsciously as well as in institutionalized forms in a political community. The Dutch had the good fortune that their trading interests led them to accommodate themselves to a life of peaceful coexistence. Although – one should add – they were sometimes ready for long-standing and cruel fights for their interests or independence, and – to be sure – they were ready to take their part from what came to be called global imperialism. Yet, the crucial point was their acceptance of the rule of a rather strict legal regime taking care of the order of society. What is more, they interiorized this legal regime, and identified themselves with its values.

Certainly, Temple's description of the Netherlands is characteristically from the other side of the channel: instead of being an unbiased account, it serves both as a warning and a support to his British readers. In other words, it is more a normative account and less a story in which each and every detail is historically correctly deciphered. Hont, in his interpretation of Temple's Dutch model, is of course much more critical than Temple was, yet he seems to side with the Dutch, although in a very complex and indirect manner.

Let me refer here to a third author whose interpretation of the Dutch golden age is even more influential than Temple's seventeenth-century or Hont's present-day interpretations. This is Johan Huizinga and his *Dutch Civilisation in the Seventeenth Century*, the last volume published in the famous historian's lifetime, in 1941. Huizinga's aim is here (in the midst of the German occupation of his country) to summarize what he regards as the specifically Dutch way of life, the manners and *moeurs* characteristic of the people of the Netherlands. His choice of presenting his case of a characteristically Dutch way of life in the context of the seventeenth century, the Dutch golden age, is proof that what he is after is not simply a detached historical account, but an effort to outline a paradigm, a Weberian kind of ideal type. Although by now historians proved some of his faults, Huizinga is quite useful for us in our search for the identification of what we call conservative urban republicanism, the more so as his work during the German occupation in the Second World War had an obviously critical overtone.[43]

Among the basic characteristics of life in the early modern United Provinces, Huizinga refers to the dominantly urban nature of human settlements: due to their extended far distance trade and intensive shipping, he claims that mercantile centres were already established here before the appearance of medieval urbanization: 'The Netherlands could, in fact, boast important trading centres even before the emergence of medieval towns.'[44] Their inclinations to enterprise led Dutch merchants to establish trade routes and develop economic partnerships on a continental and later on a global scale. Even more interestingly, this spirit of enterprise developed without any central authorities encouraging it; on the contrary, the urban elites capitalized on the freedom they enjoyed as far as laws and regulations were concerned in the field of merchant enterprise.

In Huizinga's interpretation, the Dutch success story in economic enterprise did not follow from modernization and a new set of ideas. As he puts it: 'Prosperity flowed quite naturally from the medieval system and there was never a point where the old was deliberately shaken off and the new warmly embraced.'[45] His view of the patrician urban elites is that of different tradition-driven communities pursuing their own initiatives, in accordance with the members' own individual and the community's communal interests, and making use of the special freedoms and privileges they owned since medieval times. Huizinga claims that this is not to be conceptualized as decentralization, but rather it should be labelled as a certain form of particularism: 'The division of the country into a host of legal and administrative districts was bound to go hand in hand with a conservative attitude.'[46] These units could take care of their own affairs, without the constraints of a central power. The preserved medieval ideal of freedom led to a status quo: 'Each region enjoyed autonomy, passed laws for its own benefit, and sought to impose restrictions on outsiders.'[47]

Even the uprising against Spanish rule was, in this interpretation, a conservative revolution. What the Dutch wanted to regain by their revolt was their medieval liberties, understood as privileges and immunities. Yet, they fought for them together, the small circles in this way gaining an experience of fighting together for what Huizinga calls in the Roman sense: the '*patria*'. In this way, the continuity between the past and the present was unbroken even in those years of armed conflicts, when the war of independence was fought to return to normality, to 'business as usual'.

This grand narrative of defending traditional liberties and cooperating to defend peace and order, according to Huizinga, led to a very specific way of life, and a rather characteristic system of values. This way of life consisted of a certain common sense and reserve: 'Modesty and moderation went hand in hand with tradition and great dignity.'[48] Huizinga quotes Huygens, who spoke about 'Holland's glorious simplicity.'[49] Huizinga calls cleanliness, so familiar from seventeenth-century Dutch interior paintings, 'a homely virtue', and he denies that it would resemble anything like materialism. Rather, it is a sense of reality: 'Cleanliness went hand in hand with a strong feeling for reality.'[50] And this reality check (let us recall the concept from Pieper's Thomistic realism) and cleanliness express a certain ethical balance, which is also characteristic of the Dutch way of piety, the Protestant manners of worshipping God. This Aristotelian ethical interpretation of Dutch manners is coloured by Huizinga with a list of concepts about Dutch manners, including 'simplicity, frugality, cleanliness, sobriety, a prosaic spirit, ordinariness'.

The point to be made here is that Huizinga's Dutch seventeenth-century burghers embody the practical wisdom this book is searching for: their way of life is pragmatically oriented, which makes them realistic people, who are moved by their self-interests but who learnt to cooperate within small circles to achieve the common good so visible in the streets of their towns. They are also conservative-minded people, which means that they do not hunt innovation for its own sake, but they are in tune with their age and react adequately to the demands of the moment. They prefer to run their affairs on their own, and they are ready to fight for their traditional freedoms. The particular way of life they live expresses a system of values in which practical wisdom has a crucial role: their attitude is to solve urgent present dilemmas, and they are ready to rely on traditional knowledge and cooperation to achieve these aims.

It is at this point that we can generalize our thesis. Huizinga insists that this Dutch golden age mentality is not an invention of the Reformation, but that it has deep roots in the medieval Dutch experience. The generalized point to be made about how to act properly in a political context is that the embodiment of the prudent political agent is close to the middle-class merchant of the Dutch cities and even more to the medieval burgher in his[51] capacity as a citizen of his town, and part of his guild economically and socially. In this respect, the conservative political philosophy of the city is a corrective of the extremities of globalization. The claim here is that a proper political act by a political agent presupposes a social embeddedness, which is hardly possible in the atomistic models of individualism, which substantiate the theories of the state and the global order.

A good but limited amount of individual and communal liberty, institutional economy, constitutional arrangement, a wise tradition – all are required as preconditions, if prudence is to appear in individual and common political judgements and actions. But one should not forget about the soft requirement of moderation as far as antagonistic passions are concerned nor about honouring tradition in an appropriate political culture. Politics is, after all, part of the culture of a community. A political decision or act is appropriate if it fits the given culture. In this sense, political prudence is not simply an individual's private success, but it will always remain a common achievement of a political community.

Summary: A conservative political philosophy of prudence

Constraints

Politics as practice

In the Aristotelian tradition, politics is a crucial field of human practice. Politics is done by political agents (individuals and communities), who talk, decide and act in order to influence their political environment, and to change the world around them as far as it can be changed by human, political means. They interact with their natural and social environment, and by this praxis try to have an impact on both. To achieve success in these interactions, they need a kind of applied, embodied knowledge, which is unlike *epistémé*, *scientia* or *sophia*, in our terms, unlike abstract, conceptual knowledge. What they need is not necessarily reflected, but rather experience-based, practice-oriented, pragmatic knowledge. This sort of knowledge is called 'prudence' (Latin *prudentia*, Greek *phronesis*, English practical wisdom). Practical knowledge may have different forms, not all of them politically oriented. This book is interested in practical political knowledge. Practical knowledge is a topic for practical philosophy. This book aimed to join the Aristotelian tradition of practical philosophy. Key authors of this tradition include Socrates, Plato, Aristotle, Cicero, Aquinas, the Italian Christian and non-Christian humanists, early modern moral theorists such as Montaigne and Lipsius, and late modern philosophers of practical philosophy, including Gadamer and Ricoeur. The Aristotelian tradition was revived in virtue ethics and virtue politics from Anscombe on, and got its inspiration from the political realism of Williams and Geuss.

Individuals and communities

One of the most important presuppositions of Aristotelian practical philosophy is that individuals are born into their communities. They interact with this community, and this interaction determines the two key players of politics: individuals and their communities. Individuals' character (including their sense of politics) is largely determined by the political culture of their communities. Even if the basic unit of political action remains the individual, the interaction between the political agent and his or her community remains all-important in politics.

Agency-constraint

There are three basic impediments which confine human creativity in politics. This book identified the first of these impediments as agency-constraint. This constraint means that whatever idea, will or intention is taking form in a political community, it can only be realized by the solitary or cooperative actions of individual agents. As was pointed out, human beings have a natural tendency to remain alone, as well as an inclination to mix with their kind. The key to solving the problem of how to balance these two contradictory inclinations is the Kantian term 'asocial sociability', which shows that, indirectly, even the most egoistic impulses can turn to serve the common good. The Kantian concept of asocial sociability is taken over by the political philosophy of prudence as the first step to tackle agency-constraint, even if the balance between the individual's and the community's interest is a dynamic and therefore precarious one.

The second step to tackle agency-constraint is the social teaching of the (Catholic) church. It is based on the same duality of human nature, its parallel sociability and asociability. The concept of the person plays a central role in this teaching, which unites features of individual responsibility and communal belonging. In *The Compendium of the Social Doctrine of the Church*, the person is described the following way: he (and she) is 'a free and responsible being who recognizes the necessity of integrating himself in cooperation with his fellow human beings, and who is *capable of communion* with them on the level of knowledge and love'.[1] The Catholic idea of the person unites the two halves of the human being, the egoistic and the sociable in a different way than Kantian anthropology, but the result is the same: both present a human being who has an egoistic inclination, but who is able to cooperate with others, as well. Prudence, therefore, cannot be seen only as an egoistic impulse. In the Christian teaching it is a virtue. This virtue, however, is community dependent. The agency-constraint of the individual is balanced by communal wisdom.

Time-constraint

The time-constraint of politics is the problem that the political agent does not have enough time to get informed about the details of the political issue that needs to be solved. Titian's *Allegory of Prudence* illustrates in visual form the insight that to be able to make the right decision in the present moment, the political agent needs to remember or learn the past and to investigate future prospects. It is only this temporal three-dimensionality that can help the individual to handle the time-constraint of politics.

A further element of the time-constraint is the fact that there are no isolated individual cases, as one present situation is the consequence of an earlier one, and it continues with ever new ones. In this respect, a narrative account is crucial for a right understanding of politics. A further issue of the temporal dimension of prudence is right timing (*kairos*). If you want to act prudently, you need to have a sense of rhythm (tact), to hit the right moment when to perform the action, otherwise you will miss the occasion (*occasio*).

Knowledge-constraint

Given the fact that politics is about handling the human and non-human environment on a practical level, the knowledge required needs to be practical as well. Yet, humans are severely handicapped as far as a full acquaintance with the practical situations they are involved in are concerned. This book looks at three of these epistemological handicaps: perspectival distortion, situational mutability and value dependence. Perspectival distortion means that one cannot fully grasp the situation because of the specific viewpoint one holds, from where certain things are simply not visible and other things are seen in a distorted form. Situational mutability means that political situations are not closed and stable, they are in constant transformation, and therefore there is no knowledge that could cover them once and for all. Finally, value dependence means that facts in politics are loaded with values attributed to them by observers, which is why there is no chance of gaining pure knowledge of such facts.

These constraints on knowledge, however, do not exclude the possibility of obtaining the level of practical knowledge required for political survival. Explaining how this is possible, the relevant chapter refers to the concept of tacit knowledge (Polanyi), spontaneous order (Hayek) and practical knowledge (Oakeshott).

Resources

Individual resources: virtue, character and moderation

In preparation for the serious constraints on the practical knowledge of the individual and the community, individuals have their own toolkit. Among them, the most important are virtue and character. Virtue is understood here analogously with a practical skill. It is like the example of learning to play (artistically) the piano. The difference between the two is that virtues suppose the presence of each other, the unity of virtues, which leads to character formation, in this way connecting the process of acquiring virtues with self-fashioning, the ability to work on one's self. The individual's virtues, taken together, and a well-formed character are the basic tools for the individual to balance the constraints of prudence on the individual level, enabling him or her to become a virtuous political actor. To achieve political virtue, one also needs to acquire the virtue of moderation, or self-control, which is analysed in the book through the conceptual building blocks of civility, balance and the art of trimming.

Communal resources: rule of law, tradition, political culture

An individual's resources are not sufficient to counterbalance the constraints on human political prudence. The individual, therefore, needs to rely on the wisdom of the community, which had a longer trial-and-error learning period, thereby accumulating a larger reservoir of common practical knowledge. The first level of common sense is the arrangement of political institutions, which can serve as a procedural safeguard against moral corruptibility (because, as Lord Acton said, power tends to corrupt) and the misuse of power. The argument in favour of the separation of powers, of checks and balances and other techniques of institutional balancing of internal powers in present-day constitutional democracies claims, in the footsteps of Aristotle, that political virtues cannot be guaranteed due to the fallible nature of men, and that is why institutional safeguards and the rule of law are required. It is safer if laws rule, than the rule of men, who seek power for its own sake.

Yet, institutions are operated by men. It is therefore crucial that the community has further means to influence individuals beyond the institutional barriers. It is here that customs and other informal systems of norms are taken into account, including tradition, the wisdom of the forefathers inherited by the present generation. Through honouring and preserving tradition, conservatism presents itself as vital for the flourishing of human communities.

Yet, customs and tradition are only parts of a larger whole. A political community is unconsciously coordinated by what is called 'political culture'. Political culture is nothing less than the organically coordinated ways of life within a political community, which respects both the rule of law and the operation of tradition, but which is itself a complex of implicit and unreflected standards and norms, the bases of individual and communal political decision-making. It is only through educating the next generations in our political culture that our constitutional systems can be sustained, and therefore political culture requires a certain programme of education, based on Ciceronian *decorum* and appropriateness, and the humanistic programme of *Bildung*, so characteristic of the Aristotelian–Ciceronian tradition.

Political prudence in the context of urban republicanism

Politics is the art of the imperfect. The conservative political philosophy of prudence, therefore, does not aim to find the perfect act of the political agent in a given political situation, but only the proper one. To find what is appropriate is itself an art, called *prepon* by the Greek and *decorum* by Cicero. In the Ciceronian paradigm, to achieve it entails 'a sense of shame (*verecundia*) and what one might call the ordered beauty of a life, restraint and modesty, a calming of agitations of the spirit, and due measure in all things'.[2] This ideal of order and proportion is subverted by Machiavelli's advice book to the prince, introducing the demand to be able to accept 'dirty hands' in politics. This Machiavellian revolution gave rise to political realism, emphasizing the conflictual dimension of politics. The political philosophy of prudence tries to negotiate the Aristotelian paradigm and the political realist position. The most important point in this respect is to bring together once again the individual political agent (let it be the prince or a simple citizen) and his or her community, after Machiavelli's move has cut them away from each other. In this respect, the only excuse for a politics of 'dirty hands' is if it is in the interest of the common good, and not just to preserve the power of the prince, or of the particular interest of the political agent. In this respect, the conservative political philosophy of prudence provides a historical lesson of good practices: the example of the early modern republican Holland, governed by bodies of its own citizenry. The early modern Dutch Republic is presented as a model of the conservative politics of prudence, understood as political participation and cooperation in the affairs of the community (*res publica*) in the interest of the individual and of his or her community.

The self-control of philosophy

In order to avoid the danger of idealizing a past that has never existed, the political philosophy of prudence is based on the assumption that such a venture needs to be based on existing practices, such as the examples mentioned, and not on abstract norms. Yet, of course, abstracting a political philosophy from actual historical cases will always remain somewhat lifeless and thus risky; therefore, the conservative politics of prudence has to confine itself and its findings to what has been written so far and, for the moment, give up digging any deeper or further.

Notes

Introduction: Prudence and conservatism

1. Ferenc Hörcher, *Prudentia Iuris. Towards a Pragmatic Theory of Natural Law* (Budapest: Akadémia Publishing House, 2000).
2. In addition to law and politics, there is a third realm of human social activity where prudence might have a role: this is aesthetics, or the philosophy of art, where the early modern period brought aesthetic judgement, or taste as it is called in that context, to the forefront. In this respect, Kant's *The Critique of Judgement* (1790) is both the completion of a tradition and the farewell to it. The present author wrote a historical account of the early modern discourse of taste in Hungarian: *Esztétikai gondolkodás a felvilágosodás korában 1650-1800. Az ízlésesztétika paradigmája* (Aesthetic Thought in the Age of Enlightenment 1650-1800. The Paradigm of the Aesthetics of Taste, Gondolat, Budapest, 2013).
3. Richard Bourke, 'Theory and Practice: The Revolution in Political Judgement', in *Political Judgement: Essays for John Dunn*, eds. Richard Bourke and Raymond Geuss (Cambridge: Cambridge University Press, 2009), 79.
4. One should not forget that the volume came out the year after Raymond Geuss's own *Philosophy and Real Politics* (Princeton; Oxford: Princeton University Press, 2008).
5. Richard Bourke and Raymond Geuss, 'Introduction', in *Political Judgement*, eds. Raymond Bourke and John Geuss (Cambridge: Cambridge University Press, 2009), 4.
6. John Dunn, 'Introduction', in Dunn, *Interpreting Political Responsibility. Essays 1981-1989* (Oxford: Polity Press, 1990), 3.
7. Dunn, 'Introduction', 3. See also the general claim: 'To offer prudence as the intellectual fulcrum of a modern political theory is to reject the sufficiency of a heavily moralized conception of personal agency, a fetishization of routine, or an essentially autonomous governmental practice of domestic or geopolitical manipulation as approaches to the understanding of modern politics' (Dunn, 'Introduction', 8).
8. This introduction does not allow a more substantial account of this relationship. For a more detailed picture of the views of the present author on the issue, see Ferenc Hörcher, 'Skinner and Rosanvallon: Reconciling the History of Political Thought with Political Philosophy', *Przeglad Politologiczny* no. 4 (2015): 177–90.
9. John Dunn, 'The History of Political Theory', in *The History of Political Theory and Other Essays*, ed. John Dunn (Cambridge: Cambridge University Press, 1996), 11.
10. As Geuss explains, for Lenin politics is practically answering the question 'Who whom?' (*kto kogo?*), which as Geuss interprets it, means that to give social statements political relevance is to ensure that they are about 'particular concrete people doing things to other people'. For example, the Underground regulation 'Non-payment of fare will be punished' has the following sense for Lenin: 'a policeman may arrest and fine you, if you fail to buy a ticket'. Geuss, *Philosophy and Real Politics*, 24.
11. See John Sellars's article on Marcus Aurelius, in *The Internet Encylopaedia of Philosophy*, https://www.iep.utm.edu/marcus/

12 Max Weber, *Science as a Vocation*, eds. Peter Lassman, Irving Velody and Herminio Martins (London and New York: Routledge, 2015).
13 Richard Tuck, *Philosophy and Government, 1572–1651 (Ideas in Context)* (Cambridge: Cambridge University Press, 1993).
14 Tuck describes the Ciceronian tradition still valid in the high Renaissance the following way: 'the requirement of one's *respublica* was that one lived a life defined by the cardinal virtues of prudence, justice, temperance and fortitude, and Cicero in general denied that the interests of the state could be in any other kind of conduct'. (*Philosophy and Government*, 7.) As he saw it, this harmony was broken as a result of the tumults of sixteenth-century politics, in the stoically coloured philosophical scepticism of authors such as Lipsius and Montaigne. The emerging new term *raison d'état* conceptually means an autonomous political prudence distinguished from the cardinal moral virtue of prudence as originally understood in the Ciceronian tradition.
15 István Hont, *Jealousy of Trade: International Competition and the Nation-State in Historical Perspective* (Cambridge, MA and London: Harvard University Press, 2005).
16 Yelena Baraz, *A Written Republic. Cicero's Philosophical Politics* (Princeton; Oxford: Princeton University Press, 2012), 137.
17 In Kant's Idea for a Universal History with a Cosmopolitan Aim: A Critical Guide, eds. Amelie Oksenberg Rorty and James Schmidt (Cambridge: Cambridge University Press, 2009).
18 See for what is called 'the personalist principle': *Compendium of the Social Doctrine of the Church, Chapter Three, The Human Person and Human Rights*, http://www.vatican.va/roman_curia/pontifical_councils/justpeace/documents/rc_pc_justpeace_doc_20060526_compendio-dott-soc_en.html#CHAPTER%20THREE

Chapter 1

1 Aristotle, *Nicomachean Ethics*, VI.3 1139b.
2 Aristotle, *Metaphysics*, I.2 982b7–10.
3 Here, I rely on C. D. C. Reeve's note in Aristotle, *Nicomachean Ethics*, trans., intr. and notes C. D. C. Reeve (Indianapolis/Cambridge: Hackett Publishing Company, 2014), 227, n108, which refers to NE VI.12 1144a1–3 and NE VI.7 1141a9–b8.
4 Reeve, n108, in Aristotle, *Nicomachean Ethics*, 227, referring to NE X.7–8.
5 C. D. C. Reeve, 'Introduction', in Aristotle, *Politics*, tr., intr. and notes C. D. C. Reeve (Indianapolis/Cambridge: Hackett Publishing Company, 1998), xlii–xliii.
6 Aristotle, 'The Constitution of Athens', in Aristotle, *The Politics and The Constitution of Athens*, ed. Stephen Everson (Cambridge: Cambridge University Press, 1996), IX.2., 216.
7 Aristotle, *Nicomachean Ethics*, VI.11 1143b, 109.
8 Reeve, *Introduction*, in Aristotle, *Politics*, xxxviii.
9 Aristotle, *Nicomachean Ethics*, X.9 1179b16–18. Reeve's later revised translation is 'it is not possible – or not easy – to alter by argument what has long since been locked up in traits of character'. Aristotle, *Nicomachean Ethics*, X.9 1179b16–18, 191. In a note, the translator adds that the difference is due to a philologically different reading of the Greek text.
10 Aristotle, *Politics*, II.8. 1269a20–21.

11 Aristotle, *The Constitution*, xxxiv 2–3.
12 Ibid., xxxix 6.
13 Aristotle, *Nicomachean Ethics*, VI.5 1140b7–10.
14 Ibid., VI.5 1140b7–10.
15 Ibid., VI.12 1144b35.
16 Aristotle, *Politics*, I.2 1253a1–2.
17 Aristotle, *The Constitution*, xxvii 1, 230.
18 Ibid., xxvii 5, 231.
19 Ibid., xxviii 1, 231.
20 Ibid., xviii 1, 223.
21 The immediate context is this: when both sides of the political struggle turned against him, and the 'civic consensus' that was built up by Cicero was disrupted, in the crisis situation he was first exiled in 58 BC. On his return in 57 BC, he had to realize that most of his influence and respect had disappeared and thus he had to withdraw from public life. It is in this context that he started to write once again. Unfortunately, this decision to withdraw did not save his life. For this interpretation of the context see Zetzel, 1–2.
22 Neal Wood, *Cicero's Social & Political Thought* (Berkeley: University of California Press, 1988), 179.
23 The reference to the ideal statesman is to be found in Cicero's philosophical and rhetorical works, including *De Oratore* (1.211), Rep. and Fin.
24 For Cicero's terms used to describe the political agent, see Jonathan Zarecki, 'Cicero's Definition of Politikos', *Arethusa* 42, no. 3 (2009): 251–70.
25 In what follows, I rely heavily on Zarecki.
26 His example in this respect is Pompey.
27 Zarecki, *Politikos*, 256–7.
28 Zetzel, *Cicero*, 4. The quote is from a letter to his brother in October 54 BC (Q.fr. 3.5.1–2. quoted by Zetzel, *Cicero*, 3).
29 Zarecki, *Politikos*, 262.
30 Att. 9.11.2, quoted by Zarecki, *Politikos*, 262. Another translation of the same locus is: 'I only wish I could effect and carry through some politic move (πολιτικὸν) in the present distressing circumstances of the state!', Cicero, *Epistulae ad Atticum*, http://perseus.uchicago.edu/perseus-cgi/citequery3.pl?dbname=PerseusLatinTexts&query=Cic.%20Att.%209.11&getid=1
See this other locus: 'Should he attempt to give aid to his fatherland through every possible opportunity and through words rather than through war' (Att. 9.4.2.).
31 From a letter to his brother Quintus, quoted by H. J. Haskell, *This was Cicero* (Greenwich, CT: Fawcett Premier Books, 1964), 201–2.
32 Quoted by Augustine, *City of God*, 2.21. See Cicero, *On the Commonwealth*, V.I.1.
33 Cicero, *On the Commonwealth*, V.I.2.
34 One should note that Roman law attributed a rather specific meaning to the concept of tradition. I do not have the professional knowledge to tell if it has something to do with this political meaning of the term. The Roman law meaning of the concept of tradition (from *tradere*) was 'the transfer of ownership ... through the handing over of it to the transferee by the owner' (*Encyclopedic Dictionary of Roman Law*, 739).
35 Nicgorski, *Cicero's Skepticism*, 217.
36 Cicero, *Republic*, 2.2.
37 I am aware of the risks of using anachronistic terms such as 'judgement of taste' in an ancient Roman context. I dare to use it because this connection between moral and what will be called aesthetic categories will be important in the early modern

Ciceronian tradition. For the early modern Ciceronian context, see the present author's 'Judgement and Taste: From Shakespeare to Shaftesbury', in *Aspects of the Enlightenment: Aesthetics, Politics and Religion*, ed. Ferenc Hörcher and Endre Szécsényi (Budapest: Akadémiai Kiadó, 2004), 111.
38 Nicgorski, *Cicero's Skepticism*, 110.
39 This is a reference to the anachronistic German term *Mitgefühl* or the English one of 'compassion'. On this basis, Adam Smith and his Scottish contemporaries will be working out the elaborate teaching of sympathy.
40 Nicgorski, *Cicero's Skepticism*, 111, referring to Off. 1.148; 2.15; Rep. 5.6, Amic. 82.
41 This is, once again, a reference to Scottish moral sense theory.
42 Once again, I use this term for its early modern resonance, in the work of authors such as Adam Smith, a connection that will be returned to later in this book.
43 Nicgorski, *Cicero's Skepticism*, 111.
44 Ibid., 119.
45 *Offices* 1.153 See also *Offices* 3.71: 'The function of wisdom is to discriminate between good and evil.'
46 Nicgorski, *Cicero's Skepticism*, 209, referring to *Offices* 3.71, 1.153.
47 Cicero, *On the Commonwealth*, 2.45.
48 Nicgorski, *Cicero's Skepticism*, 209.
49 Ibid.
50 Janet Coleman, *The History of Political Thought: From Ancient Greece to Early Christianity* (Oxford: Blackwell, 2000), 295.
51 In what follows, I rely on the following two secondary sources of the *Cambridge Texts in the History of Political Thought*: Margaret Atkins and Robert Dodaro: 'Introduction', in *Augustine: Political Writings*, ed. E. M. Atkins and R. J. Dodaro (Cambridge: Cambridge University Press, 2001), xi–xxvii; R. W. Dyson, 'Introduction', in *Augustine: The City of God against the Pagans*, ed. and trans. R. W. Dyson (Cambridge: Cambridge University Press, 1998), x–xxix.
52 'Augustine exploits Cicero and Sallust to argue that the great pagan Romans had themselves acknowledged the civic value of the gentler virtues (Letters 91 and 98).' Atkins and Dodaro, *Introduction*, xxi.
53 Augustine, *The City of God*, xiv, 28, quoted by Dyson, *Introduction*, xix.
54 About Augustine on prudence, I rely on Gerd Van Riel, 'Augustine on Prudence', *Augustinian Studies* 41, no. 1 (January 2010): 219-40.
55 Quoted by Van Riel, 'Augustine', 235.
56 'Letter 91, Augustine to Nectarius', in Augustine, *Political Writings*, 2-8, 3, quoted in Atkins and Dodaro, *Introduction*, xx.
57 Atkins and Dodaro, *Introduction*, xxv.
58 Ibid., xxvi, xviii.
59 Ibid., xviii.
60 Ibid., xxv.
61 Ibid., xxvi.
62 Ibid., xxvii.
63 'Letter 91, Augustine to Nectarius', in Augustine, *Political Writings*, 2-8, 5.
64 Here and in what follows, I rely on Donald Roche, 'Prudence in Aristotle and St Thomas Aquinas' (MA thesis, National University of Ireland, Maynooth, 2005), 62-9.
65 C. H. Lohr, 'The Medieval Interpretation of Aristotle', in *The Cambridge History of Later Medieval Philosophy*, ed. Norman Kretzmann, Anthony Kenny and Jan Pinborg (Cambridge: Cambridge University Press, 1982), 80-98.

66 James Doig, *Aquinas's Philosophical Commentary on the Ethics. A Historical Perspective* (Dordrecht, The Netherlands: Kluwer Academic Publishers, 2001), 20, quoted by Roche, *Prudence*, 67.
67 Doig, *Aquinas's*, quoted by Roche, *Prudence*, 68.
68 Doig, *Aquinas's*, 22, quoted by Roche, *Prudence*, 67.
69 St Thomas Aquinas, 'On Kingship', in Aquinas, *On Law, Morality, and Politics*, ed. William P. Baumgarth and Richard J. Regan SJ (Indianapolis, IN: Hackett Publishing, 2003), 263.
70 Ibid., 264.
71 Ibid., 271. The Aristotelian locus is: Aristotle, *NE*, VI.8 1141b23.
72 William P. Baumgarth and Richard J. Regan SJ, 'Introduction', in Aquinas, *On Law*, xiii–xxii, xix.
73 Aquinas, *On Law*, 272. See also 'On the contrary, political prudence, which is directed to the common good of the political community and domestic economy, which is of such things as relate to the common good of the household or family, and personal economy, which is concerned with things affecting the good of one person, are all distinct sciences', Obj. 3. in Aquinas, *On Law*, 271.
74 Ibid., 272.
75 Ibid. A similar point is found in Aristotle, *Politics*, III.4 1277a20, where we read: 'The virtue of a good ruler is the same as a good man', although the sentence comes to the conclusion, '"The virtue of a ruler and that of a citizen would not be the same".
76 Aquinas, *On Law*, 272.
77 Ibid., 266.
78 Aquinas, *Summa*, II–II, Q. 50, Second Article, in Saint Thomas Aquinas, *On Law*, 274.
79 Ibid.
80 Aquinas, *On Law*, 267.
81 Ibid.
82 Ibid.
83 It is remarkable that the late Augustine also found the lack of moderation a kind of moral corruption.
84 Quoted in Aquinas, *Summa*, Q.50, Art. 1, http://www.newadvent.org/summa/3050.htm
85 Aquinas, *Summa Theologica*, Q.50, Art. 1, http://www.newadvent.org/summa/3050.htm

Chapter 2

1 Richard Tuck, *Philosophy and Government 1572-1651* (Cambridge: Cambridge University Press, 2011), 6.
2 For an overview of the importance of the impact of Hans Baron, see James Hankins, 'The "Baron Thesis" after Forty Years and Some Recent Studies of Leonardo Bruni', *Journal of the History of Ideas* 56, no. 2 (1995): 309-38.
3 Here, I rely on Coleman, *The History of Political Thought*.
4 See the English version of James Hankins, 'Coluccio Salutati e Leonardo Bruni, chapter for Il contributo italiano alla storia del pensiero', ed. Michele Ciliberto (Rome: Treccani, 2012). As only the typescript of Professor Hankins's paper was available to me (https://www.academia.edu/31374214/The_political_thought_of_

Coluccio_Salutati_and_Leonardo_Bruni), I can provide page numbers in brackets only to this version of the paper: (1). For further reading see Robert Black, 'The Political Thought of the Florentine Chancellors', *The Historical Journal* 29, no. 4 (1986): 991–1003. Reprinted in revised form in Robert Black, 'Studies in Renaissance Humanism and Politics: Florence and Arezzo', in *Variorum Collected Studies* Series CS969, no. XIV (Farnham: Ashgate Variorum, 2011).
5 For this phrase, and much of the following story, see Hankins, 'Coluccio Salutati', 1.
6 Ibid., 4.
7 I rely on the writings of Professor Hankins in the following paragraphs on Bruni.
8 See Hans Baron and Leonardo Bruni, '"Professional Rhetorician" or "Civic Humanist"'? *Past & Present*, 36 no. 1 (1967): 21–37.
9 Arendt's mature views of the relevance of ancient democracy for contemporary politics is to be found in Hannah Arendt, *The Human Condition* (Chicago: University of Chicago Press, 1958). A later, revised version of the book is published in German: *Vita Activa oder Vom tätigen Leben* (Stuttgart: Piper, 1960).
10 Hankins, 'Coluccio Salutati', 5.
11 Ibid., 6.
12 Clare Guest, *Figural Cities. Bruni's Laudatio Urbis Florentinae and its Greek Sources in Rhetoric. Theatre and the Arts of Design*, ed. Guest (Oslo: Novus, 2008).
13 Hankins, 'Coluccio Salutati', 6.
14 Leonardo Bruni, *In Praise of Florence. The Panegyric of the City of Florence and an Introduction to Leonardo Bruni's Civil Humanism*, intr. and trans. Alfred Scheepers (Amsterdam: Olive Press, c2005), 78.
15 Ibid., 80.
16 Ibid., 79.
17 Ibid.
18 Ibid., 92.
19 The terms virtue and humanity return later in Burni's text, for example on page 97.
20 Ibid., 91.
21 See, for example, 'I do not speak about the virtue or excellence of private persons but of that of the whole republic', 102.
22 Ibid., 93.
23 Ibid.
24 Ibid., 102.
25 Ibid., 104.
26 Ibid., 105.
27 Ibid., 106.
28 Ibid., 108.
29 Ibid., 113.
30 Ibid., 119.
31 Ibid., 119–20.
32 Eugene Garver, *Machiavelli and the History of Prudence* (Madison, WI: The University of Wisconsin Press, 1987), 3.
33 Ibid., 16.
34 Ibid., 12.
35 Ibid., 14. Garver is careful to delineate the similarities and dissimilarities as well, between his own tripartite classification (algorithmic, heuristic and prudent ethics) and that of Cicero, in his *De Officiis* (*honestum utile* and his own interpretation of prudence in the third book of *De Officiis*). Garver, *Machiavelli*, 177–8, n18.

36 Ibid., 16.
37 Ibid.
38 Victoria Kahn, *Rhetoric, Prudence, and Skepticism in the Renaissance* (Ithaca; London: Cornell University Press, 1985).
39 Ibid., 184.
40 Ibid., 186.
41 Ibid.
42 Ibid.
43 Harvey C. Mansfield, Jr., 'Machiavelli's Political Science', *The American Political Science Review* 75, no. 2 (1981): 293–305, 299.
44 J. G. A. Pocock, *Machiavellian Moment, Florentine Political Thought and the Atlantic Republican Tradition* (Princeton; Oxford: Princeton University Press, 1975).
45 Ibid., 156.
46 Ibid., 161.
47 Ibid., 163.
48 Ibid., 167.
49 Unfortunately, in the recent Cambridge edition of Machiavelli, *The Prince*, ed. Quentin Skinner and Russel Price, prudence does not receive a separate entry among the Notes on the vocabulary of *The Prince*.
50 This is the insight of Andrea Polegato, who gave a talk on Machiavelli's prudence in Sorrento, at the Annual Conference of the American Association for Italian Studies, in 2018. I am grateful to Dr Polegato for sending me the typescript of his unpublished talk.
51 Pocock, *Machiavellian*, 179, quoting Machiavelli, *The Prince*, Ch. 25.
52 Mansfield claims that Machiavelli, in fact, intends *The Prince* as an advice book to 'the prudent, private man who wants to become prince'. Mansfield, *Machiavelli's*, 295.
53 Here I follow Polegato.
54 Pocock, *Machiavellian*, 167.
55 Ibid., 185.
56 Ibid., 194.
57 Ibid., 197., n39.
58 Valentina Lepri, 'The Spread of Italian Political Culture during the Renaissance: Remarks on the First Fortunes of Guicciardini's Works', *Studia Historica Brunensia* 58, no. 2 (2011): 3–12.
59 Pocock, *Machiavellian*, 219.
60 This conceptual pair returns in Pocock's analysis of Guicciardini. See, for example 256, 263.
61 Pocock, *Machiavellian*, 221.
62 Ibid., 225.
63 Ibid., 226.
64 Ibid., 232.
65 Francesco Guicciardini, 'Dialogo del Reggiemento di Firenze', in Guicciardini, *Dialogo e Discorsi del Reggimento di Firenze*, ed. Roberto Palmarocchi (Bari: Giu. Laterza e Figli, Tipografi-editori-librai, 1932), 60–1. Pocock uses a different translation to that available in the Guicciardini edition of the Cambridge Texts, edited and translated by Alison Brown in 1994. I used the second edition of this selection, where the Dialogue is to be found on pages 1–169, and the quote is on page 58. This translation has the following phrase: 'To prevent new things beginning.' Guicciardini, *Dialogo*.
66 Pocock, *Machiavellian*, 238.

67 Ibid., 251 (*la natura, la qualità, le considerazioni, la inclinazione... gli umori, della città e de' citadini ...*) D. e D., 99.
68 Guicciardini, *Dialogo*, 158.
69 Ibid., 159. '*secondo la ragione ed uso degli stati*', *Dialogo e Discorsi*, 163. *Uso* is translated in Tuck's version as custom.
70 Tuck, *Philosophy and Government*, 39.
71 I used in this case, too, the Cambridge Texts series, Giovanni Botero, *The Reason of State*, trans. and ed. Robert Bireley (Cambridge: Cambridge University Press, 2007), in order to make double-checking easier for the reader.
72 Harro Höpfl, *Jesuit Political Thought. The Society of Jesus and the State, c. 1540–1630* (Cambridge: Cambridge University Press, 2004), 165.
73 Wolfgang Theodore. However, as Bireley points out, 'Some editions have different dedicatees', for example the Prince of Peidmont, the Royal Fiscal for His Catholic Majesty in the State of Milan. Botero, *The Reason*, 1, n1.
74 Ibid., 2.
75 Ibid., 4.
76 Ibid., 34.
77 Ibid.
78 Ibid., 37. Quoted in the 'Introduction' by Robert Bireley, in Botero, *The Reason*, xxvi.
79 Ibid., 38.
80 Ibid., 40.
81 Ibid., 41.
82 Ibid.
83 Ibid., 43. Michael Oakeshott's description of the conservative disposition is to be found, for example, in his essay *On Being Conservative* (1956). See for example the following list: 'To be conservative, then, is to prefer the familiar to the unknown, to prefer the tried to the untried, fact to mystery, the actual to the possible, the limited to the unbounded, the near to the distant, the sufficient to the superabundant, the convenient to the perfect, present laughter to utopian bliss.'
84 Botero, *The Reason*, 50.
85 Ibid., 48.
86 Ibid., 62.
87 Robert Bireley, 'Introduction', in Botero, *The Reason*, xix.
88 Bireley, 'Introduction', xvii. Further relevant authors include the Jesuit Juan de Mariana (1536–1624) and the Spanish Jesuit author, Pedro de Ribadeneira (1527–1611).
89 Höpfl characterizes their own political experiences as coming from their 'own life-experience as confessors, fundraisers, preachers, pastors, teachers, ecclesiastical politicians, and organizers'. He also adds that they also served as 'confessors of princes'. Höpfl, *Jesuit*, 88–9.
90 Ibid., 107.
91 Ibid.
92 Ibid., 164.
93 Ibid., 164–5.
94 Ibid., 165.
95 Friedrich Meinecke, *Machiavellism: The Doctrine of Raison d'état and Its Place in Modern History*, trans. D. Scott (New Haven: Yale University Press, 1957).
96 Quentin Skinner, *The Foundations of Modern Political Thought* (Cambridge: Cambridge University Press, 1978), I. 253.

97 Ibid., I. 253.
98 Ibid., quoting from Montaigne, *Essais*, 600.
99 Francis Goyet, 'Montaigne and the Notion of Prudence', in *The Cambridge Companion to Montaigne*, ed. Ullrich Langer (Cambridge: Cambridge University Press, 2005).
100 Ibid., 121.
101 Ibid., 123.
102 Ibid.
103 Ibid., 125.
104 Ibid., 129.
105 Ibid.
106 Ibid., 130.
107 Pierre Hadot, *Philosophy as a Way of Life: Spiritual Exercises from Socrates to Foucault*, ed. and intr. Arnold I. Davidson (Hoboken, NJ: Wiley-Blackwell, 1995).
108 Cicero's expression (Cicero, *Tusc. Quaes.*, iv. 3.) was quoted in Montaigne's essay *Of the Education of Children*.
109 Stephen Greenblatt, *Renaissance Self-Fashioning: From More to Shakespeare* (Chicago; London: The University of Chicago Press, 1980).
110 Marc Fumaroli, *Preface to Michael A. Screech: Montaigne et la melancolie* (Paris: Presses Universitaires de France, 1992), ix, xi.
111 I used the following English language edition: Justus Lipsius, *Politica, Six Books of Politics or Political Instruction*, ed. and trans. Jan Waszink (Assen: Royal Van Gorcum, 2004).
112 See, for example, Erasmus's famous work on the Christian monarch. However, Waszink rightly calls our attention to the fact that 'the mirrors-for-princes literature grew out of the Italian humanism of the fifteenth century, which had produced many advice-books for city magistraters and podestà'. Waszink, 'Introduction', in Lipsius, *Politica*, 36.
113 Waszink, 'Introduction', 55.
114 About Tacitus, Lipsius confesses: 'On his own, he has contributed more to my work than all the others. The reason lies in his prudence, and in the fact that he is the richest in maxims.' *Politica, auctorum syllabus*, quoted by Waszink, 'Introduction', 53.
115 In what follows, I rely on Waszink, 'Introduction', 49–50.
116 Ibid., 82.
117 These are the terms used not by Lipsius, but by Waszink, 'Introduction', 84.
118 Ibid., 84.
119 Lipsius, *Politica*, 261.
120 Ibid., 283.
121 Ibid., 285. The expression is quoted from Cicero, *De Finibus*, english translation by H. Rackham (Cambridge: Harvard University Press, 1931), 5.16.
122 Lipsius, *Politica*, 333.
123 Ibid., 377.
124 Ibid., 383.
125 Ibid., 387.
126 Ibid., 425.
127 Ibid., 507.
128 Cicero, *De Officiis*, 3.31.
129 Lipsius, *Politica*, 509. Tacitus, *Agric.*, 8.1.
130 Lipsius, *Politica*, 509.
131 Ibid., 511, quoting Plutarch's *Lysander* and *Apopht Reg.*

132 Lipsius, *Politica*, 511.
133 Waszink, *Introduction*, 184.
134 Aristotle, *Nicomachean Ethics*, 1095a3, quoted in Lipsius, *Politica*, 511.
135 Waszink, 'Introduction', in Lipsius, *Politica*, 102. He positions himself close to De Landtsheer and Van Houdt, who wrote: 'Lipsius' aim was to develop a political doctrine which was no less pragmatic or realistic than that of his Italian predecessor, but at the same time more in agreement with the morality formulated by the ancient philosophers and historians, and adopted by the subsequent Christian Mirrors-for-Princes.' (G. Tournoy, J. Papy and De Landtsheer, *Lipsius en Leuven, Catalogus van de tentoonstelling in de Centrale Bibliotheek te Leuven, 18 September–17 Oktober 1997* (Leuven: Leuven University Press, 1997), 209. Translation by Waszink.)

Chapter 3

1 In what follows, I use Gadamer's summary of the movement in a piece entitled 'On the Origins of Philosophical Hermeneutics', in Hans-Georg Gadamer, *Philosophical Apprenticeships*, trans. Robert R. Sullivan (Cambridge, MA; London: The MIT Press, 1985).
2 Ibid., 178.
3 Ibid.
4 Ibid., 179.
5 Ibid.
6 Ibid., 180.
7 Ibid., 182.
8 Ibid., 184.
9 Ibid., 185.
10 Hans-Georg Gadamer, *Truth and Method*, 2nd rev. edn (London: Sheed & Ward, 1996).
11 Ibid., 14.
12 Let us refer here to Michael Polanyi's *Tacit Knowledge* (1958).
13 Gadamer, *Truth and Method*, 14.
14 Ibid., 15.
15 Ibid.
16 Ibid., 18.
17 In what follows, I analyse the following chapter in the book: 'The Hermeneutic Relevance of Aristotle', in Gadamer, *Truth and Method*, 309–20. All quotes used about this topic will come from this chapter.
18 Ibid., 312.
19 Ibid., 313.
20 Ibid.
21 Ibid., 320.
22 Ibid.
23 Ibid., 324.
24 Ibid., 337.
25 In what follows, I will rely on the entry by David Pellauer and Bernard Dauenhauer, 'Paul Ricoeur', *Stanford Encyclopedia of Philosophy*, ed. Edward N. Zalta (Winter 2016), https://plato.stanford.edu/archives/win2016/entries/ricoeur/

26 Paul Ricoeur, *Oneself as Another*, trans. Kathleen Blamey (Chicago: University of Chicago Press, 1992), 171.
27 Alasdair MacIntyre, *After Virtue: A Study in Moral Theory* (Notre Dame, IN: University of Notre Dame Press, 1981), referred to by Ricoeur at 176.
28 Gadamer, *Truth and Method*, referred to by Ricoeur at 177.
29 Ricoeur also refers to Martha C. Nussbaum, Charles Taylor and Heidegger.
30 Both of these quotes are from Ricoeur, *Oneself as Another*, 179.
31 Paul Ricoeur, *Le Juste* (Paris: Éditions Esprit, 1995). Translated as *The Just* (Chicago; London: The University of Chicago Press, 2000).
32 Ibid., xii.
33 Ibid., xiii.
34 The last two quotes are from Ricoeur, *The Just*, xv.
35 Ibid., xvi.
36 Ricoeur, 'Le Juste entre le légal et le bon' (The Just between the Legal and the Good), in *Lectures I, autour du politique* (Paris: Seuil, 1991).
37 Ricoeur, *The Just*, xxi.
38 Ibid.
39 Ibid.
40 Ibid.
41 Ibid., xxii.
42 Ibid.
43 Ibid.
44 A possible exception is MacIntyre, if one regards him as belonging to the trend labelled as virtue ethics.
45 Of this tradition, Williams is particularly interested in the work of Plato, Aristotle, Kant, Mill, Nietzsche and Hobbes. See his *Man Without Qualities*. 'Interview with Bernard Williams', *Cogito*, 28 March 2015, 13.
46 Both claims are from Mark P. Jenkins, *Bernard Williams* (Chesham: Acumen, 2006), 149.
47 Williams, *Man without Qualities*, 2.
48 Bernard Williams, *Ethics and the Limits of Philosophy* (London: Fontana Press/Collins, 2005), 34.
49 Ibid., 35.
50 Bernard Williams, *In the Beginning Was the Deed. Realism and Moralism in Political Argument*, sel., ed. and intro. Geoffrey Hawthorn (Princeton; Oxford: Princeton University Press, 2005).
51 Williams, 'Realism and Moralism in Political Theory', in *In the Beginning Was the Deed*, 1–17, 1.
52 Ibid., 2.
53 Ibid., 12.
54 Ibid., 2.
55 Ibid., 3.
56 Ibid., 5.
57 Ibid., 11.
58 Ibid., 12.
59 Ibid., 16.
60 Williams, 'In the Beginning was the Deed', in *In the Beginning Was the Deed*, 18–28.
61 Ibid., 21.
62 Ibid., 25.

63 On this topic see Colin Koopman and Bernard Williams, 'Philosophy's Need for History', *The Review of Metaphysics* 64, no. 1 (September 2010): 3–30.
64 Ibid.
65 Ibid.
66 Bernard Williams, 'Replies', in *World, Mind, and Ethics: Essays on the Ethical Philosophy of Bernard Williams*, ed. J. E. J. Altham and R. Harrison (Cambridge: Cambridge University Press, 1995), 201.
67 Mark P. Jenkins, *Bernard Williams* (Philosophy Now Series) (Montréal: McGill-Queen's University Press, 2006), 156.
68 Bernard Williams, *Ethics and the Limits of Philosophy* (Cambridge, MA: Harvard University Press, 1985), 52–3.
69 'A Mistrustful Animal: An Interview with Bernard Williams', *The Harvard Review of Philosophy* XII, no. 1 (2004): 84.
70 Bernard Williams, *Shame and Necessity* (Berkeley, CA: University of California Press, 2008), 163.
71 Williams, *Man Without Qualities*, 5.
72 Ibid., 13.
73 Ibid., 12–13.
74 Ibid.
75 Williams, *A Mistrustful Animal*, 90.
76 Ibid., 91.
77 Alasdair MacIntyre, *Raymond Geuss, Outside Ethics* (Princeton; Oxford: Princeton University Press, 2005); *Notre Dame Philosophical Reviews*, 5 March 2006, https://ndpr.nd.edu/news/outside-ethics/
78 Raymond Geuss, 'Thucydides, Nietzsche, and Williams', in *Outside Ethics* (Princeton: Princeton University Press, 2005), 230.
79 Geuss, 'Thucydides', 231, quoted by MacIntyre, *Raymond Geuss*.
80 Geuss, *Philosophy*, 1.
81 Ibid., 2.
82 Ibid.
83 Ibid., 6.
84 Ibid., 9.
85 Ibid., 10.
86 Ibid., 11.
87 Ibid., 15.
88 Ibid., 22.
89 Ibid., 25.
90 Ibid., 29.
91 Ibid., 36.
92 Friedrich Nietzsche, 'Zur Genealogie der Moral', Zweite Abhandlung, §8, in *Nietzsches Werke: Kritische Studien-Ausgabe*, ed. Giorgio Colli and Mazzino Montinari (Kusterdingen: De Gruyter, 1967), 5:306, quoted by Geuss, *Philosophy*, 39.
93 Neo-Leninism is not only unacceptable in terms of the background suppositions of its intellectual history (what else is communism if not the realization of highly theoretical principles, instead of making practical judgements) but it is also a gross political (and historical) misjudgement. After all, the decisions of Lenin directly led to the death and humiliation of hundreds of thousands of people in Russia and elsewhere. Geuss's final misjudgement illustrates a very important point, which also has theoretical relevance: that a realist account of politics in itself does not guarantee either a historically correct account of the past or right political judgements.

94 Geuss, *Philosophy*, 97.
 95 Ibid., 90.
 96 Ibid., 94.
 97 Ibid., 97.
 98 Ibid.
 99 Ibid. 'The successful exercise of this skill is often called "political judgment".'
100 Ibid., 98.

Preliminary remarks

1 Glen Newey, 'Ruck in the Carpet', *London Review of Books* 31, no. 13 (2009), 15–17.
2 Carl Schmitt, *Political Theology: Four Chapters on the Concept of Sovereignty* (Chicago: Chicago University Press, 2005). The original German version of the sentence was: '*Souverän ist, wer über den Ausnahmezustand entscheidet.*'
3 John Rawls, *A Theory of Justice* (Cambridge, MA; London: The Belknap Press of Harvard University Press, 1971), 3.
4 Geuss, *Philosophy*, 72–3.
5 Ibid., 9.
6 Paul Ricoeur, 'Is a Purely Procedural Theory of Justice Possible? John Rawls's Theory of Justice', in Ricoeur: *The Just*, 37.
7 Ricoeur: *Procedural Theory*, 56.

Chapter 4

1 I use the following English language translation of the book: Carl Schmitt, *The Concept of the Political* (Chicago: University of Chicago Press, 2007).
2 Ibid., 45.
3 The concept is discussed in the fourth thesis of Immanuel Kant, *Idea for a Universal History from a Cosmopolitan Point of View* (1784). Trans. Lewis White Beck. From Immanuel Kant, *On History* (Indianapolis, IN: The Bobbs-Merrill Co., 1963).
4 Cicero, *Cicero: On Duties (Cambridge Texts in the History of Political Thought)*, eds. M. T. Griffin and E. M. Atkins (Cambridge: Cambridge University Press), xlvi.
5 Anthony Ashley-Cooper, 3rd Earl of Shaftesbury, *Characteristics of Men, Manners, Opinion and Times* (Indianapolis, IN: Liberty Fund, 2001), 2.16.
6 David Hume, *A Treatise of Human Nature* (1738–1740), Book I, Part IV, Section VII.
7 Pierre Hadot, *Philosophy as a Way of Life*, ed. Arnold I. Davidson, trans. Michael Chase (Oxford: Blackwell, 1995).
8 Kant, *On History*, 15.
9 Ibid.
10 The phrase *methodische Individualismus* comes from Weber's student, Joseph Schumpeter (1908, new English language edition, 1980). However, Schumpeter refers back to the work of his master in the explanation of the term.
11 Joseph Cardinal Höffner, *Christian Social Teaching* (Cologne, Bratislava: Ordo Socialis, 1997), 15. https://ordosocialis.de/pdf/jhoeffner/Christl.%20Gesellschaftsl/cglenga4neu.pdf

12 Pius XII, 23 February 1944 (UG94).
13 Catechism of the Catholic Church, http://www.vatican.va/archive/ccc_css/archive/catechism/p1s2c1p6.htm. Paragraph 6. Man – Section I 'In the Image of God', article 357.
14 Höffner, *Christian Social Teaching*, 20.
15 Ibid., 22.
16 Lawrence E. Klein, *Shaftesbury and the Culture of Politeness, Moral Discourse and Cultural Politics in Early Eighteenth-Century England* (Cambridge: Cambridge University Press, 1994), 31.
17 Höffner's reconstruction of the social teaching of the church claims to speak in 'socio-theological terms'. (Höffner, *Christian Social Teaching*, 22.)
18 Ibid.
19 Henri de Lubac, *Catholicisme. Aspects sociaux du dogme*, cited in G Thils, *Theologie et Réalité sociale* (Paris: Tournai, 1952), 259, quoted by Höffner, *Christian Social Teaching*, 23.
20 Höffner, *Christian Social Teaching*, 23.
21 John 1 King James Version.
22 Höffner, *Christian Social Teaching*, 29, referring to Gustav Gundlach, 'Solidarismus', in *Staatslexikon*, ed. Hermann Sacher (Bonn: Görres Gesellschaft, 1931), IV. 1614.
23 'The image of man that Basic Law represents is not that of an isolated, sovereign individual. Basic Law has rather settled the tension between individual and community in the sense of the person's relatedness to the community and dependence on the community, without thereby violating his or her intrinsic value.' *Entscheidungen des Bundesverfassungsgerichts*, 4, 120 (20 July 1954).

Chapter 5

1 Also known as *Allegory of Time*. Presently held in the National Gallery, in London.
2 See the classic essay by Erwin Panofsky, 'Titian's Allegory of Prudence: A Postscript', in Panofsky, *Meaning in the Visual Arts* (Chicago: University of Chicago Press, 1982). For further interpretations, see also the recent essay by Simona Cohen, 'Titian's London Allegory and the Three Beasts of his Selva Oscura', *Renaissance Studies* 14, no. 1 (2000), 46; and Erin J. Campbell, 'Old Age and the Politics of Judgment in Titian's Allegory of Prudence', *Word and Image: A Journal of Verbal/Visual Poetry* 19, no. 4 (2003), 261. For the present author's contribution to the Titian interpretation, see 'Prudencia, kairosz, decorum: a konzervativizmus időszemléletéről' (Prudence, kairos, decorum: conservatism's view of time), *Információs társadalom: Társadalomtudományi folyóirat* 4 (2006): 61–80.
3 Panofsky, 'Titian's Allegory', 184.
4 Macrobius, *Saturnalia*, I, 20, 13ff, quoted by Panofsky, 'Titian's Allegory', 189.
5 Pierio Valeriano, *Hieroglyphica* (Frankfurt edition, 1678), 192.
6 Panofsky, 'Titian's Allegory', 197, quoting from Valeriano, *Hieroglyphica*, 192.
7 Panofsky, 'Titian's Allegory', 184.
8 Gary Wills, *Venice: Lion City. The Religion of Empire* (New York: Simon & Schuster, 2001), 83–4.
9 Josef Pieper, *Das Viergespann* (München: Kösel-Verlag, 1964). English translation: *The Four Cardinal Virtues* (New York: A Helen and Kurt Wolff Book, Harcourt, Brace and World, Inc., 1965).

10 Josef Pieper, *No One Could Have Known: An Autobiography, the Early Years, 1904–1945* (San Francisco: Ignatius Press, 1979).
11 Pieper, *Viergespann*, 3. Later, he also gives the Latin quote: '*Omnis virtus moralis debet esse prudent.*' Pieper, *Viergespann*, 5.
12 Ibid., 4.
13 Ibid., 8–9.
14 Ibid., 9.
15 Ibid., 10.
16 Ibid., 11.
17 Ibid.
18 Ibid., 14.
19 Ibid., 15.
20 Ibid.
21 Ibid.
22 Ibid., 16.
23 Ibid., 17.
24 Ibid.
25 Ibid., 18.
26 Ibid., 25.
27 Ibid.
28 Ibid., 26.
29 Ibid.
30 Ibid., 27.
31 Ibid., 28.
32 Ibid., 31.
33 In what follows, I rely on the collection of essays in the following collected volume: Phillip Sipiora and James S. Baumlin, *Rhetoric and Kairos. Essays in History, Theory, and Praxis* (Albany, NY: State University of New York Press, 2002).
34 Aristotle, *NE*, I.6 1096a32.
35 Ibid., II.2 1096a32.
36 Ibid., II.2 1104a8–9.
37 Ecclesiastes 3:1.
38 John E. Smith, 'Time and Qualitative Time', in Sipiora and Baumlin, *Rhetoric and Kairos*, 47.
39 James L. Kinneavy, 'Kairos: A Neglected Concept in Classical Rhetoric', in Sipiora and Baumlin, *Rhetoric and Praxis: The Contribution of Classical Rhetoric to Practical Reasoning*, ed. Jean Dietz Moss (Washington, DC: The Catholic University of America Press, 1986), 82.
40 Douglas L. Peterson, *Time, Tide, and Tempest: A Study of Shakespeare's Romances* (San Marino, CA: Huntington Library, 1973), 1.
41 John Foxe, *Time and the End of Time* (1664), 1–2, quoted by James Baumlin, 'Ciceronian Decorum and the Temporalities of Renaissance Rhetoric', in Sipiora and Baumlin, *Rhetoric and Kairos*, 145.
42 Job 7:1 King James Version.
43 Frank Kermode, *The Sense of an Ending* (New York: Oxford University Press, 1967), 47, quoted by Gregory Mason, 'In Praise of Kairos in the Arts. Critical Time, East and West', in Sipiora and Baumlin, *Rhetoric and Kairos*, 202.
44 This is the translation provided by James S. Baumlin, who analysed the emblem in his chapter: 'Ciceronian Decorum and the Temporalities of Renaissance Rhetoric',

151–2. Baumlin left out the word 'prudently' from his translation, as he relied on the inscription above the picture, and did not look at the chapter-long explanation that follows it (117–43), and in the title of which prudently (*prudentes*) already appears.

45 This is the list of related terms in Sipiora, 'Introduction. The Ancient Concept of Kairos', in Sipiora and Baumlin, *Rhetoric and Kairos*, 1. For an alternative list, see Baumlin, 'Ciceronian Decorum', 157: 'Due measure, harmony, fitness, appropriateness, proportionality, timing, timeliness'.

Chapter 6

1 Matthew 15:14 King James Version.
2 Luke 6:39 King James Version.
3 'Abiding in the midst of ignorance, thinking themselves wise and learned, fools go aimlessly hither and thither, like blind led by the blind', *The Upanishads*, ed. Juan Mascaró (Penguin Classics, 1965), 58.
4 Erasmus, *In Praise of Folly* (London: Reeves & Turner, 1876). https://www.gutenberg.org/files/30201/30201-h/30201-h.htm
5 In this respect, a key text for the political philosophy of prudence is Michael Oakeshott's famous collection of essays: *Rationalism in Politics and Other Essays* (London: Methuen, 1962).
6 Descartes, *Meditations on First Philosophy, With Selections from the Objections and Replies*, ed. and trans. John Cottingham, rev. edn (Cambridge: Cambridge University Press, 1996, 2003), 18.
7 Edmund Burke, *Reflections on the Revolution in France* (1790), ed., intr. and notes J. G. A. Pocock (Indianapolis/Cambridge: Hackett Publishing Company, 1987), 54.
8 Burke, *Reflections*, 52–3.
9 John Rawls, *A Theory of Justice*, rev. edn (Cambridge, MA: The Belknap Press of Harvard University Press, 1971, 1999), xii.
10 Ibid., 230.
11 Ibid., 231.
12 The form of Brexit, and whether it will actually take place, was still not clear when I was reading the proofs in August 2019.
13 Philip S. Gorski, 'Beyond the Fact/Value Distinction: Ethical Naturalism and the Social Sciences', *Society* 50 (2013): 543, https://doi.org/10.1007/s12115-013-9709-2
14 Michael Polanyi, *Personal Knowledge: Towards a Post-Critical Philosophy* (London, New York: Routledge, 1958), vii.
15 Maurice Merleau-Ponty, *Phenomenology of Perception* (London: Routledge, 1945/2005), 166. He also calls this form of knowledge '*savoir de familiarité*'.
16 Polanyi, *Personal*, vii.
17 Ibid., viii.
18 Ibid., 49.
19 Ibid., 50.
20 Michael Polanyi, *The Tacit Dimension* (Chicago: University of Chicago Press, 1966), 4.
21 This is the title of chapter 13. See F. A. Hayek: *The Road to Serfdom, Text and Documents, The Definitive Edition*, ed. Bruce Caldwell (Chicago: The University of Chicago Press, 1944, 2007), 193.

22 Benjamin Disraeli, *Vindication of the English Constitution in a Letter to a Noble and Learned Lord* (1835), reprinted in Disraeli, *Whigs and Whiggism*, ed. William Hutcheon (New York: Macmillan, 1914), 119, quoted by Bruce Caldwell, in F. A. Hayek, *The Road to Serfdom*, 138n4.
23 Friedrich A. Hayek, *Laws, Legislation, Liberty*, vol. 1, Rules and Order (London: Routledge, 1973, 1998), 10.
24 Ibid., 12.
25 The last three quotes are from Hayek, *Laws*, 12.
26 Andrew Gamble, 'Hayek on Knowledge, Economics, and Society', in *The Cambridge Companion to Hayek* (Cambridge: Cambridge University Press, 2006), 115.
27 Friedrich A. Hayek, 'The Facts of the Social Sciences', in *Individualism and Economic Order* (Chicago: University of Chicago Press, 1980), 64.
28 On Pocock's recapitulation of manners, see Deborah Madden, 'Education and Manners', in *A Companion to Intellectual History*, ed. Richard Whatmore and Brian Young (Chichester: Wiley-Blackwell, 2016), 264. According to Madden, it was Pocock 'who first initiated a thoroughgoing investigation into precisely how English politeness and manners came to redefine classical virtù'.
29 The last two quotes are from J. G. A. Pocock, 'Virtues, Rights, and Manners: A Model for Historians of Political Thought', in *Virtue, Commerce, and History. Essays on Political Thought and History, Chiefly in the Eighteenth Century* (Cambridge: Cambridge University Press, 1985, 1988), 48.
30 Madden, *Manners*, 273.
31 Edmund Burke, 'Letters on a Regicide Peace 1796', in *The Works of the Right Honorable Edmund Burke*, vol. VIII (London: Printed for C. and J. Rivington, 1826), 172. quoted by Pocock, 'Virtues', 49.
32 J. G. A. Pocock, 'The Political Economy of Burke's Analysis of the French Revolution', in *Virtue, Commerce, and History. Essays on Political Thought and History, Chiefly in the Eighteenth Century* (Cambridge: Cambridge University Press, 1985, 1988), 209–10.
33 For a description of Hume on the role of manners in coordinating commercial societies, see Ferenc Hörcher, *From Reason of State to Coordination by Trade, Societate Si Politica* 10, no. 1 (2016): 5–23.
34 Pocock, 'The Political', 210.
35 Hayek, *Laws*, 37.
36 Aeon J. Skoble, 'Hayek the Philosopher of Law', in *The Cambridge Companion to Hayek*, ed. Edward Feser (Cambridge: Cambridge University Press, 2006), 176.
37 Hayek, *Laws*, 123.
38 Marquis de Vauvenargues Luc de Clapiers, *The Reflections and Maxims of Luc de Clapiers Marquis of Vauvenargues*, trans. F. G. Stevens (London: Humphrey Milford, 1940), 71.
39 Michael Oakeshott, 'Rationalism in Politics', in *Rationalism in Politics and Other Essays* (Carmel, IN: Liberty Fund Inc., 1962, 1991), 11.
40 As we explained in Chapter 1 on ancient *phronesis*, Aristotle's description of *techné* can be found in Book 6 of *Nicomachean Ethics*, where he lists and describes five 'states by virtue of which the soul possesses truth'. *NE* Book 6, 1139b.
41 Oakeshott, *Rationalism*, 12.
42 Ibid., 12.
43 As we saw in Chapter 1 on ancient prudence, Aristotle discusses the concept of *phronesis* also as a form of knowledge in Book 6 of the *Nicomachean Ethics*. 'On

being Conservative' was originally published in 1956, and republished in the volume 'Rationalism in Politics', in Oakeshott, *Rationalism*, 412.
44   Oakeshott, *Rationalism*, 12.
45   Ibid., 13. 'Some excellent observations on this topic are to be found in M. Polanyi, Science, Faith and Society.' This book was published by the University of Chicago Press in 1946.
46   Oakeshott, *Rationalism*, 17.
47   Ibid., 15.
48   Ibid.

Chapter 7

1   G. E. M. Anscombe, 'Modern Moral Philosophy', *Philosophy* 33, no. 124 (1958): 1–19, see also Rosalind Hursthouse, *On Virtue Ethics* (Oxford: Oxford University Press, 2002).
2   Julia Annas, *Intelligent Virtue* (Oxford: Oxford University Press, 2011). Her earlier elaborations of the term can be found in: Julia Annas, 'Virtue as a Skill', *International Journal of Philosophical Studies* 3, no. 2 (1995): 227–43; Julia Annas, 'Moral Knowledge as Practical Knowledge', in *Moral Knowledge*, ed. E. F. Paul, F. D. Miller, Jr. and J. Paul (Cambridge: Cambridge University Press, 2001), 236–56; Julia Annas, 'The Structure of Virtue', in *Intellectual Virtue*, ed. M. DePaul and L. Zagzebski (Oxford: Clarendon Press, 2003), 15–33; Julia Annas, 'Virtue Ethics', in *The Oxford Handbook of Ethical Theory*, ed. D. Copp (Oxford: Oxford University Press, 2006), 515–36.
3   See Catherine Zuckert: 'Do "Virtue Ethics" Require "Virtue Politics?"' *Hungarian Philosophical Review*, guest ed. Ferenc Hörcher and Péter Lautner, *The Politics of Aristotle: Reconstructions and Interpretations* 57, no. 4 (2013): 95–108.
4   For an overall view of the skill analogy of virtue, and Annas's own interpretation of virtue as skill in particular, see Matthew Stichter, 'The Skill of Virtue' (DPhil thesis, Bowling Green State University, 2007), https://etd.ohiolink.edu/!etd.send_file?accession=bgsu1181851300&disposition=inline, on Annas in particular, 25–45.
5   Annas, *Intelligent Virtue*, 3.
6   Ibid., 8.
7   Ibid.
8   Ibid., 9.
9   Ibid., 13.
10 Ibid.
11 Ibid., 14.
12 Aristotle, *NE*, VI. 13.
13 Annas, *Intelligent Virtue*, 89.
14 Zuckert, *Virtue Ethics*. Elisabeth Anscombe's famous essay was entitled 'Modern Moral Philosophy', published in 1958.
15 Zuckert, *Virtue Ethics*, 95.
16 Ibid., 95.
17 Ibid., 96.
18 Ibid., 97.

19 Ibid.
20 Ibid., 99.
21 Ibid., 101.
22 Ibid.
23 Ibid.
24 Janet Coleman, MacIntyre and Aquinas, in *After MacIntyre: Critical Perspectives on the Work of Alisdair MacIntyre*, ed. John Horton and Susan Mendus (Oxford: Polity Press, 1994), 65–90.
25 Douglas B. Rasmussen and Douglas J. Den Uyl, 'Liberalism in Retreat', *The Review of Metaphysics* 62, no. 4 (2009): 875–908; Douglas B. Rasmussen and Douglas J. Den Uyl, *Norms of Liberty: A Perfectionist Basis for Non-Perfectinist Politics* (University Park: The Pennsylvania State University Press, 2005).
26 Zuckert, *Virtue Ethics*, 103.
27 Ibid., 104.
28 Rassmussen, Den Uyl, *Norms of Liberty*, 139.
29 Zuckert, *Virtue Ethics*, 105.
30 Ibid., 105.
31 Rassmussen, Den Uyl, *Norms of Liberty*, 159.
32 Zuckert, *Virtue Ethics*, 107.
33 James Hankins, 'The Virtue Politics of the Italian Humanists', to be published in *Beyond Reception: Renaissance Humanism and the Transformation of Classica Antiquity*, ed. Patrick Baker, Johannes Helmrath, Craig Kallendorf. The paper is 'part of a book-length project on humanist virtue politics'.
34 I use the manuscript available on the homepage of James Hankins at academia.edu. I am unable give the page numbers as, to date, proper pagination has not been implemented.
35 Cicero, *Politics* 1.2, 1252a31, *De legibus* 3.4.
36 Caroli Poggi, *De nobilitate liber disceptatorius, et Leonardo Chiensis De vera nobilitate tractatus apologeticus cum eorum vita et annotationibus abbatis Michaelis Justiniani* (Avellino: heredes Camilli Caballi, 1657).
37 Cicero, *Pro Sestio*, 137.
38 Letter of Guarino to Gian Nicola Salerno (1419), in *Epistolario di Guarino Veronese*, ed. R. Sabbadini, vol. 1 (Venice: C. Ferrari, 1915), 263–4. (Epistola 159).
39 Ibid.
40 In this respect, Hankins relies on A. A. Long: 'Cicero's Politics in the De Officiis', in *Justice and Generosity: Studies in Hellenistic Political Philosophy*, ed. Andrew Laks and Malcolm Schoefield (Cambridge: Cambridge University Press, 1995).
41 See, in this respect, Martha Nussbaum's works on the morally formative impact of ancient tragedies, modern novels and music.
42 Cicero, *De Officiis*, 2.23.
43 James Hankins, *The Virtue Politics of Italian Humanists*, typescript.
44 Aurelian Craiutu, *Faces of Moderation, The Art of Balance in an Age of Extremes* (Philadelphia: University of Pennsylvania Press, 2017).
45 In addition to *Faces of*, see Craiutu's *Liberalism under Siege: The Political Thought of the French Doctrinaires* (2003), *Elogiul moderației* (in Romanian, 2006), *A Virtue for Courageous Minds: Moderation in French Political Thought, 1748–1830* (2012).
46 Craiutu, *Faces of*, 2.
47 Ibid., 2.
48 Ibid., 3.

49 Ibid.
50 Ibid., 5.
51 Simone Weil, *Gravity and Grace*, trans. Arthur Wills (Lincoln: University of Nebraska Press, 1997), 211.
52 Craiutu, *Faces of*, 16.
53 Ibid., 16.
54 Ibid.
55 Ethan H. Shagan, *The Rule of Moderation. Violence, Religion, and the Politics of Restraint in Early Modern England* (New York: Cambridge University Press, 2011).
56 Peter Berkowitz, *Constitutional Conservatism: Liberty, Self-Government and Political Moderation* (Stanford: Hoover Institution Press, 2013); Paul Carrese, *Democracy in Moderation* (New York: Cambridge University Press, 2016).
57 Friedrich Nietzsche, *The Will to Power*, trans. Walter Kaufmann (New York: Vintage, 1967), 159.
58 Craiutu, *Faces of*, 20, referring to Michel Montaigne, *The Complete Essays*, trans. M. A. Screech (London: Penguin, 1991), 1261.
59 Craiutu, *Faces of*, 20.
60 Baltasar Gracián, *The Art of Worldly Wisdom*, trans. Jospeh Jacobs (Boston: Shambala, 1993), 74.
61 Aristotle, *NE*, II. 6. 1107a.
62 Ibid., II. 6. 1106b.
63 Both of these quotes are from Michael Oakeshott, *The Vocabulary of a Modern European State*, ed. Luke O'Sullivan (Exeter: Imprint Academic, 2008), 184.
64 Oakeshott, 'Political Education', in Oakeshott, *Rationalism in Politics*, 60.
65 Oakeshott, 'Rationalism in Politics', in Oakeshott, *Rationalism in Politics*, 8.
66 Oakeshott, *Rationalism*, 9.
67 Oakeshott, 'Introduction to Leviathan', in Oakeshott, *Rationalism in Politics*, 247.
68 Oakeshott, *On Human Conduct* (Oxford: Clarendon, 1991), 122.
69 Edward Shils, *The Virtue of Civility*, ed. Steven Grosby (Indianapolis, IN: Liberty Fund, 1997), 340.
70 Ibid., 4.
71 Ibid.
72 Ibid.
73 Ibid.
74 In addition to Craiutu's *Faces of*, a further paper by him on this topic is Aurelian Craiutu, 'Political Moderation and the Lost Art of Trimming', *The Island* (Tasmania, Australia) 140 (2015): 38–43. See also Cass Sunstein, 'Trimming', *Harvard Law Review* 122, no. 4 (2009): 1051–95, and Eugene Goodheart, *Holding the Center: In Defense of Political Trimming* (New Brunswick, NJ: Transaction, 2013).
75 Craiutu, *Faces of*, 25.
76 Marquis of Halifax, *Complete Works*, ed. J. P. Kenyon (London: Penguin, 1969), 50.
77 Craiutu, *Faces of*, 26.
78 Ibid., 28.
79 Ibid., 170.
80 Henry Adams, *The Education of Henry Adams* (New York: Modern Library, 1960), 192.
81 Craiutu, *Faces of*, 66.
82 Ibid., 65. He refers to Raymond Aron, *Liberté et égalité* (Paris: EHESS, 2013).

Chapter 8

1. Pocock, *Virtues*, 39.
2. Pocock's interpretation of Hobbes as a rule of law thinker is closer to that of Oakeshott than to Skinner, which concentrates on the rhetorical dimension of Hobbes's texts.
3. Ibid., 44.
4. Albert O. Hirschman, *The Passions and the Interests: Political Arguments for Capitalism before Its Triumph* (Princeton, NJ: Princeton University Press, 1977); C. B. MacPherson, *The Political Theory of Possessive Individualism: From Hobbes to Locke* (Oxford: Oxford University Press, 1962).
5. For the quotes of the last two sentences, see Pocock, *Virtues*, 49, 50.
6. Burke, *Regicide Peace*, 172.
7. Pocock, *Virtues*, 210.
8. Ibid., 210.
9. The last two quotes are from Jeremy Waldron, 'The Rule of Law', ed. Edward N. Zalta, *The Stanford Encyclopedia of Philosophy* (Fall 2016). https://plato.stanford.edu/archives/fall2016/entries/rule-of-law. (As this is a digital encyclopedia, its text does not have page numbers to identify the quotes in such a detailed way.) The concept of the rule of law is often traced back to Dicey, and we have an up-to-date, book-length, English language exposition of the concept, see Thomas Bingham, *The Rule of Law* (London: Penguin, 2010).
10. Ibid.
11. Ibid.
12. Aristotle, *Politics*, 1292a5.
13. Waldron, *The Rule of Law*.
14. Aristotle, *Politics*, 1282b.
15. The term 'invisible hand' comes from the authors of the Scottish Enlightenment, and in particular, from Adam Smith, who used the term three times, but whose approach to commerce is based on an understanding of the mutually advantageous interaction between self-interest and public benefits. He must have been influenced also by Bernard Mandeville.
16. Friedrich Hayek, 'The Legal and Political Philosophy of David Hume (1711–1776)', in *The Collected Works of F. A. Hayek, The Trend of Economic Thinking. Essays on Political Economists and Economic History*, ed. W. W. Bartley, III and Stephen Kresge (Chicago: University of Chicago Press, 1991). Hayek's article was first presented as a talk at Freiburg University in July 1963.
17. David Hume, 'Of the Origin of Government', in Hume, *Essays, Moral, Political, and Literary*, rev. edn (Indianapolis, IN: Liberty Classics, 1985, 1987), 40–1.
18. David Hume, 'Of the Rise and Progress of the Arts and Sciences', in Hume, *Essays*, 116.
19. Aristotle, *NE*, 1180a.
20. Francis Wormuth, 'Aristotle on Law', in Wormuth, *Essays in Law and Politics*, ed. Dalmas H. Nelson and Richard L. Sklar (Port Washington, NY: Kennikat Press, 1978), 17.
21. James Bernard Murphy, 'Habit and Convention at the Foundation of Custom', in *Customary Law, Legal, Historical and Philosophical Perspectives*, ed. Amanda Perrau-Saussine and James Bernard Murphy (Cambridge: Cambridge University Press, 2009), 63.
22. James Bernard Murphy, *The Philosophy of Customary Law* (Oxford: Oxford University Press, 2014), 6.

23 For a general overview from the perspective of the social sciences, see Edward Shils, *Tradition* (Chicago: University of Chicago Press, 1981).
24 For the Christian concept of tradition, see Yves Congar, *The Meaning of Tradition* (San Francisco: Ignatius Press, 2004).
25 Ernst-Wolfgang Böckenförde, *Staat, Gesellschaft, Freiheit* (Frankfurt/Main: Suhrkamp, 1976), 60.
26 'Freiheit ist ansteckend', *Frankfurter Rundschau*, 1. November 2010 online, 2. November 2010, 32. https://web.archive.org/web/20101104053317/; http://www.fr-online.de/kultur/debatte/-freiheit-ist-ansteckend-/-/1473340/4795176/-/index.html#
27 For an overview of the present-day relevance of the Böckenförde paradox for constitutional interpretation, see Ferenc Hörcher, 'Prepolitical Values? Böckenförde, Habermas and Ratzinger and the use of the Humanities in Constitutional Interpretation', in *A bölcsészettudományok hasznáról/Of the Usefulness of the Humanities* (Budapest: L'Harmattan, 2014), 87–101.
28 F. A. Hayek, 'Kinds of Order in Society (1964)', in *The Politicization of Society*, ed. Kenneth Templeton, Jr. (Indianapolis, IN: Liberty Press, 1979), 509.
29 C. D. C. Reeve: 'Introduction', in Aristotle, *Politics*, xlvi.
30 Hannah Arendt, 'The Crisis in Culture', in *Judgement, Imagination, and Politics*, ed. Ronald Beiner and Jennifer Nedelsky (Lanham: Rowman and Littlefield Publishers, 2001), 14.
31 Alasdair MacIntyre, 'Rival Aristotles: Aristotle against Some Modern Aristotelians', in MacIntyre, *Ethics and Politics, Selected Essays*, vol. 2 (Cambridge: Cambridge University Press, 2006), 39.
32 Ibid., 39.
33 Ibid.
34 Ibid.
35 This distinction was made by Ferdinand Tönnies in his *Gemeinschaft und Gesellschaft* (Leipzig: Fues's Verlag, 1887).
36 David Wiles, *Greek Theatre Performance. An Introduction* (Cambridge: Cambridge University Press, 2000), 48.
37 Pierre Hadot, *Philosophy as a Way of Life: Spiritual Exercises from Socrates to Foucault*, ed. and intr. Arnold I. Davidson (Hoboken, NJ: Wiley-Blackwell, 1995).
38 Alasdair MacIntyre, *Dependent Rational Animals. Why Human Beings Need the Virtues* (London: Duckworth, 1999), 156.
39 MacIntyre, however, did not accept the label 'communitarian' to describe his own position.
40 Jenő Szűcs, Julianna Parti, 'The Three Historical Regions of Europe: An Outline', *Acta Historica Academiae Scientiarum Hungaricae* 29, no. 2/4 (1983): 131–84.
41 For a more detailed account of the historical background behind the V4 countries' coming together, see the present author's paper: 'The V4 Cooperation and the European Schism Over the Migration Crisis: The History of Political Thought in the Service of Political Analysis', in *Central and Eastern European Socio-Political and Legal Transition Revisited*, ed. Balázs Fekete and Fruzsina Gárdos-Orosz (Frankfurt am Main: Peter Lang GmbH, Internationaler Verlag der Wissenschaften, 2017).
42 Nora Berend, Przemysław Urbańczyk and Przemysław Wiszewski, *Central Europe in the High Middle Ages* (Cambridge: Cambridge University Press, 2013), 37.
43 Aristotle, *Politics*, 1328a.
44 Reeve, *Introduction*, lxvii.

45 Hörcher, 'Dramatic Mimesis and Civic Education in Aristotle, Cicero and Renaissance Humanism', *Aisthesis: Pratiche linguaggi e saperi dell'estetico rivista online del seminario permanente di estetica* 10, no. 1 (2017): 87–96.

Chapter 9

1 Baron Anthony Quinton, *The Politics of Imperfection: The Religious and Secular Traditions of Conservative Thought in England from Hooker to Oakeshott* (London, Boston: Faber and Faber, 1978).
2 Ibid., 11.
3 Ibid., 17.
4 Ibid., 16.
5 Ibid.
6 We relate this time to the writings of Daniel Kapust, and especially his paper, Kapust, 'Cicero on Decorum and the Morality of Rhetoric', *European Journal of Political Theory* 10, no. 1 (2011): 92–112.
7 Cicero, *Orator*, tr. H. M. Hubbell, in Cicero, *Brutus and Orator*, 7, 8 (Cambridge, MA: Harvard University Press, 1952), 70.
8 Cicero, *Orator*, 74. In his discussion of Ciceronian decorum, Kapust gives the original Latin terms: '*aptum esseconsentaneumque tempori et personae*'. Kapust, 'Cicero on Decorum', 98.
9 Cicero, *Orator*, 99.
10 Ibid., 44.
11 Cicero, *On the Ideal Orator*, tr. James M. May and Jakob Wisse (Oxford: Oxford University Press, 2001), 3. 195–7.
12 This is a term suggested by Kapust, 'Cicero on Decorum', 101.
13 Cicero, *On Duties*, ed. M. T. Griffin and E. M. Atkins (Cambridge: Cambridge University Press, 1991), 1. 14–15.
14 Ibid., 1.93. Cicero's virtuous person, the one who behaves with decorum, is in search of this measure in his relationships to all things; he never gets tired of judging appropriateness, and relating things and persons to each other and to himself.
15 Robert A. Kaster, *Emotion, Restraint, and Community in Ancient Rome* (Oxford: Oxford University Press, 2005), 19.
16 For an assessment of early modern political realism and its relationship with prudence, see Hörcher, 'The Renaissance of Political Realism in Early Modern Europe: Giovanni Botero and the Discourse of "Reason of State"', *Krakowskie Studia z historii panstwa prawa*, 9, no. 2 (2016): 187–210.
17 About the continuity between his activity and way of thinking as statesman and philosopher, and between theory and practice, see Nicgorski, *Cicero's Skepticism*, 4.
18 Numa Denis Fustel De Coulanges, *The Ancient City. A Study on the Religion, Laws, and Institutions of Greece, and Rome* (Kitchener, ONT: Batoche Books, 2001).
19 For a more recent account of the religious origins of Roman law, and of the survival and transformation of it in republican Rome, see J. Rüpke, *Religion in Republican Rome: Rationalization and Ritual Change* (Philadelphia: The University of Pennsylvania Press, 2012).
20 For a claim that both Cicero and Machiavelli belonged to what could be labelled conservative republicanism, see Manjeet Ramgotra, 'Conservative Roots of

Republicanism', *Theoria: A Journal of Social and Political Theory* 61, no. 139 (2014): 22–49.
21. It was Carl Schmitt who made the case that theology played a crucial role in the birth of our modern political vocabulary. See his *Political Theology. Four Chapters on the Concept of Sovereignty* (1922), tr. G. Schwab (Chicago: University of Chicago Press, 2005).
22. Fustel De Coulanges, *The Ancient City*, 8.
23. Saskia T. Roselaar, 'Cicero and the Italians: Expansion of Empire, Creation of Law', in *Cicero's Law: Rethinking Roman Law of the Late Republic*, ed. Paul J. du Plessis (Edinburgh: Edinburgh University Press, 2016), 155, relying on Emma Dench, 'Cicero and Roman Identity', in *The Cambridge Companion to Cicero* (Cambridge: Cambridge University Press, 2013), 122.
24. Jed W. Atkins, *Roman Political Thought* (Cambridge: Cambridge University Press, 2018), 121.
25. Ibid., 121–2.
26. Ibid., 122. One should not forget, however, that compared to Roman law, Greek *nomos* is much closer to customs and mores than to law, in the sense of a whole system of explicit legal norms.
27. Brad Inwood and Fred D. Miller, 'Law in Roman Philosophy', in *A Treatise of Legal Philosophy and General Jurisprudence*, ed. Fred D. Miller, Carrie-Ann Biondi (Dordrecht: Springer, 2015), abstract.
28. Maurizio Viroli, 'Machiavelli and the Republican Idea of Politics', in *Machiavelli and Republicanism*, ed. Gisela Bock, Quentin Skinner, Maurizio Viroli (Cambridge: Cambridge University Press, 1990, 1993), 162–3.
29. Ibid., 162–3.
30. Ibid., 162.
31. Ibid., 165.
32. Ibid.
33. Ibid., 169.
34. Caroline Robbins, *The Eighteenth-Century Commonwealthman: Studies in the Transmission, Development, and Circumstance of English Liberal Thought from the Restoration of Charles II until the War with the Thirteen Colonies* (1959) (Indianapolis, IN: Liberty Fund, 2004).
35. The root of the concept of the modern republic was, of course, Latin *res publicae*, which was also the title of Cicero's famous work in the Platonic tradition of the *Politeia*.
36. Franco Venturi, *Utopia and Reform in the Enlightenment* (Cambridge: Cambridge University Press, 1971), 41.
37. E. H. Kossmann, 'Dutch Republicanism', in *Political Thought in the Dutch Republic, Three Studies*, ed. E. H. Kossmann (Amsterdam: Koninklije Nederlandse Akademie van Wetenshappen, 2000), 171.
38. Ibid., 180.
39. William Temple, *Observations upon the United Provinces of the Netherlands* (London: Maxwell, 1673). I used the 2011 print of the 1932 edition of the work (Cambridge: Cambridge University Press, 2011).
40. István Hont, 'Free Trade and the Economic Limits to National Politics: Neo-Machiavellian Political Economy Reconsidered', in *Jealousy of Trade. International Competition and the Nation-State in Historical Perspective*, ed. I. Hont (Cambridge, MA: The Belknap Press of Harvard University Press, 2005), 197.

41 Temple, *Observations*, 131.
42 This is Hont's collection, Hont, *Jealousy*, 197, n.17.
43 My approach to Huizinga is close to that of Willem Otterspeer, in his *Orde en trouw. Over Johan Huizinga*. I used the English translation *Order and Loyalty. About Johan Huizinga* (Amsterdam: De Bezige Bij, 2006). This author associates Huizinga's achievement with Ranke's conservative or rather conserving manner – in his reading, Ranke's aim was to help the reconstruction of an earlier form, *Romanitas*, the harmonic unity of the earlier Roman–Christian Europe. Otterspeer supposes the same motivation behind Huizinga's approach to history.
44 Johan Huizinga, *Dutch Civilisation in the Seventeenth Century* (London: Collins, 1968), 16.
45 Ibid., 25.
46 Ibid., 26.
47 Ibid., 23.
48 Ibid., 62.
49 Ibid., 61.
50 Ibid., 63.
51 Although women could become citizens of medieval towns, they were very rarely active members of the urban magistracy.

Summary: A conservative political philosophy of prudence

1 *The Compendium of the Social Doctrine of the Church* http://www.vatican.va/roman_curia/pontifical_councils/justpeace/documents/rc_pc_justpeace_doc_20060526_compendio-dott-soc_en.html
2 Cicero, *On Duties*, 1.93.

Bibliography

Adams, Henry. *The Education of Henry Adams*. New York: Modern Library, 1960.
André, J.-M. *L'otium dans la vie morale et intellectuelle romaine, des origines à l'époque augustéenne*. Paris: University of Paris, 1966.
Annas, Julia. *Intelligent Virtue*. Oxford: Oxford University Press, 2011.
Annas, Julia. 'Moral Knowledge As Practical Knowledge'. In *Moral Knowledge*, edited by Ellen Frankel Paul, Fred D. Miller, Jr, and Jeffrey Paul, 236–56. Cambridge: Cambridge University Press, 2001.
Annas, Julia. 'The Structure of Virtue'. In *Intellectual Virtue*, edited by M. DePaul and L. Zagzebski, 15–33. Oxford: Clarendon Press, 2003.
Annas, Julia. 'Virtue Ethics'. In *The Oxford Handbook of Ethical Theory*, edited by D. Copp, 515–36. Oxford: Oxford University Press, 2006.
Annas, Julia. 'Virtue as a Skill'. *International Journal of Philosophical Studies* 3, no. 2 (1995): 227–43.
Anscombe, Gertrude Elizabeth Margaret. 'Modern Moral Philosophy'. *Philosophy* 33, no. 124 (1958): 1–19.
Aquinas, Saint Thomas. 'On Kingship'. In *Aquinas. On Law, Morality, and Politics*, edited by William F. Baumgarth and Richard J. Regan, S.J. Indianapolis: Hackett Publishing, 2003.
Arendt, Hannah. 'The Crisis in Culture'. In *Judgement, Imagination, and Politics*, edited by Ronald Beiner and Jennifer Nedelsky. Lanham: Rowman and Littlefield Publishers, 2001.
Arendt, Hannah. *The Human Condition*. Chicago: University of Chicago Press, 1958.
Aristotle. 'The Constitution of Athens'. In Aristotle, *The Politics and The Constitution of Athens*, edited by Stephen Everson. Cambridge: Cambridge University Press, 1996.
Aristotle. *Metaphysics*, edited by W. D. Ross, 2 vols. Oxford: Clarendon Press, 1924. Reprinted 1953 with corrections.
Aristotle. *Nicomachean Ethics*, translated, introduction and notes by C. D. C. Reeve. Indianapolis/Cambridge: Hackett Publishing Company, 2014.
Aristotle. *Politics*, translated, introduction and notes by C. D. C. Reeve. Indianapolis/Cambridge: Hackett Publishing Company, 1998.
Aron, Raymond. *Liberté et égalité:Cours au Collège de France*. Paris: EHESS, 2013.
Ashley-Cooper, Anthony, 3rd Earl of Shaftesbury. *Characteristics of Men, Manners, Opinion and Times*. Indianapolis: Liberty Fund, 2001.
Atkins, Jed W. *Roman Political Thought*. Cambridge: Cambridge University Press, 2018.
Atkins, Margaret and Robert Dodaro. 'Introduction'. In *Augustine: Political Writings*, edited by E. Margaret Atkins and Robert J. Dodaro. Cambridge: Cambridge University Press, 2001.
Augustine, St. *The City of God against the Pagans*, translation by R. W. Dyson. New York: Cambridge University Press, 1998.
Baraz, Yelena. *A Written Republic: Cicero's Philosophical Politics*. Princeton, Oxford: Princeton University Press, 2012.

Baumlin, James S. 'Ciceronian Decorum and the Temporalities of Renaissance Rhetoric'. In *Rhetoric and Kairos: Essays in History, Theory, and Praxis*, edited by Phillip Sipiora and James S. Baumlin, 138–64. Albany: State University of New York Press, 2002.

Berend, Nora, Przemysław Urbańczyk and Przemysław Wiszewski. *Central Europe in the High Middle Ages*. Cambridge: Cambridge University Press, 2013.

Berger, Adolf. *Encyclopedic Dictionary of Roman Law*. Clark: The Lawbook Exchange, Ltd, 2004.

Berkowitz, Peter. *Constitutional Conservatism: Liberty, Self-Government and Political Moderation*. Stanford: Hoover Institution Press, 2013.

Bireley, Robert. 'Introduction'. In Giovanni Botero, *The Reason of State, 1589*, translated and edited by Robert Bireley. Cambridge: Cambridge University Press, 2007.

Black, Robert. 'The Political Thought of the Florentine Chancellors'. *The Historical Journal* 29, no. 4 (1986): 991–1003.

Böckenförde, Ernst-Wolfgang. *Staat, Gesellschaft, Freiheit*. Frankfurt/Main: Suhrkamp, 1976.

Böckenförde, Ernst-Wolfgang. 'Freiheit ist ansteckend', *Frankfurter Rundschau*, 1. November 2010 online, 2. November 2010, 32. https://web.archive.org/web/2010110 4053317/

Botero, Giovanni. *The Reason of State*, 1589, translated and edited by Robert Bireley. Cambridge: Cambridge University Press, 2007.

Bourke, Richard. 'Theory and Practice: The Revolution in Political Judgement'. In *Political Judgement. Essays for John Dunn*, edited by Richard Bourke and Raymond Geuss, 73–110. Cambridge: Cambridge University Press, 2009.

Bruni, Leonardo. *In Praise of Florence: The Panegyric of the City of Florence*, translated and introduction by Alfred Scheepers. Syracuse: Olive Press, 2005.

Burke, Edmund. 'Letters on a Regicide Peace'. 1796. In *The Works of the Right Honorable Edmund Burke*, vol. VIII. London: Printed for C. and J. Rivington, 1826.

Burke, Edmund. *Reflections on the Revolution in France (1790)*, edited, introduction and notes by J. G. A. Pocock. Indianapolis and Cambridge: Hackett Publishing Company, 1987.

Caldwell, Bruce. *The Road to Serfdom: Text and Documents – The Definitive Edition (The Collected Works of F. A. Hayek, Volume 2)*. Chicago: The University of Chicago Press, 1944, 2007.

Campbell, Erin J. 'Old Age and the Politics of Judgment in Titian's Allegory of Prudence'. *Word and Image: A Journal of Verbal/Visual Poetry* 19, no. 4 (2003): 261–70.

Carrese, Paul. *Democracy in Moderation*. New York: Cambridge University Press, 2016.

Cathechism of the Catholic Church, http://www.vatican.va/archive/ENG0015/_INDEX.HTM

Cicero, Marcus Tullius. *De Inventione*, translated by H. M. Hubbell. Cambridge: Harvard University Press, 1960.

Cicero, Marcus Tullius. *De Officiis*, edited by Walter Miller, Loeb Classical Library. Cambridge: Harvard University Press, 1913.

Cicero, Marcus Tullius. 'De Oratore'. In Cicero, *Rhetorica. Vol. I (De Oratore)*, edited by Augustus Samuel Wilkins. Oxford: Clarendon Press, 1963.

Cicero, Marcus Tullius. *De Re Publica*, edited by J. E. G. Zetzel. Cambridge: Cambridge University Press, 1995.

Cicero, Marcus Tullius. *On the Commonwealth and On the Laws*, edited and translated by James E. G. Zetzel. Cambridge: Cambridge University Press, 1999.

Cicero, Marcus Tullius. *On Duties*, edited by Miriam Tamara Griffin and E. Margaret Atkins. Cambridge: Cambridge University Press, 1991.
Cicero, Marcus Tullius. *On the Ideal Orator*, translated by James M. May and Jakob Wisse. Oxford: Oxford University Press, 2001.
Cicero, Marcus Tullius. *Orator*, translated by Harry Morator Hubbell. In Cicero: Brutus and Orator, 7, 8. Cambridge: Harvard University Press. 1952.
Cicero, Marcus Tullius. *Pro Sestio. In Vatinium*, translated by R. Gardner. Loeb Classical Library 309. Cambridge: Harvard University Press, 1958.
Cicero, Marcus Tullius. *Tusculan Disputations*, edited by J. E. King Loeb Classical Library. Cambridge: Harvard University Press, 1927.
Clapiers, Luc de, Marquis de Vauvenargues. *The Reflections and Maxims of Luc de Clapiers Marquis of Vauvenargues*, translated by F. G. Stevens. London: Humphrey Milford, 1940.
Cohen, Simona. 'Titian's London Allegory and the Three Beasts of His Selva Oscura'. *Renaissance Studies* 14, no. 1 (2000): 46–69.
Coleman, Janet. *The History of Political Thought: From Ancient Greece to Early Christianity*. Oxford: Blackwell, 2000.
Coleman, Janet. 'MacIntyre and Aquinas'. In *After MacIntyre: Critical Perspectives on the Work of Alasdair MacIntyre*, edited by John Horton and Susan Mendus, 65–90. Oxford: Polity Press, 1994.
Compendium of the Social Doctrine of the Church, available at: http://www.vatican.va/roman_curia/pontifical_councils/justpeace/documents/rc_pc_justpeace_doc_20060526_compendio-dott-soc_en.html
Congar, Yves. *The Meaning of Tradition*. San Francisco: Ignatius Press, 2004.
Coulanges, Numa Denis Fustel De. *The Ancient City: A Study on the Religion, Laws, and Institutions of Greece, and Rome*. Kitchener: Batoche Books, 2001.
Craiutu, Aurelian. *Faces of Moderation, The Art of Balance in an Age of Extremes*. Philadelphia: University of Pennsylvania Press, 2017.
Craiutu, Aurelian. *Liberalism Under Siege: The Political Thought of the French Doctrinaires*. Lanham: Lexington Books, 2003.
Craiutu, Aurelian. 'Political Moderation and the Lost Art of Trimming'. *The Island (Tasmania, Australia)* 140 (2015): 38–43.
Craiutu, Aurelian. *A Virtue for Courageous Minds: Moderation in French Political Thought, 1748–1830*. Princeton, Oxford: Princeton University Press, 2012.
De Landtsheer, Jeannine, Gilbert Tournoy, and Jan Papy, eds. *Lipsius en Leuven: Catalogus van de tentoonstelling in de Centrale Bibliotheek te Leuven, 18 September–17 Oktober, 1997*, Supplementa Humanistica Lovaniensia, 13. Leuven: Leuven University Press, 1997.
Dench, Emma. 'Cicero and Roman Identity'. In *The Cambridge Companion to Cicero*, edited by Catherine Steel, 122–47. Cambridge: Cambridge Univerity Press, 2013.
Descartes, René. *Meditations on First Philosophy, With Selections from the Objections and Replies*, edited and translated by John Cottingham, rev. edn. Cambridge: Cambridge University Press, 1996, 2003.
Disraeli, Benjamin. *Vindication of the English Constitution in a Letter to a Noble and Learned Lord* (1835), reprinted in Disraeli: *Whigs and Whiggism*, edited by William Hutcheon. New York: Macmillan, 1914.
Doig, James. *Aquinas's Philosophical Commentary on the Ethics. A Historical Perspective*. Dordrecht: Kluwer Academic Publishers, 2001.

Dunn, John. 'Introduction'. In Dunn, *Interpreting Political Responsibility. Essays 1981–1989*, 1–8. Oxford: Polity Press, 1990.
Dyson, Robert W. 'Introduction'. In *Augustine: The City of God against the Pagans*, edited and translated by Robert W. Dyson. Cambridge: Cambridge University Press, 1998.
Entscheidungen des Bundesverfassungsgerichts 4, no. 120 (20 July 1954).
Erasmus, Desiderius. *In Praise of Folly*. London: Reeves & Turner, 1876.
Flower, Harriet I. *Consensus and Community in Republican Rome*. The twentieth Todd Memorial Lecture delivered in the University of Sydney 18 July 2013, available at: https://www.academia.edu/10982077/Consensus_and_Community_in_Republican_Rome, downloaded in June 2019.
Foxe, John. *Time and the End of Time*, 1–2. London, 1664.
Fumaroli, Marc. Preface to Michael A. Screech: *Montaigne et la melancolie*. Paris: Presses Universitaires de France, 1992.
Gadamer, Hans-Georg. *Philosophical Apprenticeships*, translated by Robert R. Sullivan. Cambridge and London: The MIT Press, 1985.
Gadamer, Hans-Georg. *Truth and Method*. New York: Crossroad, 1986.
Gamble, Andrew. 'Hayek on Knowledge, Economics, and Society'. In *The Cambridge Companion to Hayek*, 111–31. Cambridge: Cambridge University Press, 2006.
Garver, Eugene. *Machiavelli and the History of Prudence*. Madison: The University of Wisconsin Press, 1987.
Geuss, Raymond. *Outside Ethics*, reviewed by Alasdair MacIntyre, University of Notre Dame. *Notre Dame Philosophical Reviews*, 2006.
Geuss, Raymond. *Philosophy and Real Politics*. Princeton and Oxford: Princeton University Press, 2008.
Geuss, Raymond. 'Thucydides, Nietzsche, and Williams'. In Raymond Geuss, *Outside Ethics*, 219–33. Princeton and Oxford: Princeton University Press, 2005.
Goodheart, Eugene. *Holding the Center: In Defense of Political Trimming*. New Brunswick, NJ: Transaction, 2013.
Gorski, Philip S. 'Beyond the Fact/Value Distinction: Ethical Naturalism and the Social Sciences'. *Society* 50 (2013): 543.
Goyet, Francis. 'Montaigne and the Notion of Prudence'. In *The Cambridge Companion to Montaigne*, edited by Ullrich Langer. Cambridge: Cambridge University Press, 2005.
Gracián, Baltasar. *The Art of Worldly Wisdom*, translated by Jospeh Jacobs. Boston: Shambala, 1993.
Greenblatt, Stephen. *Renaissance Self-Fashioning. From More to Shakespeare*. Chicago and London: The University of Chicago Press, 1980.
Guest, Clare. 'Figural Cities. Bruni's Laudatio Urbis Florentinae and Its Greek Sources in *Rhetoric*'. *Theatre and the Arts of Design*, edited by C. Guest, 126–45. Oslo: Novus, 2008.
Guicciardini, Francesco. 'Dialogo del Reggiemento di Firenze'. In Guicciardini, *Dialogo e Discorsi del Reggimento di Firenze*, edited by Roberto Palmarocchi. Bari: Giu. Laterza e Figli, Tipografi-editori-librai, 1932.
Gundlach, Gustav. 'Solidarismus'. In *Staatslexikon*. Bonn: Görres Gesellschaft, 1931, IV: 1614.
Hadot, Pierre. *Philosophy as a Way of Life: Spiritual Exercises from Socrates to Foucault*, edited and introduction by Arnold I. Davidson. Oxford: Wiley-Blackwell, 1995.
Hankins, James. 'The "Baron Thesis" after Forty Years and Some Recent Studies of Leonardo Bruni'. *Journal of the History of Ideas* 56, no. 2 (1995): 309–38.

Hankins, James. 'Coluccio Salutati e Leonardo Bruni'. In *Il contributo italiano alla storia del pensiero*, edited by Michele Cilibert. Rome: Treccani, 2012.

Hankins, James. 'The Virtue Politics of the Italian Humanists'. In *Beyond Reception: Renaissance Humanism and the Transformation of Classica Antiquity*, edited by Patrick Baker, Johannes Helmrath and Craig Kallendorf, 95–114. Berlin and Boston: De Gruyter, 2019.

Haskell, H. J. *This was Cicero*. Greenwich: Fawcett Premier Books, 1964.

Hayek, Friedrich A. 'The Facts of the Social Sciences'. In *Individualism and Economic Order*, ed. Friedrich A. Hayek, 57–76. Chicago: University of Chicago Press, 1980.

Hayek, Friedrich A. 'Kinds of Order in Society (1964)'. In *The Politicization of Society*, edited by Kenneth Templeton, Jr. Indianapolis: Liberty Press, 1979.

Hayek, Friedrich A. *Laws, Legislation, Liberty*, Volume 1: Rules and Order. London: Routledge, 1973, 1998.

Hayek, Friedrich A. 'The Legal and Political Philosophy of David Hume (1711–1776)'. In *The Collected Works of F. A. Hayek. Volume 3: The Trend of Economic Thinking. Essays on Political Economists and Economic History*, edited by W. W. Bartley, III. and Stephen Kresge, 101–8. Chicago: University of Chicago Press, 1991.

Hayek, Friedrich A. *The Road to Serfdom, Text and Documents*, The Definitive Edition, edited by Bruce Caldwell. Chicago: The University of Chicago Press, 1944, 2007.

Hirschman. Albert O. *The Passions and the Interests: Political Arguments for Capitalism before Its Triumph*. Princeton: Princeton University Press, 1977.

Höffner, Joseph Cardinal. *Christian Social Teaching*. Cologne, Bratislava Ordo Socialis, 1997, available on the following link: https://ordosocialis.de/pdf/jhoeffner/Christl.%20Gesellschaftsl/cglenga4neu.pdf, downloaded June 2019.

Hont, István. 'Free trade and the Economic Limits to National Politics: Neo-Machiavellian Political Economy Reconsidered'. In Hont, *Jealousy of Trade. Internatonal Competition and the Nation-State in Historical Perspective*, 185–266. Cambridge: The Belknap Press of Harvard University Press, 2005.

Höpfl, Harro. *Jesuit Political Thought. The Society of Jesus and the State, c. 1540–1630*. Cambridge: Cambridge University Press, 2004.

Hörcher, Ferenc. 'Dramatic Mimesis and Civic Education in Aristotle, Cicero and Renaissance Humanism'. *Aisthesis: Pratiche linguaggi e saperi dell'estetico rivista online del seminario permanente di estetica* 10, no. 1 (2017): 87–96.

Hörcher, Ferenc. 'From Reason of State to Coordination by Trade'. *Societate si Politica* 10, no. 1 (2016): 5–23.

Hörcher, Ferenc. 'Judgement and Taste: From Shakespeare to Shaftesbury'. In *Aspects of the Enlightenment: Aesthetics, Politics and Religion*, edited by Ferenc Hörcher and Endre Szécsényi, 111–66. Budapest: Akadémiai Kiadó, 2004.

Hörcher, Ferenc. 'Prudencia, kairosz, decorum: a konzervativizmus időszemléletéről' (Prudence, Kairos, Decorum: Conservatism's View of Time). *Információs társadalom: Társadalomtudományi folyóirat* 4 (2006): 61–80.

Hörcher, Ferenc. *Prudentia Iuris: Towards a Pragmatic Theory of Natural Law*. Budapest: Akadémia Publishing House, 2000.

Hörcher, Ferenc. 'The Renaissance of Political Realism in Early Modern Europe: Giovanni Botero and the Discourse of "Reason of State"'. *Krakowskie Studia z historii panstwa prawa* 9, no. 2 (2016): 187–210.

Hörcher, Ferenc. 'Skinner and Rosanvallon: Reconciling the History of Political Thought with Political Philosophy'. *Przeglad Politologiczny*, XX, no. 4 (2015): 177–89.

Hörcher, Ferenc. 'The V4 Cooperation and the European Schism over the Migration Crisis: The History of Political Thought in the Service of Political Analysis'. In *Central and Eastern European Socio-Political and Legal Transition Revisited*, edited by Balázs Fekete and Fruzsina Gárdos-Orosz, 231–47. Frankfurt am Main: Peter Lang GmbH, Internationaler Verlag der Wissenschaften, 2017.
Huizinga, Johan. *Dutch Civilisation in the Senteenth Century*. London: Collins, 1968.
Hume, David. 'Of the Origin of Government'. In Hume, *Essays, Moral, Political, and Literary*, revised edition, 37–41. Indianapolis: Liberty Classics, 1985, 1987.
Hume, David. 'Of the Rise and Progress of the Arts and Sciences'. In Hume, *Essays, Moral, Political, and Literary*, rev. edn, edited by Eugene F. Miller, 111–37. Indianapolis: Liberty Classics, 1985, 1987.
Hume, David. *A Treatise of Human Nature*. London: John Noon, 1739.
Hursthouse, Rosalind. *On Virtue Ethics*. Oxford: Oxford University Press, 2002.
Inwood, Brad, and Fred D. Miller. 'Law in Roman Philosophy'. In *A Treatise of Legal Philosophy and General Jurisprudence*, edited by Fred D. Miller, and Carrie-Ann Biondi, 133–65. Dordrecht: Springer, 2015.
Jenkins, Mark P. 'Bernard Williams'. In *Philosophy Now Series*. Montréal: McGill-Queen's University Press, 2006.
Kahn, Victoria. *Rhetoric, Prudence, and Skepticism in the Renaissance*. Ithaca and London: Cornell University Press, 1985.
Kant, Immanuel. *Critique of the Power of Judgment*, edited by Paul Guyer, translated by Paul Guyer and Eric Mathews. Cambridge and New York: Cambridge University Press, 2000. The Cambridge Edition of the Works of Immanuel Kant.
Kant, Immanuel. 'Idea for a Universal History from a Cosmopolitan Point of View, translated by Lewis White Beck'. In *On History*, edited by Lewis White Beck, 11–26. New York: MacMillan, 1986.
Kapust, Daniel. 'Cicero on Decorum and the Morality of Rhetoric'. *European Journal of Political Theory* 10, no. 1 (2011): 92–112.
Kaster, Robert A. *Emotion, Restraint, and Community in Ancient Rome*. Oxford: Oxford University Press, 2005.
Kennedy, Geoff. 'Cicero, Roman Republicanism and the Contested Meaning of Libertas', *Political Studies* 62, no. 3 (2014): 488–501.
Kermode, Frank. *The Sense of an Ending*. New York: Oxford University Press, 1967.
Kinneavy, James L. 'Kairos: A Neglected Concept in Classical Rhetoric'. In *Rhetoric and Praxis: The Contribution of Classical Rhetoric to Practical Reasoning*, edited by Jean Dietz Moss, 79–105. Washington DC: The Catholic University of America Press, 1986.
Klein, Lawrence E. *Shaftesbury and the Culture of Politeness, Moral Discourse and Cultural Politics in Early Eighteenth-Century England*. Cambridge: Cambridge University Press, 1994.
Koopman, Colin and Bernard Williams. 'Philosophy's Need for History'. *The Review of Metaphysics* 64, no. 1 (2010): 3–30.
Kossmann, Ernst Heinrich. 'Dutch Republicanism'. In Kossmann, *Political Thought in the Dutch Republic, Three Studies*, 167–94. Amsterdam: Koninklije Nederlandse Akademie van Wetenshappen, 2000.
Lepri, Valentina. 'The Spread of Italian Political Culture during the Renaissance: Remarks on the First Fortunes of Guicciardini's Works'. *Studia Historica Brunensia* 58, no. 2 (2011): 3–12.

Lévy, Carlos. 'Philosophical Life versus Political Life: An Impossible Choice for Cicero?' In *Cicero's Practical Philosophy*, edited by Walter Nicgorski, 58–78. Notre Dame: University of Notre Dame Press, 2012.

Lipsius, Justus. *Politica, Six Books of Politics or Political Instruction*, edited and translated by Jan Waszink. Assen: Royal Van Gorcum, 2004.

Lohr, C. H. 'The Medieval Interpretation of Aristotle'. In *The Cambridge History of Later Medieval Philosophy*, edited by Norman Kretzmann, Anthony Kenny and Jan Pinborg, 80–98. Cambridge: Cambridge University Press, 1982.

Long, A. A. 'Cicero's Politics in the De Officiis'. In *Justice and Generosity: Studies in Hellenistic Political Philosophy*, edited by Andrew Laks and Malcolm Schoefield, 213–40. Cambridge: Cambridge University Press, 1995.

Lubac, Henri de. *Catholicisme. Aspects sociaux du dogme*, cited in G Thils, *Theologie et Réalité sociale*. Paris: Tournai, 1952.

Macchiavelli, Niccolo. *The Prince*, edited by Quntin Skinner and Russell Price, second edition. Cambridge: Cambridge University Press, 1988, 2019.

MacIntyre, Alasdair. *After Virtue: A Study in Moral Theory*. Notre Dame: University of Notre Dame Press, 1981.

MacIntyre, Alasdair. *Dependent Rational Animals: Why Human Beings Need the Virtues*. London: Duckworth, 1999.

MacIntyre, Alasdair. 'Rival Aristotles: Aristotle against some Modern Aristotelians'. In MacIntyre, *Ethics and Politics, Selected Essays*, vol. 2, 22–41. Cambridge, Cambridge University Press, 2006.

MacPherson, C. B. *The Political Theory of Possessive Individualism: From Hobbes to Locke*. Oxford: Oxford University Press, 1962.

Macrobius. *The Saturnalia*, translated by Percival Vaughan Davies. The Records of Civilization, Sources and Studies, No. LXXIX. New York: Columbia University Press, 1969.

Madden, Deborah. 'Education and Manners'. In *A Companion to Intellectual History*, edited by Richard Whatmore and Brian Young, 262–75. Chichester: Wiley Blackwell, 2016.

Mansfield, Harvey C., Jr. 'Machavelli's Political Science'. *The American Political Science Review* 75, no. 2 (1981): 293–305.

Marquis of Halifax. *Complete Works*, edited by J. P. Kenyon. London: Penguin, 1969.

Mason, Gregory. 'In Praise of Kairos in the Arts: Critical Time, East and West'. In *Rhetoric and Kairos. Essays in History, Theory, and Praxis*, edited by James S. Baumlin and Phillip Sipiora, 199–210. Albany: State University of New York Press, 2002.

Meinecke, Friedrich. *Machiavellism: The Doctrine of Raison D'état and Its Place in Modern History*, translated by D. Scott. London, 1957.

Merleau-Ponty, Maurice. *Phenomenology of Perception*. London: Routledge, 1945, 1962.

Montaigne, Michel. *The Complete Essays*, translated by M. A. Screech. London: Penguin, 1991.

Murphy, James Bernard. 'Habit and Convention at the Foundation of Custom'. In *Customary Law, Legal, Historical and Philosophical Perspectives*, edited by Amanda Perreau-Saussine and James Bernard Murphy, 53–78. Cambridge: Cambridge University Press, 2009.

Murphy, James Bernard. *The Philosophy of Customary Law*. Oxford: Oxford University Press, 2014.

Newey, Glen. 'Ruck in the Carpet'. *London Review of Books* 31, no. 13 (2009): 15–17.

Nicgorski, Walter. 'Cicero on Aristotle and Aristotelians'. *Hungarian Philosophical Review* 57, no. 4 (2013): 34–56.
Nicgorski, Walter, ed. *Cicero's Practical Philosophy*, Notre Dame: University of Notre Dame Press, 2012.
Nicgorski, Walter. *Cicero's Skepticism and His Recovery of Political Philosophy*. New York: Palgrave Macmillan, 2016.
Nietzsche, Friedrich. *The Will to Power*, translated by Walter Kaufmann. New York: Vintage, 1967.
Nietzsche, Friedrich. 'Zur Genealogie der Moral' In *Nietzsches Werke: Kritische Studien-Ausgabe*, edited by Giorgio Colli and Mazzino Montinari, 245–412. Berlin: De Gruyter, 1967.
Oakeshott, Michael. 'Introduction to Leviathan'. In Oakeshott, *Rationalism in Politics and Other Essays*, 221–94. Carmel: Liberty Fund Inc., 1962, 1991.
Oakeshott, Michael. *On Human Conduct*. Oxford: Clarendon, 1991.
Oakeshott, Michael. 'Political Education'. In Oakeshott, *Rationalism in Politics and Other Essays*, 43–69. Carmel: Liberty Fund Inc., 1962, 1991.
Oakeshott, Michael. 'Rationalism in Politics'. In Oakeshott, *Rationalism in Politics and Other Essays*, 5–42. Carmel: Liberty Fund Inc., 1962, 1991.
Oakeshott, Michael. *The Vocabulary of a Modern European State*, edited by Luke O'Sullivan. Exeter: Imprint Academic, 2008.
Oksenberg Rorty, Amelie and James Schmidt. *Kant's Idea for a Universal History with a Cosmopolitan Aim: A Critical Guide*. Cambridge: Cambridge University Press, 2009.
Otterspeer, Willem. *Orde en trouw. Over Johan Huizinga* (Order and Loyalty. About Johan Huizinga). Amsterdam: De Bezige Bij, 2006.
Panofsky, Erwin. 'Titian's Allegory of Prudence: A Postscript'. In Panofsky, *Meaning in the Visual Arts*, 181–205. Chicago: University of Chicago Press, 1982.
Pellauer, David and Bernard Dauenhauer. 'Paul Ricoeur'. In *The Stanford Encyclopedia of Philosophy* (Winter 2016 Edition), edited by Edward N. Zalta, Peterson Douglas L. *Time, Tide, and Tempest: A Study of Shakespeare's Romances*. San Marino: Huntington Library, 1973.
Pieper, Josef. *Das Viergespann*. München: Kösel-Verlag, 1964. English translation: *The Four Cardinal Virtues*. Notre Dame, Indiana: University of Notre Dame Press, 1966. https://www.google.com/search?hl=en&q=Wolff+Book%2C+Harcourt%2C+Brace+and+World%2C+Inc.%2C+1965
Pieper, Josef. *No One Could Have Known: An Autobiography, the Early Years, 1904–1945*. San Francisco: Ignatius Press, 1979.
Pocock, John G. A. *Machiavellian Moment, Florentine Political Thought and the Atlantic Republican Tradition*. Princeton and Oxford: Princeton University Press, 1975.
Pocock, John G. A. 'The Political Economy of Burke's Analysis of the French Revolution'. In Pocock, *Virtue Commerce, and History: Essays on Political Thought and History, Chiefly in the Eighteenth Century*, 215–310. Cambridge: Cambridge University Press, 1985, 1988.
Pocock, John G. A. 'Virtues, Rights, and Manners'. In Pocock, *Virtue, Commerce, and History: Essays on Political Thought and History, Chiefly in the Eighteenth Century*, 37–50. Cambridge: Cambridge University Press, 1985, 1988.
Poggi, Caroli. *De nobilitate liber disceptatorius, et Leonardo Chiensis De vera nobilitate tractatus apologeticus cum eorum vita et annotationibus abbatis Michaelis Justiniani*. Avellino: heredes Camilli Caballi, 1657.

Polanyi, Michael. *Personal Knowledge. Towards a Post-Critical Philosophy*. London and New York: Routledge, 1958.

Polanyi, Michael. *Science, Faith and Society*. Chicago: University of Chicago Press, 1946.

Polanyi, Michael. *The Tacit Dimension*. Chicago: University of Chicago Press, 1966.

Quinton, Sir Anthony. *The Politics of Imperfection: The Religious and Secular Traditions of Conservative Thought in England from Hooker to Oakeshott*. London and Boston: Faber and Faber, 1978.

Ramgotra, Manjeet. 'Conservative Roots of Republicanism'. *Theoria: A Journal of Social and Political Theory* 61, no. 139 (2014): 22–49.

Rasmussen, Douglas B. and Douglas J. Den Uyl. 'Liberalism in Retreat'. *The Review of Metaphysics* 62, no. 4 (2009): 875–908.

Rasmussen, Douglas B. and Douglas J. Den Uyl. *Norms of Liberty: A Perfectionist Basis for Non-Perfectinist Politics*. University Park: The Pensylvania State University Press, 2005.

Rawls, John. *A Theory of Justice*. Cambridge and London: The Belknap Press of Harvard University Press, 1971, 1999.

Reeve, C. David C. 'Introduction'. In Aristotle, *Nicomachean Ethics*, translated and introduced by C. D. C. Reeve. Indianapolis: Hackett Publishing Company, 2014.

Reeve, C. David C. 'Introduction'. In Aristotle, *Politics*, translated by C. D. C Reeve. Indianapolis, Cambridge: Hackett Publishing Company, 1998.

Ricoeur, Paul. 'Is a Purely Procedural Theory of Justice Possible? John Rawls's Theory of Justice'. In Ricoeur, *The Just*, 36–57. Chicago and London: The University of Chicago Press, 2000.

Ricoeur, Paul. *Le Juste*. Paris: Éditions Esprit, 1995. Translated: *The Just*. Chicago and London: The University of Chicago Press, 2000.

Ricoeur, Paul. *Oneself as Another*, translated by Kathleen Blamey. Chicago: University of Chicago Press, 1992.

Robbins, Caroline. *The Eighteenth-Century Commonwealthman: Studies in the Transmission, Development, and Circumstance of English Liberal Thought from the Restoration of Charles II until the War with the Thirteen Colonies* (1959). Indianapolis: Liberty Fund, 2004.

Roche, Donald. 'Prudence in Aristotle and St Thomas Aquinas'. MA Thesis, National University of Ireland, Maynooth, 2005.

Roselaar, Saskia T. 'Cicero and the Italians: Expansion of Empire, Creation of Law'. In *Cicero's Law: Rethinking Roman Law of the Late Republic*, edited by Paul J. du Plessis, 145–65. Edinburgh: Edinburgh University Press, 2016.

Rüpke, Jörg. *Religion in Republican Rome: Rationalization and Ritual Change*. Philadelphia: The University of Pennsylvania Press, 2012.

Sabbadini, R. *Epistolario di Guarino Veronese*, vol. 1. Venice: C. Ferrari, 1915.

Schmitt, Carl. *The Concept of the Political*. Chicago: University of Chicago Press, 2007.

Schmitt, Carl. *Political Theology: Four Chapters on the Concept of Sovereignty*, edited and translated by George Schwab. Chicago: University of Chicago Press, 2005.

Schumpeter, Joseph. *Methodological Individualism*, introduction by F. A. Hayek. Brussels: European Institute, 1980.

Sellars, John. 'Marcus Aurelius'. In *The Internet Encylopaedia of Philosophy*, https://www.iep.utm.edu/marcus/

Seneca, Lucius Annaeus. *De Otio*, edited by G. D. Williams. Cambridge Greek and Latin Classics Cambridge: Cambridge University Press, 2003.

Shagan, Ethan H. *The Rule of Moderation. Violence, Religion, and the Politics of Restraint in Early Modern England*. New York: Cambridge University Press, 2011.

Sharples, Robert W. 'Cicero's Republic and Greek Political Theory'. *Polis* 5, no. 2 (1986): 30–50.
Shils, Edward. *Tradition*. Chicago: University of Chicago Press, 1981.
Shils, Edward. *The Virtue of Civility*, edited by Steven Grosby. Indianapolis: Liberty Fund, 1997.
Sipiora, Phillip. 'Introduction: The Ancient Concept of Kairos'. In *Rhetoric and Kairos: Essays in History, Theory, and Praxis*, edited by Phillip Sipiora and James S. Baumlin, 1–22. Albany: State University of New York Press, 2002.
Sipiora, Phillip and James S. Baumlin, *Rhetoric and Kairos: Essays in History, Theory, and Praxis*. Albany: State University of New York Press, 2002.
Skinner, Quentin. *The Foundations of Modern Political Thought*. Cambridge: Cambridge University Press, 1978.
Skoble, Aeon J. 'Hayek the Philosopher of Law'. In *The Cambridge Companion to Hayek*, edited by Edward Feser, 171–181. Cambridge: Cambridge University Press, 2006.
Smith, John E. 'Time and Qualitative Time'. In *Rhetoric and Kairos: Essays in History, Theory, and Praxis*, edited by Phillip Sipiora and James S. Baumlin, 46–57. Albany: State University of New York Press, 2002.
Stichter, Matthew. *The Skill of Virtue*. DPhil Thesis, 2007, available at: https://etd.ohiolink.edu/!etd.send_file?accession=bgsu1181851300&disposition=inline
Sunstein, Cass. 'Trimming'. *Harvard Law Review* 122, no. 4 (2009): 1051–95.
Szűcs, Jenő and Julianna Parti. 'The Three Historical Regions of Europe: An Outline'. *Acta Historica Academiae Scientiarum Hungaricae* 29, no. 2/4 (1983): 131–84.
Tacitus, Cornelius. *Germany and Agricola: The Oxford Translation*, revised with notes, with a brief introduction by James Kendrick. New York: Translation Publishing, 1922.
Temelini, Mark A. 'Cicero's Concordia: The Promotion of a Political Concept in the Late Roman *Republic*'. DPhil Thesis, McGill University, Montreal, 2002.
Temple, William. *Observations upon the United Provinces of the Netherlands*. London: Maxwell, 1673.
Tönnies, Ferdinand. *Gemeinschaft und Gesellschaft*. Leipzig: Fues's Verlag, 1887.
Tuck, Richard. *Philosophy and Government*. *1572–1651*. Cambridge: Cambridge University Press, 1993.
The Upanishads, edited by Juan Mascaró. Penguin Classics, 1965.
Valeriano, Pierio. *Hieroglyphica*. Frankfurt edition, 1678.
Venturi, Franco. *Utopia and Reform in the Enlightenment*. Cambridge: Cambridge University Press, 1971.
Viroli, Maurizio. 'Machiavelli and the Republican Idea of Politics'. In *Machiavelli and Republicanism*, edited by Gisela Bock, Quentin Skinner and Maurizio Viroli, 143–71. Cambridge: Cambridge University Press, 1990, 1993.
Waldron, Jeremy. 'The Rule of Law'. *The Stanford Encyclopedia of Philosophy* (Fall 2016 Edition), edited by Edward N. Zalta, https://plato.stanford.edu/entries/rule-of-law/
Weil, Simone. *Gravity and Grace*, translated by Arthur Wills. Lincoln: University of Nebraska Press, 1997.
Wiles, David. *Greek Theatre Performance. An Introduction*. Cambridge: Cambridge University Press, 2000.
Williams, Bernard. *Ethics and the Limits of Philosophy*. Cambridge: Harvard University Press, 1985.
Williams, Bernard. *In the Beginning Was the Deed. Realism and Moralism in Political Argument*, selected, edited and with an introduction by Geoffrey Hawthorn. Princeton, Oxford: Princeton University Press, 2005.

Williams, Bernard. *Man Without Qualities*. 'Interview with Bernard Williams'. *Cogito*, 28 March 2015.
Williams, Bernard. *A Mistrustful Animal*. 'An Interview with Bernard Williams'. *The Harvard Review of Philsoophy* XII, no. 1 (2004): 80–91.
Williams, Bernard. 'Replies'. In *World, Mind, and Ethics: Essays on the Ethical Philosophy of Bernard Williams*, edited by J. E. J. Altham and R. Harrison, 185–224. Cambridge: Cambridge University Press, 1995.
Williams, Bernard. *Shame and Necessity*. Berkeley: University of California Press, 2008.
Wills, Gary. Venice: Lion *City. The Religion of Empire*, New York: Simon and Schuster, 2001.
Wood, Neal. *Cicero's Social & Political Thought*. Berkeley: University of California Press, 1988.
Wormuth, Francis. 'Aristotle on Law'. In Wormuth, *Essays in Law and Politics*, edited by Dalmas H. Nelson and Richard L. Sklar. Port Washington, New York: Kennikat Press, 1978.
Zarecki, Jonathan. 'Cicero's Definition of Politikos'. *Arethusa* 42, no. 3 (2009): 251–70.
Zuckert, Catherine. 'Do "Virtue Ethics" Require "Virtue Politics"?' In Hungarian *Philosophical Review*, 57, no. 14: *The Politics of Aristotle: Reconstruxctions and Interpretations*, guest edited by Ferenc Hörcher and Péter Lautner (2013): 95–108.

Index of Names

Adams, Henry   132, 186
Adorno   71
Agricola, Rudolph   53
Alberti   106
Albert the Great   28
Althusser   132
Anaxagoras   125
Annas, Julia   7, 117, 118, 119, 120, 121, 127, 184
Anscombe   117, 121, 162, 184
Antony   22
Apollonius   125
Aquinas   5, 6, 28, 29, 30, 31, 32, 33, 34, 47, 48, 75, 79, 85, 95, 96, 98, 99, 122, 162, 170, 171, 185
Aristides   36
Aristophanes   54
Aristotle   1, 5, 6, 8, 13, 14, 15, 16, 17, 18, 19, 24, 28, 29, 30, 31, 32, 33, 34, 35, 36, 37, 39, 40, 44, 47, 50, 53, 54, 55, 58, 59, 60, 62, 65, 66, 69, 75, 79, 81, 82, 84, 91, 98, 100, 111, 117, 120, 121, 122, 123, 124, 125, 128, 129, 132, 136, 138, 139, 142, 143, 144, 145, 146, 147, 156, 162, 165, 168, 169, 170, 171, 176, 177, 181, 183, 184, 186, 187, 188, 189
Aron, Raymond   127, 132, 186
Athenodorus   125
Atticus   22
Augustine   26, 27, 28, 33, 55, 70, 75, 86, 169, 170, 171

Baron, Hans   34, 35, 36, 171, 172
Bellarmine, Robert   48
Berkowitz, Peter   128, 186
Berlin, Isaiah   114, 136
Böckenförde   140, 141, 145, 147, 188
Bodin   49, 56
Boethius   28
Borgia, Cesare   41
Botero   45, 46, 47, 48, 174, 189

Bourke, Richard   1, 2, 3, 167
Bruegel, Pieter   104
Bruni, Leonardo   13, 35, 36, 37, 38, 171, 172
Burke, Edmund   105, 106, 111, 112, 113, 114, 128, 132, 135, 182, 183, 187

Caesar, Julius   22, 23, 125
Capponi   43
Carrese, Paul   128, 186
Castiglione, Baldassare   39, 40, 46, 47, 51
Cato   23, 25, 37, 125, 157
Cicero   1, 4, 5, 6, 8, 9, 19, 20, 21, 22, 23, 24, 25, 26, 27, 28, 30, 33, 34, 35, 36, 37, 44, 47, 51, 53, 54, 55, 56, 57, 75, 79, 86, 101, 115, 124, 125, 126, 130, 132, 134, 140, 142, 143, 147, 150, 151, 152, 153, 154, 155, 156, 157, 162, 165, 168, 169, 170, 172, 175, 179, 181, 182, 185, 189, 190, 191
Clodius   22
Coke, Edward   140
Craiutu, Aurelian   8, 127, 128, 131, 132, 185, 186
Crassus   22

Den Uyl   121, 122, 123, 185
Descartes   39, 57, 105, 111, 112, 139, 182
Dion   125
Disraeli, Benjamin   111, 183
Dunn, John   1, 2, 4, 167
Dworkin   6, 68

Eliot, T. S.   139
Epictetus   3
Erasmus   104, 175, 182

Ferguson, Adam   138
Foucault   132, 175, 188
Foxe, John   101, 181
Fumaroli   50, 52, 175

Fustel De Coulanges, Numa Denis   153, 189, 190

Gadamer, Hans-Georg   1, 6, 24, 40, 57, 58, 59, 60, 61, 62, 63, 64, 65, 66, 75, 84, 139, 162, 176, 177
Garrigou-Lagrange, Réginald   86
Garver, Eugene   39, 40, 172
Geertz, Clifford   146
Geuss, Raymond   1, 2, 6, 66, 68, 71, 72, 73, 74, 75, 80, 81, 82, 152, 162, 167, 178, 179
Goethe   68, 95
Goyet, Francis   50, 175
Gracián, Baltasar   1, 128, 186
Greenblatt Stephen   51, 175
Guarino of Verona   125, 185
Guicciardini, Piero   39, 40, 41, 42, 43, 44, 45, 47, 48, 54, 56, 173, 174

Habermas   67, 70, 188
Hadot, Pierre   51, 89, 144, 175, 185, 188
Hamlet   51, 131
Hankins, James   6, 7, 35, 36, 118, 123, 124, 125, 126, 127, 171, 172, 185
Harrington   134, 157
Hayek, Friedrich August von   7, 109, 111, 112, 113, 114, 133, 137, 138, 141, 164, 182, 183, 187, 188
Hegel   59, 63, 68, 89
Heidegger, Martin   40, 57, 60, 62, 65, 97, 177
Helmholtz   59
Henri de Navarre   50
Hobbes   67, 72, 73, 79, 81, 86, 87, 130, 134, 149, 177, 187
Höffner   90, 91, 92, 179, 180
Hont, István   4, 158, 159, 168, 190, 191
Höpfl   45, 48, 174
Huizinga, Johan   159, 160, 191
Hume, David   87, 88, 89, 109, 111, 112, 113, 132, 135, 137, 138, 179, 183, 187
Huygens   160

Isocrates   36

John of Salisbury   35

Kahn, Victoria   39, 40, 173
Kant, Immanuel   2, 7, 24, 57, 59, 60, 63, 64, 65, 66, 68, 70, 71, 72, 86, 89, 90, 91, 109, 125, 139, 143, 163, 167, 168, 177, 179
Konrad, Joseph   70
Kossmann, E. H.   158, 190

Lenin   3, 4, 71, 72, 73, 167, 178
Leonardo da Vinci   13
Leonardo of Chios   124
Lipsius, Justus   1, 6, 49, 52, 53, 54, 55, 56, 75, 162, 168, 175, 176
Livy   47
Locke   81, 122, 168, 187
Luther   48, 70, 89

Machiavelli, Niccolo   1, 6, 9, 35, 38, 39, 40, 41, 42, 43, 44, 45, 46, 48, 49, 50, 51, 52, 53, 54, 55, 56, 60, 61, 81, 82, 98, 116, 120, 123, 124, 125, 126, 152, 153, 154, 155, 165, 172, 173, 174, 189, 190
MacIntyre, Alasdair   60, 63, 64, 71, 72, 121, 122, 123, 139, 143, 144, 145, 177, 178, 185, 188
Macrobius   94, 180
Mandeville, Bernard   87, 88, 111, 187
Marco Vecellio   93
Marcus Aurelius   3, 167
Maritain, Jacques   86
Marx   68, 73
Merleau-Ponty   110, 111, 132, 182
Montaigne   6, 49, 50, 51, 52, 75, 128, 129, 131, 132, 158, 162, 175, 186
Montesquieu   8, 44, 89, 128, 133
Murphy, James Bernard   138, 139, 187

Nicgorski, Walter   24, 25, 169, 170, 189
Nietzsche   1, 57, 68, 71, 72, 73, 128, 177, 178, 186
Nussbaum, Marth C.   64, 70, 121, 122, 123, 143, 144, 145, 177, 185

Oakeshott, Michael   1, 6, 7, 47, 86, 109, 111, 113, 114, 115, 116, 127, 129, 130, 132, 164, 174, 182, 183, 184, 186, 187, 189
Octavian   22

Index of Names

Orazio Vecellio 93
Orwell, George 111

Panaetius 125
Panofsky 94, 95, 180
Pascal 70, 86, 99
Pericles 18, 19, 33, 82, 125, 153, 157
Peterson, Douglas L. 101, 181
Petrarch 35
Phaedrus 132
Pieper, Josef 7, 95, 96, 97, 98, 99, 160, 172, 180, 181
Plato 1, 5, 8, 13, 14, 15, 16, 20, 21, 24, 25, 28, 32, 33, 40, 54, 58, 62, 66, 71, 81, 115, 125, 132, 162, 177, 190
Pocock, J. G. A. 40, 41, 42, 43, 112, 113, 133, 134, 135, 158, 173, 182, 183, 187
Polányi, Michael 110, 111, 115, 164, 176, 182, 184
Pompey 22, 23, 169
Pope Julius II 13
Popper, Karl 114
Ptolemy of Lucca 35
Pythagoras 125

Quinton, Anthony, Baron 148, 149, 150, 189

Rahner, Karl 86
Raphael 13, 14
Rasmussen 121, 122, 185
Rawls, John 1, 2, 6, 64, 67, 68, 71, 73, 74, 81, 82, 106, 120, 133, 179, 182
Reeve, C. D. C 15, 17, 100, 168, 182, 188
Richelieu 157
Ricoeur, Paul 1, 6, 60, 62, 63, 64, 65, 66, 82, 84, 162, 176, 177, 179
Ryle, Gilbert 146

St Francis 86
St Theresa 86
Sallust 56, 126, 170
Sartre 132, 156
Savile, George, Marquis of Halifax 131
Schmitt, Carl 1, 12, 80, 81, 83, 84, 86, 121, 179, 190
Scipio 125
Seneca 56

Shaftesbury, third earl of 86, 87, 88, 90, 170, 179, 180
Shakespeare 51, 131, 170, 175, 181
Shils, Edward 130, 131, 139, 186, 188
Skinner, Quentin 49, 50, 134, 167, 173, 174, 187, 190
Smith, Adam 107, 113, 135, 170, 187
Smith, John E. 101, 181
Socrates 5, 14, 21, 36, 40, 58, 62, 66, 81, 162, 175, 188
Soderini 43
Solon 19
Sophocles 69, 70, 153
Suarez, Francisco 48

Tacitus 4, 6, 45, 55, 56, 175
Taylor, Charles 64, 177
Temple, William 158, 159, 190, 191
Thucydides 69
Titian 93, 94, 95, 163, 180
Tocqueville 127, 128, 132, 133, 157
Tönnies 188
Trump, Donald 79
Tuck, Richard 4, 6, 44, 45, 134, 168, 171, 174

Valeriano, Pierio 94, 180
Vauvenargues, de 114, 116, 183
Venturi, Franco 158, 190
Vico 58, 59
Viroli, Maurizio 155, 156, 190
Vitoria, Francisco de 48
Voltaire 114, 129

Waldron, Jeremy 135
Walzer, Michael 156
Waszink, Jan 53, 56, 175, 176
Weber, Max 3, 4, 67, 72, 109, 159, 168, 179
Williams, Bernard 6, 66, 67, 68, 69, 70, 71, 72, 74, 75, 144, 145, 152, 156, 162, 177, 178
Wittgenstein 58, 68, 91

Zetzel 20, 169
Zuckert, Catherine 7, 118, 121, 122, 123, 127, 184, 185

Index of Subjects

agency-constraint 6, 83, 85, 92, 105, 123, 136, 138, 163
ancient constitution 17, 135, 140
art of governing (*techne politike*) 20
art of the city 155, 156, 157
art of trimming 131, 132, 133, 164, 186
asociability 86, 163
asocial sociability 7, 88, 89, 163
Athens 13, 14, 15, 16, 19, 21, 26, 37, 70, 71, 75, 143, 144, 157, 158, 168

balanced 3, 13, 18, 53, 131, 155, 163
baroque 46
Bildung 59, 82, 86, 165
Brazil 79
Brexit 79, 107, 108, 182

cardinal virtue 1, 4, 5, 6, 8, 24, 31, 41, 45, 46, 47, 54, 81, 95, 96, 99, 127, 151, 155, 168, 180
casuistry 48, 98, 99
character 7, 8, 18, 21, 23, 26, 31, 32, 84, 97, 99, 107, 117, 118, 119, 120, 123, 124, 125, 129, 132, 133, 135, 136, 140, 141, 142, 147, 154, 162, 164, 168
choice 1, 16, 17, 19, 25, 26, 27, 31, 43, 47, 49, 51, 58, 60, 61, 63, 64, 69, 70, 72, 73, 84, 109, 118, 123, 130, 139, 144, 147, 156, 159
chronos 101, 102
civility 8, 127, 130, 131, 132, 133, 164, 186
cleverness (*deinotês*) 18, 47, 48, 97
commerce 38, 112, 113, 134, 135, 183, 187
commercial society 89, 134, 135
common law 137, 138, 139, 140
community 7, 8, 17, 18, 19, 25, 26, 27, 29, 30, 31, 32, 37, 38, 51, 53, 55, 58, 71, 84, 85, 87, 90, 91, 108, 112, 117, 120, 121, 122, 124, 125, 126, 128, 129, 130, 132, 135, 136, 139, 141, 142, 143, 144, 145, 146, 147, 148, 149, 152, 153, 154, 155, 156, 157, 158, 161, 162, 163, 164, 165, 166, 180, 189
compromise 8, 49, 87, 129, 131
concord 38, 42, 126, 156
concordia 126
conflict 3, 5, 7, 8, 19, 35, 42, 52, 65, 83, 86, 87, 105, 107, 115, 122, 131, 143, 144, 153, 155, 156, 158, 160
conservatism 3, 5, 6, 9, 17, 19, 23, 43, 51, 75, 79, 82, 87, 106, 111, 113, 128, 132, 135, 148, 149, 157, 165, 180, 186
conservative republicanism 9, 117, 156, 189
constitution 14, 15, 16, 17, 19, 42, 44, 64, 146, 168, 169, 183
convention 138, 139, 187
cooperation 2, 6, 8, 19, 29, 38, 44, 67, 85, 87, 88, 113, 160, 163, 166, 188
coordination 102, 113, 183
courage 1, 37, 38, 46, 128
craft 14, 72, 74
cruelty 44, 126
culture 5, 8, 21, 23, 24, 26, 33, 35, 38, 44, 59, 79, 89, 101, 126, 127, 132, 133, 135, 139, 141, 142, 143, 144, 145, 146, 147, 154, 158, 159, 161, 162, 164, 165, 173, 180, 188
customs 8, 17, 23, 47, 59, 84, 133, 135, 138, 139, 141, 147, 148, 149, 154, 159, 165, 190

decision 4, 5, 7, 15, 22, 25, 27, 36, 38, 39, 50, 51, 55, 62, 65, 67, 80, 82, 83, 84, 85, 92, 93, 96, 97, 98, 99, 100, 104, 105, 107, 108, 109, 117, 118, 129, 137, 146, 147, 149, 161, 163, 165, 169
decisionism 83, 84
decorum 8, 24, 36, 37, 102, 115, 150, 151, 156, 165, 180, 181, 182, 189

Index of Subjects

deed   2, 5, 19, 21, 22, 23, 25, 32, 38, 55, 58, 62, 63, 67, 68, 72, 120, 124, 125, 151, 177
deinos, or cunning   60, 61 / 18, 60, 97, 152
deliberation   7, 24, 25, 47, 56, 97, 99, 105, 138, 142, 143
discord   126
Docilitas   97
Dutch Republic   9, 158, 166, 190

education   8, 17, 21, 22, 23, 31, 60, 115, 123, 124, 125, 135, 140, 141, 145, 146, 147, 159, 165, 175, 183, 186, 189
egoism   87, 89
eloquence   125, 150, 151
Enlightenment   17, 57, 70, 90, 91, 141, 167, 170, 190
episteme   15, 60, 75, 100, 162
erudition   35, 54, 126
ethics   4, 7, 13, 14, 15, 16, 17, 18, 27, 28, 30, 33, 34, 35, 36, 39, 54, 57, 59, 62, 63, 64, 66, 67, 69, 70, 71, 72, 87, 96, 98, 99, 100, 101, 117, 120, 122, 123, 127, 128, 142, 143, 144, 168, 169, 171, 172, 176, 177, 178, 183, 188
ethos   16, 60, 125, 127, 140, 141, 154
eudaimonia   54, 60, 73, 120, 121, 142
European Union   79
experience   14, 15, 16, 17, 22, 23, 26, 27, 30, 31, 33, 34, 36, 43, 44, 45, 46, 47, 52, 53, 54, 58, 59, 75, 79, 82, 94, 97, 98, 99, 103, 107, 112, 125, 126, 133, 141, 142, 147, 149, 151, 154, 158, 160, 161, 162

facts and values   108, 109
fairness   73, 75, 106, 133
freedom   69, 81, 90, 111, 123, 134, 136, 137, 138, 140, 159, 160
French revolution   111, 113, 157, 183
friendship   64, 122, 123, 142

golden mean   24, 37, 50, 52, 129
good sense   68, 150

habits   8, 17, 29, 119, 121, 123, 125, 133, 138, 139, 146, 159
habitus   27, 28, 29, 51

happiness (*eudaimonia*)   15, 28, 54, 60, 73, 120, 121, 142, 146
harmony   25, 27, 37, 38, 58, 99, 135, 144, 155, 168, 182
hexis   51
historical knowledge   4, 49
Holland   158, 165
honestum   24, 25, 172
humanism   25, 34, 36, 37, 58, 59, 101, 116, 126, 134, 135, 141, 172, 175, 185, 189
humanitas   37
human nature   7, 24, 31, 32, 47, 51, 55, 69, 70, 73, 75, 79, 80, 82, 85, 86, 87, 88, 89, 91, 92, 104, 105, 121, 122, 123, 141, 144, 148, 163, 179
human sciences   59, 62

identity   63, 64, 85, 90, 100, 118, 128, 140, 142, 144, 145, 146, 147, 154, 190
imagination   65, 68, 188
imago Dei   91, 92
immoderate   87, 91
imperfection   55, 148, 149, 150, 189
inclination   7, 31, 86, 89, 91, 99, 132, 135, 163
India   79
institution   18, 111
interpersonal relationship   30, 64, 81, 82, 87, 142
interpretation   2, 3, 8, 13, 15, 17, 27, 28, 35, 39, 40, 42, 43, 45, 48, 51, 52, 61, 62, 63, 84, 86, 94, 95, 109, 118, 120, 137, 144, 145, 153, 154, 159, 160, 169, 170, 172, 180, 184, 187, 188

Jesuit   45, 47, 48, 49, 128, 174
judgement (*giudicio*)   1, 2, 7, 16, 22, 23, 24, 25, 32, 38, 59, 61, 62, 65, 74, 97, 99, 100, 105, 109, 115, 117, 119, 120, 132, 137, 138, 150, 151, 154, 167, 169, 170, 188
jurisprudence   13, 14, 136, 190
justice   1, 38, 46, 64, 65, 73, 74, 75, 81, 82, 95, 96, 106, 124, 125, 127, 133, 135, 137, 138, 168, 179, 182, 185

kairos   7, 47, 72, 100, 101, 102, 163, 180, 181, 182

kanon 50
know-how 51
knowledge-constraint 6, 92, 103, 104, 106, 108, 109, 113, 114, 137, 164
know-what 51

legitimate 8, 31, 41, 42, 72, 80, 89, 128, 131
liberties 34, 105, 106, 160
Logos / Word 58, 68, 91, 138 / 38, 44
Low Countries 49, 52

manners 59, 87, 112, 113, 133, 134, 135, 145, 149, 158, 159, 160, 179, 183
memory 59, 85, 94, 95, 97, 113, 135, 142
metaphysic rights 105
Middle Way 128, 129
mixed government 42, 44
mixed regime 42
moderation 1, 8, 9, 24, 31, 32, 47, 50, 52, 75, 87, 102, 127, 128, 129, 130, 131, 132, 133, 135, 141, 151, 160, 161, 164, 171, 185, 186
moeurs 112, 113, 135, 159
mores 8
mos maiorum 154

natural law 1, 25, 98, 112, 133, 135, 167
natural right 105
nature 3, 5, 15, 18, 22, 23, 24, 25, 26, 29, 32, 40, 44, 46, 51, 53, 58, 60, 62, 63, 69, 70, 73, 74, 79, 81, 82, 84, 85, 88, 89, 90, 91, 97, 98, 99, 105, 106, 114, 121, 122, 123, 128, 137, 138, 141, 143, 146, 154, 159, 165
negotium 5
neostoicism 52
Netherlands 104, 157, 159, 190
nomos 8, 113, 138, 139, 152, 154, 190

observer 99, 106, 108, 109, 158, 164
organicism 149
otium 5, 22

participant 2, 43, 67, 106, 108, 126, 134
pater patriae 22
patria 41, 154, 160
patrician 21, 158, 160

person 7, 18, 20, 25, 26, 30, 31, 46, 50, 51, 59, 60, 61, 62, 63, 67, 68, 84, 86, 89, 90, 91, 92, 93, 95, 98, 99, 100, 101, 106, 110, 118, 119, 120, 123, 144, 150, 151, 163, 168, 171, 172, 180, 189
persona 52, 59, 154
perspectival distortion 7, 105, 106, 108, 109, 164
philia (friendship) 123
philosophy 1, 2, 3, 4, 5, 9, 13, 14, 15, 19, 21, 24, 28, 29, 30, 33, 39, 42, 47, 51, 57, 58, 59, 62, 63, 64, 65, 66, 67, 68, 71, 72, 73, 75, 77, 79, 81, 82, 84, 85, 86, 87, 89, 90, 91, 93, 96, 97, 98, 100, 105, 109, 110, 112, 114, 121, 122, 124, 125, 126, 127, 129, 132, 136, 138, 141, 143, 144, 147, 148, 149, 150, 152, 153, 156, 157, 161, 162, 163, 165, 166, 167, 168, 170, 171, 174, 175, 176, 177, 178, 179, 182, 184, 185, 187, 188, 190
phronesis 1, 13, 15, 18, 19, 25, 33, 39, 41, 58, 59, 60, 62, 63, 64, 65, 75, 84, 100, 115, 123, 129, 138, 162, 183
phronimos 17, 18, 60, 61, 75
planned order (*taxis*) 113
poetry 13, 124, 180
"the political" 3, 6, 67, 83
political community 8, 17, 20, 23, 25, 30, 34, 45, 46, 84, 85, 89, 118, 120, 126, 127, 133, 134, 135, 136, 139, 140, 141, 142, 143, 145, 146, 155, 156, 157, 158, 159, 161, 163, 165, 171
political culture 8, 21, 23, 26, 44, 79, 126, 127, 132, 135, 139, 141, 142, 145, 146, 147, 154, 159, 161, 162, 164, 165, 173
political knowledge 105, 109, 113, 126, 130, 162
political prudence (*civilis prudentiae*) 5, 6, 25, 29, 30, 31, 50, 53, 75, 80, 82, 95, 96, 97, 100, 102, 120, 128, 145, 150, 151, 152, 155, 161, 164, 165, 168, 171
political realism 1, 6, 9, 57, 66, 67, 68, 71, 79, 80, 81, 83, 84, 86, 152, 162, 165, 189
political theology 83, 128, 179, 190
political wisdom 75, 148, 151
politikos 20, 21, 155, 169

popolo 126
power 1, 3, 8, 13, 16, 17, 19, 20, 21, 22, 26, 31, 32, 34, 38, 40, 41, 42, 43, 44, 46, 47, 48, 54, 56, 64, 66, 67, 68, 72, 73, 74, 82, 83, 89, 91, 97, 116, 131, 135, 136, 137, 138, 142, 149, 152, 155, 157, 158, 160, 164, 165, 186
practical knowledge 7, 25, 44, 54, 59, 61, 62, 103, 109, 111, 112, 113, 114, 115, 129, 162, 164, 184
practical philosophy 5, 15, 24, 28, 29, 30, 33, 39, 57, 58, 59, 62, 63, 66, 75, 87, 90, 100, 109, 162
practical wisdom 1, 5, 8, 15, 16, 18, 19, 39, 51, 52, 58, 65, 75, 100, 115, 123, 124, 125, 126, 133, 136, 138, 148, 149, 154, 160, 162
practice 1, 2, 3, 4, 5, 6, 16, 18, 23, 25, 30, 34, 36, 44, 59, 60, 63, 64, 68, 70, 71, 72, 73, 74, 75, 82, 111, 112, 113, 115, 120, 122, 125, 132, 138, 139, 141, 143, 146, 152, 162, 165, 166, 167, 189
prepon 9, 101, 150, 165
prince 32, 40, 41, 42, 43, 45, 46, 51, 52, 53, 54, 131, 149, 152, 153, 154, 155, 165, 173, 174
princeps senatus 22
privileges 34, 160
propensity 86, 89
propriety 24, 38, 101, 102, 149, 150, 151, 156
providentia / foresight 98 / 43, 48, 95, 97, 98
prudence 1, 2, 3, 5, 6, 7, 8, 9, 11, 13, 19, 23, 24, 25, 26, 27, 28, 29, 30, 31, 32, 33, 34, 35, 36, 37, 38, 39, 40, 41, 42, 43, 44, 45, 46, 47, 48, 49, 50, 51, 52, 53, 54, 55, 57, 58, 61, 62, 66, 75, 77, 80, 81, 82, 84, 85, 92, 93, 94, 95, 96, 97, 98, 99, 100, 109, 115, 116, 117, 125, 126, 127, 128, 129, 132, 136, 138, 141, 147, 148, 149, 150, 151, 152, 153, 155, 156, 157, 158, 161, 162, 163, 164, 165, 166, 167, 168, 170, 171, 172, 173, 175, 180, 182, 183, 189, 191
prudentia 1, 19, 20, 24, 27, 33, 53, 57, 94, 123, 124, 126, 150, 162, 167
prudenzia 41, 43

reality check 70, 96, 160
reality principle 7, 96
reason 2, 3, 17, 18, 23, 28, 29, 31, 32, 39, 44, 57, 59, 60, 61, 65, 66, 67, 68, 75, 88, 96, 99, 111, 112, 118, 119, 121, 122, 123, 124, 129, 132, 138, 148, 149, 174, 175
reason of state 4, 44, 45, 46, 47, 48, 49, 52, 53, 54, 56, 157, 174, 183, 189
Rechtsstaat 79
rector 20
relativism 39, 98, 99, 109
Renaissance 6, 7, 13, 24, 33, 34, 38, 39, 45, 49, 51, 53, 95, 101, 116, 118, 121, 123, 124, 125, 126, 133, 152, 155, 157, 168, 172, 173, 175, 180, 181, 185, 189
republic 1, 15, 16, 20, 22, 23, 33, 35, 47, 95, 124, 127, 137, 141, 154, 157, 158, 168, 169, 172, 190
republic, conservative 141, 151
republicanism 9, 117, 133, 134, 138, 152, 156, 157, 158, 159, 165, 189, 190. *See also* conservative republicanism; urban republicanism
Republic of Letters 126
res publica 23, 134, 154, 166
revolt 160
revolution 39, 40, 52, 80, 95, 114, 139, 157, 160, 165, 167, 182
rhetoric 5, 19, 21, 24, 26, 34, 39, 45, 46, 47, 48, 53, 58, 59, 65, 101, 102, 124, 125, 126, 142, 151, 172, 173, 181, 182, 189
Roman Law 17, 37, 139, 152, 154, 169, 189, 190
Rome 21, 22, 26, 27, 34, 37, 38, 41, 42, 43, 44, 59, 75, 125, 126, 151, 153, 157, 158, 189
rule of law 8, 43, 79, 133, 135, 136, 137, 138, 139, 140, 141, 164, 165, 187
rules 2, 17, 30, 32, 37, 39, 48, 50, 54, 65, 79, 99, 110, 112, 113, 114, 115, 125, 126, 130, 134, 136, 137, 139, 183
Russia 79, 145, 178

sapientia 124
scepticism 39, 51, 69, 71, 87, 88, 113, 149, 168

scholasticism   6, 33, 45, 48
scientia   162
Scottish enlightenment   86, 87, 89, 107, 138, 187
self-fashioning   51, 164, 175
sensus communis   25, 59, 87, 154
separation of powers   165
Sermon on the Mount   91
shame (*verecundia*)   24, 66, 71, 151, 165, 178
situational mutability   7, 105, 106, 108, 109, 164
skill analogy   117, 118, 119, 184
sociability   7, 29, 85, 86, 87, 88, 89, 90, 91, 92, 163
social constructivism   111
societas   86
sophia   15, 25, 59, 75, 100, 124, 162
sophrosune   8
Sparta   42, 43
speech   2, 19, 20, 21, 38, 58, 62, 127, 150, 151
spontaneous order (*kosmos*)   7, 111, 113, 137, 138, 141, 164
stoicism   101
studia humanitatis   124
synderesis   96

tact   59, 102, 163
taste   24, 25, 59, 65, 89, 115, 167, 169, 170
techné   15, 17, 20, 60, 114, 183
telos   64, 69
temperate   155
temporal-constraint   92, 105, 138
Ten Commandments   86, 87, 91
time-constraint   7, 93, 163
Tory   111
tradition   1, 5, 6, 7, 8, 9, 13, 14, 15, 17, 18, 22, 23, 25, 34, 35, 36, 38, 40, 41, 42, 43, 44, 45, 47, 48, 51, 54, 55, 56, 57, 58, 59, 61, 62, 63, 66, 67, 72, 75, 79, 81, 86, 89, 94, 95, 99, 101, 103, 112, 115, 120, 122, 125, 127, 128, 129, 130, 133, 137, 139, 140, 144, 145, 150, 153, 154, 155, 157, 158, 160, 161, 162, 164, 165, 167, 168, 169, 170, 173, 177, 188, 190
traditionalism   149
traditional knowledge   114, 115, 139, 160
tragic dimension   65, 70
trimming (art of)   131, 132, 133, 164, 186

urban elites   159, 160
urban republicanism   138, 157, 158, 159, 165

value   3, 5, 6, 8, 28, 35, 37, 43, 62, 82, 92, 108, 109, 120, 121, 124, 170, 180, 182
value dependence   7, 105, 108, 109, 164
Verstehen   109
via media   65, 81
viewpoint   19, 59, 106, 113, 164
violence   27, 64, 80, 186
Virtù   38, 40, 41, 42, 43, 120, 183
virtue   1, 2, 3, 4, 5, 6, 7, 8, 14, 15, 17, 18, 19, 24, 25, 26, 27, 29, 30, 31, 32, 33, 35, 36, 37, 38, 39, 40, 41, 43, 44, 45, 46, 47, 48, 50, 51, 53, 54, 55, 57, 61, 64, 65, 75, 81, 82, 84, 87, 94, 95, 96, 97, 98, 99, 100, 103, 112, 117, 118, 119, 120, 121, 122, 123, 124, 125, 126, 127, 128, 129, 130, 131, 132, 133, 134, 135, 136, 138, 139, 140, 141, 144, 149, 151, 152, 158, 160, 163, 164, 168, 171, 172, 177, 183, 184, 185, 186
virtue ethics   1, 7, 66, 117, 120, 121, 123, 124, 162, 177, 184, 185
virtue politics   55, 56, 85, 118, 121, 123, 124, 162, 184, 185
virtus   37, 53, 181
vita activa   26, 34, 36, 125, 134, 172
vita contemplativa   125

Whig   113

zoon politikon   18, 33

www.ingramcontent.com/pod-product-compliance
Lightning Source LLC
Chambersburg PA
CBHW052042300426
44117CB00012B/1935